Please check all items for damages
before leaving the Library.
Thereafter you will be held
responsible for all injuries
to items beyond reasonable wear.

Helen M. Plum Memorial Library

Lombard, Illinois

A daily fine will be charged for
overdue materials.

VERMEER

A View of Delft

ANTHONY
BAILEY

A JOHN MACRAE BOOK

Henry Holt and Company
New York

Henry Holt and Company, LLC
Publishers since 1866
115 West 18th Street
New York, New York 10011

Henry Holt® is a registered trademark of Henry Holt and Company, LLC.

Simultaneously published in the United Kingdom under the title
A View of Delft: Vermeer Then and Now
by Chatto & Windus, London.

Library of Congress Cataloging-in-Publication Data

Bailey, Anthony, 1933–
    Vermeer : a view of Delft / Anthony Bailey.—1st ed.
        p. cm.
    "A John Macrae Book."
    Includes bibliographical references and index.
    ISBN: 0-8050-6718-3
    1. Vermeer, Johannes, 1632–1675. 2. Painters—Netherlands—Biography. 3. Delft
(Netherlands)—In art. I. Title.
ND653.V5 B25 2001
759.9492—dc21   00-066366

Henry Holt books are available for special promotions and premiums.
For details contact: Director, Special Markets.

First Edition 2001

Printed in the United States of America
1   3   5   7   9   10   8   6   4   2

Contents

Illustrations

The author and publishers are grateful to the owners of the following pictures for permission to reproduce them:

Black and white illustrations

Carel Fabritius, *Self-Portrait*, 1654. The Trustees of the National Gallery, London. (p. 4)

Egbert van der Poel, *A View of Delft after the Explosion of 1654*. The Trustees of the National Gallery, London. (p. 13)

Emanuel de Witte, *The Tomb of Prince Willem I in the Nieuwe Kerk, Delft*, 1656. Musée des Beaux-Arts, Lille. (p. 32)

Attributed to Johannes Vermeer, *St Praxedis*, 1655. Barbara Piasecka Johnson Collection Foundation, Princeton, NJ. (p. 64)

Johannes Vermeer, *Diana and her Companions*, *c.* 1655–6. Royal Cabinet of Paintings, Mauritshuis, The Hague. (p. 74)

Johannes Vermeer, *Christ in the House of Martha and Mary*, *c.* 1655. The National Gallery of Scotland, Edinburgh. (p. 78)

Johannes Vermeer, *Girl asleep at a Table*, *c.* 1657. All rights reserved, the Metropolitan Museum, New York. (p. 84)

Pieter de Hooch, *Courtyard of a House in Delft*, 1658. The Trustees of the National Gallery, London. (p. 91)

Johannes Vermeer, *Girl reading a Letter at an Open Window*, *c.* 1657. Gemäldegalerie Alte Meister, Staatliche Kunstsammlungen, Dresden. (p. 94)

Johannes Vermeer, *Woman tuning a Lute*, *c.* 1664. All rights reserved, the Metropolitan Museum, New York. (p. 114)

Johannes Vermeer, *The Glass of Wine*, *c.* 1658–60. Gemäldegalerie, Berlin. (p. 117)

Colour illustrations

Carel Fabritius, *The Goldfinch*, 1654. Royal Cabinet of Paintings, the Mauritshuis, The Hague.

Johannes Vermeer, *The Procuress*, 1656. Gemäldegalerie Alte Meister, Staatliche Kunstsammlungen, Dresden.

Johannes Vermeer, *The Little Street*, *c.* 1657–8. Copyright of Rijksmuseum Stichting, Amsterdam.

Johannes Vermeer, *The Milkmaid*, *c.* 1658–60. Copyright of Rijksmuseum Stichting, Amsterdam.

Johannes Vermeer, *View of Delft*, *c.* 1660–1. Royal Cabinet of Paintings, the Mauritshuis, The Hague.

Johannes Vermeer, *Woman in Blue reading a Letter*, *c.* 1663–4. Copyright of Rijksmuseum Stichting, Amsterdam.

Johannes Vermeer, *Girl with a Pearl Earring*, *c.* 1665–6. Royal Cabinet of Paintings, the Mauritshuis, The Hague.

Johannes Vermeer, *Woman with a Pearl Necklace*, *c.* 1664. Gemäldegalerie, Berlin.

Johannes Vermeer, *The Music Lesson (A Lady at the Virginals with a Gentleman)*, *c.* 1662–4. Royal Collection, London. Copyright Her Majesty Queen Elizabeth II.

Johannes Vermeer, *A Lady writing*, *c.* 1665. Copyright of Board of Trustees, the National Gallery, Washington, DC.

Johannes Vermeer, *The Lacemaker*, *c.* 1669–70. Louvre, Paris. Photo copyright RMN – R.G. Ojeda.

Johannes Vermeer, *Girl with a Red Hat*, *c.* 1665. Copyright of Board of Trustees, the National Gallery, Washington, DC.

Johannes Vermeer, *The Concert*, *c.* 1665–6. Isabella Stewart Gardner Museum, Boston. (Stolen; present whereabouts unknown.)

Johannes Vermeer, *The Art of Painting*, *c.* 1666–7. Copyright Kunsthistorisches Museum, Vienna.

Maps (by Reginald Piggott)

Acknowledgements

The search for Johannes Vermeer has now been going on for nearly a century and a half. As mentioned in the text, the French politician and writer Théophile Thoré was one of the first explorers, but the 'Sphinx of Delft' he found was very much a ghost lacking material attributes. Another Frenchman, Henri Havard, began to look in the 1870s in the as yet uncatalogued Delft archives for facts about Vermeer's life, and his inquiries were followed by the investigations of Abraham Bredius, whose patrician standing was such that he was allowed to take original documents from the archives home to The Hague, where he occasionally underlined with blue pencil words he wanted to recall. In more recent years Vermeer's trail has been pursued by a number of scholars, Dutch and foreign, professional and amateur. The roll of honour should include L.G.N. Bouricius, P.T.A. Swillens, A.J.J.M. van Peer (a primary schoolteacher), H.W. van Leeuwen (like Bouricius a Delft archivist), J.C. Hebbers, Rob Ruurs, C.J. Matthijs, and J.M. Montias. Montias, a former professor of economics at Yale University, began looking into the activities of the Delft Guild of St Luke in 1975, and although at that point he had (so he has written) 'no special interest in Vermeer's life', gradually realised that there were new things to find out about Vermeer; he started to look more systematically for documents related to the artist and his relatives. What Montias has uncovered about Vermeer's extended family and 'milieu' greatly exceeds what he has discovered about the artist himself; but every writer on Vermeer is immensely indebted to him. Montias's *Vermeer and his Milieu* includes almost all of the extant documents.

My bibliography is an acknowledgement of my debt to many scholars and writers, but I also want to express my gratitude to those who have found things, sent me material, answered questions, translated documents, or pointed me in the right direction. They include Lief Achten; Fred Bachrach; Margot Bailey; Albert Blankert; Annette Boesveld; Christopher Brown; C.J. Fox; David Hockney; Buell Hollister; Susan Jowers; Walter Liedtke; Daniella Lokin; Jannes Meijer; Lies Meijer-Vonkeman; John Michael Montias; John Nash; Heleen Nieman; Neil Olson; Jacqueline Oud; Jenny Overton; Bridget Sojourner; Sarah Speight; Philip Steadman; Claudia Swan; Sarah Taft; John Updike; Marieke de Winkel; Graham Wrathmell; and the staffs of the archives in Delft and of the libraries in The Hague.

Author's Note

This book is an attempt to make accessible much of the research that has been done in the last century or so into the life of Johannes Vermeer. It tries to strike a balance between the questions art historians ask and the interests of the intelligent common reader. It puts Vermeer's home town of Delft in the foreground of the inquiry. It assumes that a now world-famous painter was once a local artist, an innkeeper's son who painted, a man who married and worked his way upwards while being a busy husband and a frequently harassed father of a large family. It is primarily a biography, an account of the life of an extremely elusive man, rather than a book about his paintings. However, since Vermeer was an artist, his work – a vital byproduct of his life – naturally comes in for examination, and helps us arrive at ideas about his personality. I accept the figure of thirty-five, possibly thirty-six, as the number of his known paintings.

A few points about language, time, and place. The Dutch have one word only – *stad* – for town and city, and I have used both English words when describing Delft, a small city or a large town. I have not translated the Dutch Oude and Nieuwe, since doing so in regard to, say, the Oude Kerk and Nieuwe Kerk as Old Church and New Church would beg questions when using Dutch names for streets such as the Oude Langendijk and Nieuwe Langendijk. As for dates, most of Holland (though not Utrecht) adopted the Gregorian calendar on 5 December 1582, a day which became 15 December; to travel to Utrecht from Delft was to go back ten days. England stayed on the old Julian system until 1752, when it made the change; the

American colonies did likewise. As for money and the complex matter of values, a Delft cloth-worker in 1642 got eighteen stuivers a day; there were twenty stuivers to one guilder, and a 6-pound loaf of rye bread cost about four and a half stuivers; many working people spent half their income on bread.

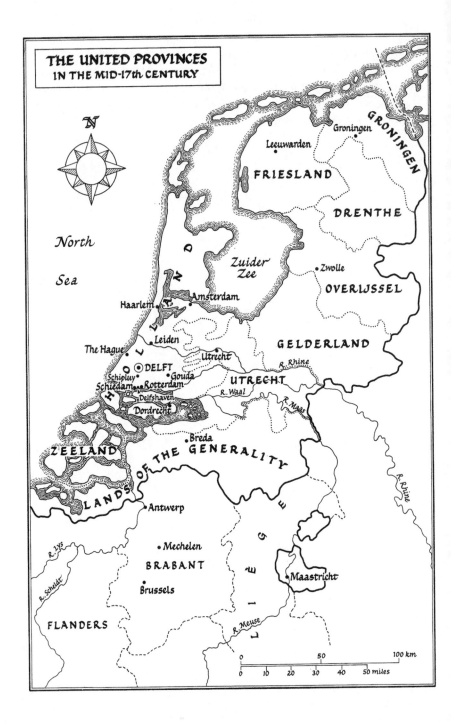

THE UNITED PROVINCES
IN THE MID-17th CENTURY

N

North

Sea

GRONINGEN

Groningen

Leeuwarden

FRIESLAND

DRENTHE

Zuider
Zee

Zwolle

OVERIJSSEL

Amsterdam

Haarlem

H O L L A N D

Leiden

GELDERLAND

The Hague

Utrecht

R. Rhine

DELFT

Gouda

UTRECHT

Schipluy

Schiedam

Rotterdam

R. Waal

R. Maas

Delfshaven

Dordrecht

Breda

LANDS OF THE GENERALITY

ZEELAND

L I E G E

R. Rhine

Antwerp

R. Lys

Mechelen

Maastricht

R. Scheldt

BRABANT

Brussels

FLANDERS

R. Meuse

0   50   100 km

0   10   20   30   40   50 miles

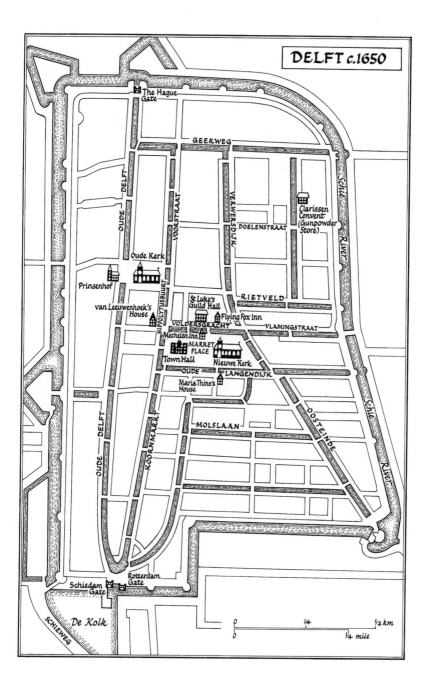

DELFT c.1650

The Hague Gate

GEERWEG

OUDE DELFT

VOORSTRAAT

VERWERSDIJK

DOELENSTRAAT

Clarissen Convent (Gunpowder Store)

Schie River

Oude Kerk

Prinsenhof

van Leeuwenhoek's House

HIPPOLYTUSBUURT

St Luke's Guild Hall

RIETVELD

Flying Fox Inn

VOLDERSGRACHT

VLAMINGSTRAAT

Mechelen Inn

MARKET PLACE

Town Hall

Nieuwe Kerk

OUDE

LANGENDIJK

Maria Thins's House

MOLSLAAN

OOSTEINDE

Schie River

OUDE DELFT

KOORNMARKT

Rotterdam Gate

Schiedam Gate

SCHIEWEG

De Kolk

0   ¼   ½ km
0   ¼ mile

Authentic art has no use for proclamations . . .
it accomplishes its work in silence.

Marcel Proust, *Le Temps Retrouvé*

1. *The World Turned Upside-Down*

Monday morning, 12 October 1654. Within the close-packed town of Delft – a long box of streets and canals surrounded by a defensive wall and a watery girdle of canal and river that served as a moat – laundry was spread to dry in several thousand back-yards. The skyline of orangey-red pan-tiled roofs was dominated by three towers: that of the Town Hall, rebuilt forty years before; that of the Nieuwe Kerk – Nieuwe to distinguish it from the Oude Kerk, though by now it was a hundred and fifty years old – which stood at the opposite end of the large Market Place from the Town Hall; and that of the Oude Kerk, which backed on a canal called the Oude Delft, across which prosperous three- and four-storey houses faced each other. The massive tower of the Oude Kerk looked as if it might any day fall on the neighbouring houses; it was at least 2 metres out of plumb but nearby residents – long used to its dangerous tilt – weren't holding their breath. At street level the usual sounds of the day could be heard. Carriages and hand-barrows rattled over the brick- and cobble-paved streets. Mallets, wedges, and saws were being used in timber-yards and coopers' workshops. Hammers clashed against anvils in smithies. The click and clack of looms rose from several hundred houses where, as was common, people worked in their own homes, making serge and worsted, silk and satin. Some trades of course were quieter; for example, those where tapestries were being woven, and canvas and clothing sewn. And some were just about silent. In fifty or sixty private houses and in a dozen or so ateliers attached to potteries, artists wielded brushes as they painted canvases and panels, plates and tiles.

So it was in a small house in the Doelenstraat, a narrow street in the north-east of the city, close to the archery butts and headquarters of the city militia and to the former convent of the Poor Clares, the Clarissen, now used as a store for army munitions. In this Doelenstraat cottage an artist named Carel Fabritius sat in front of his easel. Fabritius was thirty-two years old. He was preoccupied with a portrait, the subject of which – Simon Decker, the retired verger of the Oude Kerk, who lived not far away on the south side of the Jan Voersteeg – was sitting to one side behind the easel.

Fabritius was a highly talented artist, a good-looking man with a broad nose and full lips, the son of a schoolteacher and a midwife from Midden Beemster, a village in a reclaimed lake area just north of Amsterdam. He had ten siblings including two brothers who also took to painting. Their father was an amateur painter; their grandfather a Calvinist preacher who had come north from Ghent in Flanders in 1584.

In the not very long course of his life so far Fabritius had lost his first wife and his two children. He had been a carpenter and builder – hence the surname Fabritius, from the Latin *faber*, 'maker'. In Amsterdam he had worked in Rembrandt's studio for a year or more, and had picked up from the older man – the greatest artist in that great city – many skills in the handling of paint and in ways of considering subject-matter. He had painted among other things a biblical scene, *The Raising of Lazarus*, and a portrait of an Amsterdam silk merchant, Abraham de Potter. Delft was the home town of his second wife, Agatha, who was a widow when he met her. They lived first in her family's house on the Oude Delft canal, before moving to the Doelenstraat. By 1654 he had been in Delft for four years, and for the past two years a member of the Delft Guild of St Luke, the association which regulated the profession of painters, as well as those of faience-makers, bookbinders, glassmakers and so on. Thus Fabritius was now qualified not only to work in Delft but to sign his pictures, market them, and accept apprentices.

His reputation had been growing in his adopted city. Although a number of his pictures – some unfinished, all unsold – were stacked against the walls of his studio, others were out in the world, some with local dealers such as Reynier Vermeer, some with private patrons. One such patron was Dr Theodore Vallensis, a prominent Delft burgher and dean of the Surgeons' Guild, who had commissioned Fabritius to paint murals in his house on the Oude Delft. Fabritius's former fellow-Rembrandt pupil, the Dordrecht painter Samuel van Hoogstraten, wrote in 1678 that these 'miracles of perspective' could be compared with the frescoes of Giulio Romano in the Palazzo del Tè of Duke Vincenzo Gonzaga in Mantua, with a magical character that made the space around them look larger than it was.* Fabritius had also done murals for a Delft brewer named Nicolaes Dichter, who owned a brewery called *De Vekeerde Werelt*, 'The World Turned Upside-Down'; this name was taken from an old Netherlandish saying which artists were accustomed to illustrate with an inverted orb hung outside an inn and maybe a drunken figure or two – the world, it was suggested, could be a personal one that went topsy-turvy. Fabritius had also worked with the artist brothers Daniel and Nicolaes Vosmaer on a big sea picture. He seems to have tried out all sorts of approaches and many kinds of subject, in various sizes.

A very small creation of his was a *View in Delft* painted in 1652 – a miniature but slightly dizzymaking prospect. A man sits at an outside stall displaying two stringed instruments and contemplates the cobbled roadway where the Oude Langendijk meets the Vrouwen-recht. The road climbs steeply over a humped bridge. There's a single tree in leaf, houses, and the Nieuwe Kerk, strangely small, seen from the rear. The distorting effect is like that of an amusement arcade mirror, with different elements of the picture in irregular focus, an unnaturally wide angle of view, and disconcerting discrepancies of scale. The sunlit viola da gamba and lute loom large in the foreground, almost overwhelming the black-coated and black-hatted man sitting in the shadows, with the thumb of one hand propping up his chin. The instruments may be symbols of love (as in

---

*Regrettably, by the time van Hoogstraten wrote this in his *Inleyding tot de Hooge Schoole*, the Fabritius murals had already disappeared.

music 'the food of love'). The hanging sign may be advertising an inn; it shows a swan – perhaps a symbol denoting a happy death (as in swan song), perhaps a hostelry of dubious reputation (as with the swans that drew the chariot of Venus). The experts also disagree as to whether the man is trying to sell the instruments or is waiting for

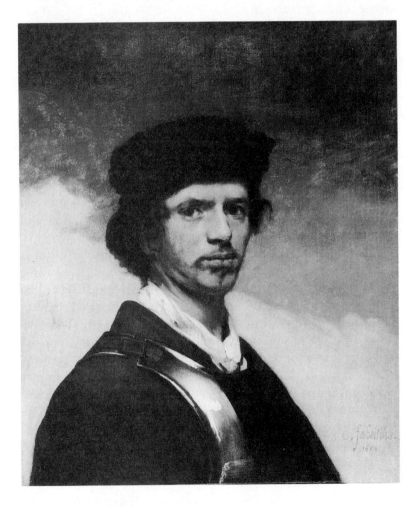

Self-Portrait, 1654, Carel Fabritius.

a young woman. Most agree that the tiny size of the picture (15.4 ×
31.6 cm, 6¹⁄₁₆ × 12⁷⁄₁₆ in.) enhances its success; it is a *tour de force*; the
view both is and isn't Delft as Fabritius's friends and colleagues
would have recognised it.

Hoogstraten said that it was a pity that Fabritius never worked on
a royal building or church, where – he implied – his ability to create
such startling illusions would have been seen to greater advantage.
But in fact the *View in Delft* is happy in its size; only its context is
unclear. Was it intended for a peepshow or perspective box, of the
kind that Hoogstraten himself made?

Other Fabritius works included two assumed-to-be self-portraits,
in which Rembrandt's influence is visible, the person being painted
looking out at the viewer with a direct, perhaps slightly disgruntled,
gaze: in one, with his black chest-hair blatantly exposed, he is set
against a wall of peeling plaster; in the other, he wears a military
breast-plate and stands against an intimidatingly stormy sky. There
was also a painting called *The Sentry*. In this, a soldier in distressed
breeches sits dozing outside a weirdly dysfunctional archway – is he
on supposed guard-duty at the Clarissen convent munitions store? –
while being watched by a much more alert dog.

A seemingly more straightforward work was *The Goldfinch* (see
colour section), painted earlier in this same year on a little panel of
thick wood that may have been once built into a cabinet. The bird –
known for its skill at drawing water from small containers – is called a
putterje in Dutch and there may have been a pun intended here on the
name of Fabritius's patron Abraham de Potter; goldfinches were also
known for liking thorns and thistles and could therefore in that
symbol-conscious age be a useful symbol of Christ's Passion. But
none of these aspects seems particularly important. The painting is
Fabritius's masterpiece. And it is also just a depiction of a goldfinch.
The little bird, chained to a curved rail on top of its box, seen against
a rough white plaster wall, looks life-size. Broad brush-strokes
become visible when the viewer gets close, but at a short distance *The
Goldfinch* – head turned inquisitively towards us – is miraculously
real. The little bird might have been a household pet, though we can

only assume, from the loving familiarity with which it is painted, that it belonged here in a small house in the Doelenstraat.

Despite portrait commissions, times weren't easy for Fabritius and Agatha. Recently, for the Delft town council, he had done two coats of arms, one large, one small, for a payment of twelve guilders; this was equal to his registration fee with the Guild of St Luke, half of which he still owed. He was in debt to a waiter at the nearby Doel inn, with 110 guilders owed for food and drink. The death of the Prince of Orange, William II, in November 1650, had apparently cut off commissions expected from that influential quarter. But debt was part of an artist's life. Fabritius's neighbour, Egbert van der Poel, who was also thirty-two, had not long ago agreed to pay off, partly with pictures, a loan of 217 guilders made to him by Arent van Straten, landlord of another inn, the Golden Fleece.* A relatively new member of the St Luke's Guild, Reynier Vermeer's twenty-two-year-old son Johannes, had only been able to afford a down payment of one and a half guilders on the six guilders' entry fee he owed as a local man who had trained outside Delft. Some of their colleagues were saying that as far as Delft was concerned, it would be all downhill from now on; it was time to move elsewhere. Egbert van der Poel had been talking of moving to Rotterdam. Adam Pick had sold up and gone to Leiden, while Emanuel de Witte and Paulus Potter had decided to try their hands in Amsterdam.

Shortly before ten-thirty on that same Monday morning, a little more than a hundred yards away, a man named Cornelis Soetens approached the old convent buildings in which the States-General, the Dutch national assembly, maintained an arsenal – one of six in Delft. Although there was now peace with Spain, both England and France – by sea and by land respectively – were still a real threat. The fact that the former Clarissen convent was jammed full with munitions and explosives was something the residents of the neighbourhood were aware of, though they kept it at the back of their

---

*Van der Poel had spent most of the loan on canvas for paintings. Fabritius had witnessed the agreement between lender and borrower.

minds. It hadn't deterred the builders of several streets of new houses between the Lakengracht and Verwersdijk, in an area known as the Raam, where the old frames for stretching cloth in the open air used to stand.

Soetens, a clerk for the States-General, had the task this morning of removing a 2-pound sample of gunpowder from the store – a sort of tower, three-quarters buried in the convent garden, that was known as *t'Secret van Holland*. It held about 90,000 pounds of gunpowder, mostly underground. Soetens was accompanied by a colleague from The Hague, wearing a red cloak, and by a servant. A lantern was lit, a door to the store was opened, and Soetens's companion handed his fine cloak to the servant so that it wouldn't get dirty on their errand and told him to take it home. The two men went in and down the dark stairs to collect their sample.

Some minutes passed. It was still an ordinary Monday morning in Delft. And then it seemed as if the heart of creation had opened up. The air filled with an immense noise that multiplied and magnified into an all-encompassing roar. Five huge successive explosions merged with one another. The earth shuddered and shuddered again. Flames rose and an intense heat fanned out in a searing wave. Walls fell and bits of houses soared upwards along with their contents: beams and floorboards, bricks and roof-tiles, glass and pottery, pans and tools, clothes and children's toys flew up and outwards; so did curtains, carpets, doors, windows, knives and spoons, loaves of bread, barrels of beer. And so, too, did once-living things, some now barely alive, many dead. Trees; plants; men; women; children; cats; dogs; pet birds. They were whole or in pieces: arms, legs, torsos, heads, rose and fell. The vibrating air was thick with smoke and dust and rubble, and strangely wet as well, for the water in the canals had been blown high.

Some thought it was the end of the world. Others believed that heaven had split asunder, that they had seen the mouth of hell gape wide. And then those who still had their hearing began to make out the cries of people from under fallen houses.

The Thunderclap radiated out from the Secret of Holland in the former convent garden. It travelled across the flat country's meadows, lanes and waterways to other towns. Doors slammed in Haarlem and Delfshaven.

Here in Delft, the shock wave passing through the ground caused houses in the first few hundred yards to fall down. The shock wave sweeping through the air made other buildings collapse and hurled pieces of them outwards into nearby structures. The rush of heat meant that trees and buildings caught fire. In the tightly packed streets around the Clarissen convent the effect was catastrophe; just about every house was flattened between the Geerweg to the north and the Doelenstraat to the south, between the city wall to the east and the Verwersdijk to the west. The guild-halls of the civic guards and the surgeons were among the buildings destroyed. Beyond this zone of total disaster, tiles were stripped and roof-timbers sent crashing down, but though the roofs and walls of the two great churches were slightly damaged and their window-glass was cracked and smashed, the churches themselves still stood above the skyline of the city. Many trees had been chopped off cleanly at ground level while those whose trunks still stood had blackened boughs bereft of leaves. Where the Secret of Holland had stood was a deep hole which soon filled with black water.

It was a little while before those outside the immediate area of calamity pulled themselves together. The rush of many to help was affected by caution – perhaps there were more explosions to come. For some, fright predominated, and they fled the city in panic. There were also many impediments in the way of those who wanted to assist: canal bridges down, streets blocked, bodies and parts of bodies everywhere, fires burning. But soon many residents of the less damaged parts of the city were there, levering beams, pulling aside clumps of brick and plaster, scrabbling and digging with their hands. Some looked for family members and friends. Some heard cries and screams and sobs, and worked to rescue strangers. Many of those killed were cloth-workers. In the house of one man who made serge, all were dead: the master, his wife, their servant-woman, their children. The neighbourhood girls' school was in ruins and twenty-eight children and their teachers fatally injured. One woman who had a clothing business had been hit on the head by a door lintel and killed, and dead too were four of her seamstress apprentices; three were more fortunate, two being pulled alive from under a wall and one from under a loom, where she had fallen. In the Doelenstraat Egbert van der Poel's daughter was one of those found dead. So, too, in Carel Fabritius's house were his mother-in-law Judith van Pruijsen, his assistant-cum-pupil, Mathias Spoors, and the verger Simon Decker. The painter himself was extricated from the wreckage badly crushed. But he was still breathing and was carried off to the hospital near the Koornmarket.

It was a wet evening. The wind went round to the south-west and strengthened; rain fell steadily. The torches of those looking for victims were frequently blown out. To assist the overstretched Delft physicians, doctors arrived from outside the city – from Schiedam, Rotterdam, and The Hague – to bandage wounds and amputate limbs. People were still being pulled alive from ruined buildings through the next day or so. Twin babies were found unharmed in their cradles in a wrecked house in which their mother lay dead. One seventy-five-year-old man was found alive, lying on his bed, in a house that had collapsed over him. A little girl just over a year old was pulled from the rubble still in her high-chair, clutching an apple in one hand, with only a scratch to show her rescuers, at whom she laughed. The record for survival apparently belonged to an elderly woman who was brought forth from the wreckage of a large house four days after the explosion, still conscious; she asked those who were lifting her, 'Has the world come to an end?' Unfortunately for many it had. There were some who had survived the Thunderclap itself but been trapped, such as two women on whom a wall fell at half-past six that evening of the 12th as rescuers tried to dig them free. Many of the victims were unidentified, but among those who were eventually named was the painter of *The Goldfinch*. Carel Fabritius had died of his wounds less than an hour after he had arrived at the hospital. No trace was found of Cornelis Soetens and his colleague from The Hague.

★

A veil is drawn over what occurred after Soetens and his companion went down into the well-named Secret of Holland that morning. Did one of them drop the lantern? Was a spark struck – say, by a metal padlock or key hitting a paving stone or a brick? Whatever the impulse, a devastating force had been suddenly released in the Second Quarter of Delft. The power that had slammed doors in Haarlem and Delfshaven broke windows in The Hague and shook them in Amersfoort and Gouda. The great *thump* was heard in Den Helder, the port on the tip of North Holland, and even, so it was claimed, a little further off, on the North Sea island of Texel, 60 miles away.* And here was a disaster which had touched almost everyone in Delft; it was hard to find a family who hadn't lost a member or hadn't had one injured. The explosion's effects had been felt by young and old, the well-to-do, the hard-working, and the poor. It had come out of the blue, without any warning whatsoever. In a war, those who enlisted knew what to expect; in a war, civilians recognised the possibility of looting and murder. This had been a total surprise. There hadn't been time even to pray.

People came from all over to gaze and wonder and of course to express sympathy. The States-General sent a letter of condolence. Among the distinguished visitors who toured the shattered city was Elizabeth Stuart, sister of the executed King of England Charles I; in 1613 at the age of seventeen she had married Frederick, the Elector Palatine, who was briefly King of Bohemia. She had lived in The Hague for the last thirty years, with the help of pensions granted by the States-General and the English Parliament, and in recent times had been surrounded by many exiled Stuart supporters to whom she was fondly known as the Queen of Hearts. She wrote to her son Charles Louis, the current Elector Palatine, on 19 October, to see if she could get his help in redeeming a diamond necklace which she had been forced to pawn, and added:

---

*Texel was sometimes used as a term to express the remotest reaches of the country. Gerbrandt Bredero, painter and writer, had said in his play *The Spanish Brabanter*, 'Go as far as Texel, Death still comes to us all.'

I am sure you hear of the blowing up of the magazine of Delft this day seven-night. I went upon Thursday to see it, you cannot imagine how the town is ruined, all the streets near the tower where it was are quite down, not one stone upon another. The host of the doole [possibly the Doel tavern] there was standing upon the threshold of his door, when the blow was. It stunned him a little, and after he turned himself to go into his house and found none, [he saw that] it was quite turned over.

To Sir Edward Nicholas, one of the aides of her nephew (who was to become Charles II), she wrote: 'It is a sad sight, whole streets quite razed . . . it is not yet known how many persons are lost, there is scarce any house in the town but the tiles are off.'

There were funerals to attend, though the Reformed Church made no great ceremony of obsequies at any time and the services were simple. Carel Fabritius was among the fifteen who were buried in the Oude Kerk two days later, as were his mother-in-law and Simon Decker. The irony may have been noticed by some that Decker's job would have included the duty of keeping the register of burials; Fabritius's father had fulfilled the same task in Midden Beemster. As the Queen of Bohemia had suggested, the death toll remained uncertain, though one report gave the number of identified dead as fifty-four (which happened to match the last figures of the year); thirteen years later the city historian Dirck van Bleyswijck put the figure between five hundred and a thousand – a wide enough margin for error. Some bodies had been dismembered or decapitated. Roughly a thousand were seriously injured, with bones broken, sight or hearing impaired, minds unhinged. More people might have been killed or injured if it hadn't been the day of the pig market in Schiedam and of the fair in Voorburg, to which many had gone from Delft.

It was easier to determine damage to property. Anyone could see directly where whole streets had been blown away, where walls had fallen and roofs had collapsed. About two hundred houses were completely wrecked and about three hundred others needed major structural repairs. The Doelen – the hall of the civic guard, named like the nearby inn after the targets on the archery butts the militia men shot at – had been destroyed, and so had been the nearby quarantine hospital where plague victims were confined. On a smaller scale the blast had flattened the summer house, standing in an orchard, which had belonged to Burgomaster Bruin Jacobsz van der Dussen. Fortunately the seventy-year-old burgomaster, a member of a distinguished brewery-owning family (like many Delft patricians), was at the Town Hall at the time of the catastrophe; all his fruit trees were also blown down or shattered. On the churches, weathervanes were dented and twisted. Splits and cracks had appeared in walls everywhere. Because thousands of tiles had been torn from roofs, and many windows broken, the rain that fell for several succeeding days did further damage. Inside houses, precious objects had fallen from shelves, pictures had dropped from walls, and furniture was ruined. In many dwellings, like those of Fabritius and van der Poel, paintings were lost for ever.

Long-term assistance was gradually rendered. Some wealthy men bought thousands of roof-tiles and gave them out to the needy. The Provincial Council of Holland and West Friesland made a grant of 100,000 guilders to help pay for repairs. A tax holiday was allowed to those most severely affected – for some, a period as long as twenty-five years free of property taxes was granted. Some victims received compensation, including six-year-old David Pieters, who had injuries that remained with him for the rest of his life; he was given a pension of twenty-five guilders a year. The list of claimants for building repair grants showed how the explosion was no respecter of occupation: it included people who were bakers, millers, shoemakers, harness-makers, barrelmakers, glass-engravers, carpenters, turfcutters, silversmiths, painters, apothecaries, tobacco buyers, schoolmasters, wagon-builders, tile-bakers, and coffin-makers; even Simon Decker, verger and sexton, turned up in the lists, presumably as the result of a claim by his surviving family. Some claimants, among them Mathijs Pomij and Huych Leeuwenhoek, had several houses which they evidently rented out. Pieter Abramse Beedam, a coffin-maker in the Geerweg, put in for replacing 1,200 pan-tiles and 40 ridge-tiles at a cost of just over nineteen guilders. Widows and foreigners who owned Delft property made claims.

The dust had scarcely settled before some realised the tragedy might have its profitable side. There was of course a lot of work for builders and carpenters and glaziers – *fabers* of all sorts – and for the crews of barges which carried away rubble and brought in building materials. A new gunpowder store was built but was erected a mile from the city centre and well outside the city walls. Before the end of the year a journalist from Amsterdam named J.P. Schabaelje had produced a sensationalist pamphlet about the *Donderslag*, 'the Thunderclap'. Two artists, Gerbrandt van den Eeckhout from Amsterdam, who had, like Fabritius, worked in Rembrandt's studio, and Herman Saftleven from Rotterdam, came to town to draw the wreckage. Van den Eeckhout's drawing showed the little girl in her high-chair being rescued and was used in the Schabaelje pamphlet.

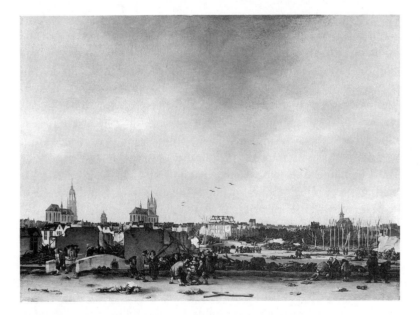

A View of Delft after the Explosion of 1654, Egbert van der Poel.

Local artists such as Daniel Vosmaer and the bereaved Egbert van der Poel began to make paintings of the scene, and, in the latter's case, to attempt to capture not just the after-effect but the very moment of the explosion. Van der Poel – whether working through the pain of loss or simply working a market for disaster pictures – painted the catastrophe over and over. Even though he moved to Rotterdam in 1655, it remained his subject; more than twenty pictures of the explosion by him still exist. Serious literary expressions about the tragedy were also published. Joost van den Vondel, the Amsterdam poet and playwright (and unofficial national laureate), composed a poem that recalled Delft's great fire of 1536 and invoked the power of Chaos: the gunpowder had been meant to be a support for the country, not its enemy, though it had buried Delft in a sea of ash. The chronicler Lieuwe van Aitzema eschewed Pompeiian metaphor but compared Delft to Jerusalem and Carthage; he said 100,000 cannons firing at the city couldn't have done more damage. Less helpful, at least to agnostic readers, were those commentators who viewed the *ontploffing* as a sign of the Almighty's wrath. The minister Petrus de Witte burst forth with a fiery pamphlet in which he explained that the explosion was a manifestation of God's displeasure at the mild, even tolerant way Delft Protestants had been treating other religious groups, rather than vehemently opposing them. The liberal Reformed, the Mennonites, and the Roman Catholics were just as much infidels as Mohammedans and other heathens. Indeed, Delft was a veritable Sodom or Gomorrah that deserved its fate. Petrus de Witte denounced the city council for allowing Catholic services to be held in the old Begijnhof chapel after the explosion. Similarly, if less obstreperously, a Jesuit priest, Arnout van Geluwe, said that he was taking comfort from the fact that neighbourhoods where 'many devout Catholic hearts dwelt' had been spared – a sure sign that God was looking after those He really cared for.

In front of the old Clarissen convent, when the rubble had been cleared, a large open space was made into a horse-market. The plague hospital was re-erected not far away, but this time outside the city walls on the east side of the Schie River. New houses were built in the wrecked streets. The Doelen of the Civic Guard and the Anatomy Chamber of the Surgeons' Guild were re-established on the Verwersdijk in a damaged building of the old St Mary Magdalen convent. Householders set to work to glue pottery and decorative tiles together and have damaged paintings restored. At the local Guild of St Luke, the crafts association to which Delft artists belonged, one of the headmen for that year pulled out a register and turned to the list of painters. He wrote after the name 'Carolus fabrycyus', *doot* ('dead'). Fabritius had joined the guild two years before and was member number 75; the final instalment of six guilders he had owed for joining went unpaid, and so – presumably – did the 110 guilders he owed at the Doel tavern. Member no. 78 was a young Delft artist, ten years younger than Fabritius, named Johannes Vermeer, who had joined the guild at the end of 1653, the year before.

Fabritius and Vermeer had other links: paintings by the former turned up in the possession of the latter, paintings of the latter seem to show the influence of the former. Moreover, they both appeared in a 1667 guide to the city's history, topography, and most eminent personalities. The author, Dirck van Bleyswijck, a youth of seventeen in 1654, eventually became a burgomaster of Delft. In his *Description of the City of Delft* he described Fabritius as 'an outstanding and excellent painter' and told of his death in the gunpowder explosion. And van Bleyswijck's publisher, Arnold Bon, who had his office and printing establishment in the Market Place and was also a poet, provided some dutiful but nevertheless poignant verses of his own on the death of 'the greatest artist that Delft or even Holland had ever known'. These concluded:

> Thus did this Phoenix, to our loss, expire,
>   In the midst and at the height of his powers,
>   But happily there arose out of his fire
> Vermeer, who masterfully trod his path.

A slightly different last stanza appeared in some copies of van Bleyswijck's *Description*, and the last two lines of this were

2. *A Visit to the Tomb*

To many in Delft, it was a miracle that the city's most celebrated possession, the monumental tomb of William I, Prince of Orange, came through the explosion unscathed within the Nieuwe Kerk. There were many cracks in the mostly fifteenth-century fabric of the church; its roof was damaged and most of the stained-glass windows – which had survived the great fire of 1536 and the attacks of iconoclasts thirty years later – were blown in; but the tomb itself, with its bronze statuary and ornate marble work, was intact. It seemed an excellent omen.

The citizenry recognised the artistic importance of the tomb but also saw its value as a magnet for patriotic Dutch visitors and foreign travellers. The tomb was known throughout Europe. One English visitor was impressed by the fact that 'You give no money to see it, only what you please to put into the poor's box.' However, poor children knew that the tomb was a good place at which to accost well-to-do tourists, with hand or hat held out for a small coin.

For a young man such as Vermeer, growing up in Delft close to the church, the tomb was a reminder of the history he had taken in at school or heard, via his parents, in stories his grandparents had told; by 1654 three generations had passed between the death of the Prince and the deaths in the Doelenstraat. The stories were now almost folk-tales – like those that English children learned about the Saxon king who burned the cakes or later young Americans were told about a youth, a future president, who could not tell a lie. There were stirring accounts of the bloody revolt against Spain that had been in many ways a civil war. It had been Lowlander against Lowlander. There had been siege and starvation, mayhem and murder. Some stories were heroic; some were like memories of a painful birth, the fierce particulars of torment scarcely recollectable but built into one's soul – in this case, the soul of the nation. Vermeer had grown up learning about the old all-Catholic seventeen provinces which by marriage and descent had come from being lands belonging to the Dukes of Burgundy to being part of the Habsburg Empire – and thus, by the second half of the sixteenth century, to being ruled by Philip II of Spain. In the 1560s the disruptive forces had been intense. Some forces were political, as provincial nobles and local oligarchies tussled with the authorities representing the central power. Other forces were religious. A profound dissatisfaction with the liturgical and moral ways of the Roman Catholic Church had seized northern Europe and inspired an opposition to Rome that led to the Reformation; new dissenting sects called Lutherans, Anabaptists or Mennonites, and – most forcefully in the Netherlands – Calvinists, had spread from France through the Walloon country and Flanders and thence northwards. Psalm-books were printed for the masses to chant from. Hedge-preachers attracted thousands to hear their fiery sermons denouncing the Pope and his minions.

Against this rising tide of Protestantism, Philip II was sworn to protect Holy Church and extirpate heresy. He had instruments for that purpose in the Inquisition (introduced in the Low Countries in 1520 by his father, Charles V) and – under the Duke of Alva, in Brussels – the Council of the Troubles, well-nicknamed the Council of Blood. Confessions to disloyalty and heretical practices were exacted by torture. Executions and martyrdoms took place by the axe, burning and drowning. Philip, unlike his father who had been raised in the Netherlands, was a thorough Spaniard and a fanatical Catholic. His policies aroused ever more active opposition. In 1566 a vengeful outbreak of iconoclasm took place: churches, including the Nieuwe Kerk in Delft, were looted; stained-glass windows and statues were smashed; vestments were desecrated and religious paintings the

Reformers thought idolatrous pulled down and kicked to pieces. The Ten Commandments were put up in their place, the second of them declaring: 'Thou shalt not make unto thee any graven image . . .' Then for a moment the governing powers in Brussels and other towns reasserted themselves. In Delft in 1568 an influential dissenting printer, Herman Schinkel, was beheaded in the Market Place for publishing 'heretical' pamphlets. In the same year a mass execution of dissident nobles and leading citizenry was ordered by the Council of Blood: many died, many were arrested and tortured, and – as Alva intended – the savagery of the repression sowed fear among some of those who might have been considering defecting to the Reformed ranks. And yet both Reformation and rebellion continued to take hold. It was certainly the wrong moment for the Spanish overlords to impose a 'tenth-penny' tax, as they did in 1569, making money as well as religion and political power a factor in the conflict.

In the Dutch chronicles of the Great Revolt, William the Silent, Prince of Orange, was the hero of heroes, the *pater patriae*. The Burgrave of Antwerp and the Stadtholder (literally 'the Placeholder') on behalf of Philip II of Spain, in the provinces of Holland, Zeeland, and Utrecht, he had been raised a Catholic and was loath to deny his loyalties to his king. But Philip's centralist, militarist, and doctrinally dogmatic ways helped push a reluctant William into the opposition leadership. In 1572 the rebels who were scoffed at as 'beggars' by Philip's aide Berlaymont showed their mettle; their fleet took Brielle. Catching the same wind, the upper-class oligarchies that ran towns such as Delft transferred their allegiance from Philip to the rebels and followed Prince William – a change called the Great Alteration.

The Spanish garrison thereupon cleared out of Delft. When William set up a commission to select a place where the States-General's arms and powder should be stored, Delft was chosen and the Prince made the town his headquarters. It was better provided with walls and gates than the unfortified Hague, and perhaps something in its quiet character appealed to his taciturn temperament. In April 1573 he joined the Reformed Church, though he never became a Calvinist zealot; his efforts were directed against Spanish hegemony rather than the Church of Rome. In the same year the city magistrates of Haarlem who had co-operated with the Spanish were brought to Delft and, on the Prince's orders, beheaded in the Market Place.

In the ensuing decade of military turmoil, Delft – unlike a number of other Dutch cities – had a charmed life. Leiden was besieged by a Spanish army for five months in 1574 and suffered terribly. Zeeland and the region of Utrecht were occupied for a time. But once again money was a factor: Spanish troops mutinied for lack of pay; Philip's royal exchequer was bankrupt. The northern provinces now had a chance to firm up their semi-independent position; a union of these provinces was agreed at Utrecht in 1579; and after that the religious divide – a Protestant-dominated north and a Catholic-dominated south – seemed as crucial as their geographical differences, with sea-water and river-water encircling and guarding the Dutch, while the Walloons, Brabanters, and Flemings went on sharing a long land boundary with the French. But neither side yet realised how fixed things were. The Spaniards took desperate measures to get at William. In 1580 he was denounced by Philip as 'chief perturber and corrupter of entire Christianity and especially of the Netherlands'. A reward of 25,000 crowns plus patents of nobility was offered to anyone who produced the rebel prince alive or dead.

In 1584 the war with Spain was sixteen years old. William was fifty-one and was living in St Agatha's, another of Delft's former convents (now called the Prinsenhof, after his stay there), on the Oude Delft across from the Oude Kerk. On Sunday 8 July, the Prince read the morning's dispatches in bed. They told of the death of the Duke of Anjou, who had been a likely French ally for the Dutch cause. The bearer of the disappointing dispatches, a man who claimed to be François Guion, son of a murdered Calvinist, was in reality a fervent Habsburg loyalist, Balthazar Gerard. He had been surprised to be allowed into the Duke's presence with his news, and was slow to act. But two days later, better prepared, Gerard was waiting on a staircase when the Prince came from his dining-room. Gerard fired several shots at him at point-blank range. The Prince, dying, exclaimed, 'Mon Dieu, mon Dieu, ayez pitié de moy et ce pauvre peuple!'*

Gerard was treated to a lingering execution: his right hand was burnt off with a red-hot iron; with pincers his flesh was torn from his bones in six places; his body was disembowelled and quartered; his no longer beating heart was pulled out; and finally his head was chopped off. The Habsburg reward was paid to his parents. Because of the Spanish occupation of Brabant, the Orange family mausoleum in Breda was inaccessible, and the Prince was buried on 3 August in the Nieuwe Kerk in Delft.

The assassination of William the Silent seemed in hindsight to mark a permanent division between north and south. Within a year the Duke of Parma, Philip's new commander, had confirmed his hold on the southern Netherlands and many dissident southerners had fled north, taking their skills and savings and energies with them. In the northern provinces the spirit of resistance was alive and increasingly buoyed up by commercial success. Perhaps seventy or eighty thousand Brabanters, Flemings, and Walloons came north, including half the population of Antwerp in the four years after it fell to Spain in 1585 and the Scheldt was closed by the Dutch to trading ships. Among the skilled workers from the south who came to Delft were weavers and potters and tile-makers. The city gave subsidies and temporary housing to the new traders. As we saw, Carel Fabritius's grandfather was one who came north. The maternal grandparents of Johannes Vermeer were from Antwerp. In 1609 the States-General concluded a truce with a financially exhausted Spain. At that semi-victorious moment, the States also decided to appease those more militant northerners who would have liked to go on fighting under the Orange banner. Although Prince William had already been commemorated in a thousand pamphlets and engravings, it was regarded as time to make a permanent monument for the founding father of the republic.

★

*He spoke in the court language which was French.

The man picked for the task was Hendrick de Keyser. He had started as a stonemason in Amsterdam but became a successful architect, the designer of the Zuiderkerk, the Westerkerk, and the Exchange in Amsterdam. He was also a sculptor, and the Prince's tomb was to be his masterpiece. De Keyser – forty-nine when work began on it in 1614 – borrowed some features from the tomb of Henri II and Catherine de' Medici at the Abbey of St Denis on the outskirts of Paris, with marble the main material and bronze statues at each corner. For the Nieuwe Kerk, de Keyser designed an opulent, canopied pavilion. On top of this structure was engraved a Latin epitaph in gold on a marble tablet. The epitaph praised the Prince as the 'Father of the Fatherland, who valued the prosperity of the Netherlands higher than his own interests or those of his family; who twice, and largely at his own expense, gathered powerful armies and led them into battle under the command of the States; who averted the tyranny of Spain, [and] brought back and restored the true religion and ancient laws'. Within the pavilion the Prince was shown twice in effigy. Alive, in bronze, he was seated on a throne, in armour, looking at once regal and paternal. Dead, in white marble, he lay in state, his loyal dog at his feet. It was said of this animal, a mastiff, that it refused food and drink after William's assassination, and thus died too.

Not satisfied with his double representation of the silent Prince, de Keyser placed in tall niches at the corners four life-sized statues, cast in bronze with the help of the Utrecht bell-founder van Meurs. These female figures personified Liberty, Justice, Religious Faith, and Fortitude – the Prince's attributes. A fifth figure, representing Fame, blew a trumpet over the recumbent effigy of the Prince. She was poised on the toes of her left foot like a ballet dancer, a pose which made for trouble when the immensely heavy statue came to be erected. Fame kept falling over, and remedial works took the monument's cost well above the large sum of 28,000 guilders budgeted for it.*

Hendrick de Keyser died a year before the tomb was completed in

---

*Fame, however, stood erect on tiptoe through the Thunderclap of 12 October 1654.

1624; it was finished by his son and his workshop assistants. As soon as they could, the townspeople of Delft came to bask in its rather florid glow. The citizens brought their wives and children and even their dogs. The visitors admired the black marble columns and obelisks. They noted how the four corner figures expressed the Prince's character. They read the inscribed mottoes: for instance, *Saevis tranquillus in undis* beside the statue of Fortitude, 'At peace amid the raging sea'. Among the Prince's heraldic devices was *Je Maintiendray*, with an emblem of two anchors showing that under his leadership the ship of state was twice as secure. In the floor nearby a stone lid with brass lifting rings gave entrance to the crypt where the Prince's coffin lay – and where, later, the bodies of most members of his House of Orange were to reside. Some visitors thought about the vanity of earthly pleasures (this was what Dirck van Bleyswijck in his *Description* of 1667 suggested they do at the tomb). Some reflected on the growing wealth and mercantile power of the country the Prince had helped bring into being – a prosperity manifest in this tomb – but also considered that even in relatively peaceful times life was risky, with any serious illness likely to snatch you away.

Tourists from abroad came, too, to gaze at the Prince's monument. A tour of Delft generally started with a visit to the Nieuwe Kerk and the Tomb, and might end at the Prinsenhof with a reverent look at the staircase wall pocked by the shot from Gerard's gun. The twenty-year-old Englishman John Evelyn came to Delft during a tour of the Netherlands in August 1641 and thought the monument was 'a piece of rare art'. But he went on to the Town Hall at the other end of the Market Place and seemed equally intrigued by the hollow wooden framework that an adulterous woman had to wear in public, with (so he wrote in his diary) 'her head coming out at the hole, & the rest hanging on her shoulders, as a penance for incontinency'.

In the half-century before the Thunderclap, while the fortunes of the House of Orange slowly waned and those of the States-General and the burgher-oligarchy gradually rose, the legend of William I had a seemingly independent life. Although some held against him his profitless attempts to get French backing for the struggle with Spain, and his failure to deliver a new nation made up of all seventeen provinces, his reputation prospered as warrior-father of the nation. The people of the northern provinces often saw themselves as the new Children of Israel, a chosen people; like the ancient Hebrews they had come out of slavery into freedom and William was *ons Moyses*, 'our Moses', and was so acclaimed by the poet Vondel:

> The one leads the Hebrews through the Red Sea flood,
> The other guides his people through a sea . . . of tears and blood.

William's immediate descendants were faced by the need for constant military action to justify their claim to the stadtholdership – a title which survived the break with the Habsburgs. Under Prince Maurice, William I's oldest surviving son and Stadtholder now of five of the seven United Provinces, the court and government of the northern provinces moved from Delft to The Hague. Prince Maurice reorganised the army, made up mostly of German mercenaries. By 1609 he had recovered much of the remaining land in the north that had been lost to the Spanish; the northern provinces went on controlling the River Scheldt, bottling up Antwerp and constricting the access of maritime trade to Brabant and Flanders.

The truce of 1609 annoyed Maurice; he would have liked to crown his military career by a knock-out blow against Spain. But in the internal struggle between the Stadtholder and the States of Holland, Maurice won several victories: Johan van Oldenbarneveldt, leading statesman of the province of Holland, was brought before a show-trial in 1619 and executed. Hugo Grotius, born in Delft, a distinguished writer on issues of war and peace and a proponent of patrician rather than absolute princely government, was imprisoned by the Orangist regime but escaped in a book-chest and had to flee the country.

Thereafter, however, the trend was towards government-by-regents, by members of burgher families, in an oligarchical arrangement that allowed the House of Orange only an occasional look-in. This caste was self-perpetuating at national, provincial, and municipal levels. The *herren*, 'lordships', as they called themselves, co-opted their fellow-burghers to vacancies on councils. It was not democratic but nor was it corrupt, by the European standards of the time. There was no ostentatious magnificence or conspicuous consumption. (The tomb of William I was probably the most extravagant thing in the United Provinces.) Instead there developed what came to be called 'regents' mentality', a rather high-and-mighty attitude among these gentlemen of seeming to know what was best for the country.

After the end of the Twelve Years Truce, besieged Bergen-op-Zoom was liberated and Breda recaptured, with consequent glory to the Prince of Orange. There were signal naval successes, too, such as in early January 1629, when the Delft-born Vice-Admiral Pieter Pieterszoon Hein, sailing on behalf of the Dutch West India Company, brought into the Zuider Zee a captured Spanish fleet of galleons from Mexico laden with silver plate and ships from Brazil carrying a costly cargo of sugar. It seemed that half the country went to Amsterdam to gawp at Spanish prisoners and cheer the heroic Dutch sailors. There was also a naval victory in 1639, when Spanish sea-power was cut down to size in the Battle of the Downs off the Kent coast. Admiral Maarten Tromp, another Delft man, with thirteen ships defeated seventy-seven Spanish vessels. (Tromp's victory was also – pleasantly for the Dutch – a blow to English pride, since it took place in English waters.)

After Spain was demoted from its position as number one enemy, other powers stepped into the ring. Britain and the United Provinces were increasingly competitors. This was so despite the close ties by marriage between the Houses of Stuart and Orange and despite the robust Protestantism that held sway in both countries, and at one point led Cromwell to propose they unite. English and Dutch ships vied for precedence through the narrow waters of the English Channel and in the North Sea. Their traders trod on each other's toes in the new worlds of Asia, Africa, and America. The stresses arising from these abrasive contacts produced naval wars three times in the century. The other international problem was France. That country under Louis XIV was keen to fill the vacuum left by Spain and to manipulate the ambitions of the Stuarts and the House of Orange. France wanted to control the Netherlands – to possess, if not all the provinces, then certainly the Habsburg southern provinces, which would make her the immediate neighbour of the United Provinces.

And yet these were pre-eminently Dutch times, at least for the first seventy years of the seventeenth century: the 'Golden Age'. The aspirations of a mere one and a half million people in the northern provinces, living on a small waterlogged chunk of land 60 miles square, brought into being a country that was for a short time the most powerful in the world. Roughly half of those people lived in two provinces, Holland and Zeeland, and most of that half in Holland, in a horseshoe of densely populated towns and intervening villages which easily communicated with one another by barge or carriage. A good deal of the country was at or just below sea-level, liable to flood if the north wind blew too long over the sea at high tide, and protected by dikes and river-banks, canals and drainage schemes that required constant investment and attention. Holland was a work of engineering science and practical art. Most Dutch people knew what it was to handle a spade for the purposes of rearranging earth and water. *Saevis tranquillus in undis.*

All kinds of industry thrived: shipbuilding; brick-making; grain-importing and -milling; thread-spinning and cloth-weaving; brewing; glass-blowing; pottery-baking and faience-glazing. Artists and scientists and religious thinkers were generally encouraged to fulfil their talents (though some went hungry as they did so).

For immigrants – for poor mechanics from Germany, Jewish merchants from Spain and Portugal, printers from England, weavers and pottery-workers from Flanders – the United Provinces seemed a freer place than those that they had left. Many Low Countries folk had their own memories of persecution which had encouraged their move to the north, where even under Spanish rule the apparatus of oppression had been less efficient. One English ambassador to The Hague, Sir William Temple, observed in 1673 how civil wars and religious troubles had helped to increase the swarm in this Country, not only by such as were persecuted at home, but great numbers of peaceable men, who came here to seek for quiet in their lives, and safety in their Possessions or Trades; like those Birds that upon the approach of a rough Winter season, leave the Countrys where they were born and bred, flye away to some kinder and softer Climate, and never return till the Frosts are past, and the Winds are laid at home.

English sailors served – for better pay – in Dutch fleets. English (and French and German) students studied at Dutch universities. There were nearly twenty English and Scottish religious communities in the Republic by 1632. A band of English Puritans found a refuge for eleven years in Leiden; although at first they had job difficulties because of guild restrictions, some became Leiden citizens. One, William Brewster, taught at Leiden University and published religious texts which annoyed James I when they were imported into Britain. However, the separatist Puritans eventually didn't like the free way of things in Holland; they found Dutch behaviour too loose, were disturbed by the hugs and kisses that Dutch parents gave their children, and feared that their adolescent sons would be corrupted by Dutch licentiousness. And they found Holland too welcoming, too absorbing: the Puritan elders were worried about losing their own English identity and concerned that if they stayed they might be unable to preserve their own Pilgrim Church. When they sailed for the New World in 1620, via England, they set off from Delfshaven, the harbour on the Maas near Rotterdam that, since the fourteenth century, had given Delft its own opening to the sea.

The intolerant Calvinism of the age often seemed toned down when filtered through the Dutch temperament. The country called the United Provinces was the first in Europe to stop persecutions for witchcraft – its last witch trial in 1610 ended in the women being acquitted. Jews poured in – Sephardim from Spain and Portugal, Ashkenazim from central and eastern Europe. Possibly because the Jews appeared to have a claim to be the real 'people of the Bible', probably because they were useful as bankers, traders, and jewellers, they were allowed more conspicuous rights to worship than, say, Catholics. Large synagogues were built. There were, of course, restrictions: Jews weren't supposed to try to convert Christians; Jewish men weren't allowed to marry Christian women; and they were barred from public office and guild membership; but there was no real ghetto in Amsterdam, where most Jews lived. Jewish scholarship flourished, though the Orthodox Jews sometimes found free-thinking Jewish colleagues hard to put up with. Baruch Spinoza, the philosopher who made lenses for a living, was excommunicated from his synagogue for heretical thoughts: he believed the universe was an organic entity in which God was expressed and that the Bible was a historical document intended only for the ancient Hebrews. But he recognised the merits of Holland and knew he had 'the rare felicity of living in a state where entire freedom of opinion prevails, where all may worship God in their own fashion, and where nothing is held sweeter, nothing more precious than such liberty'.

Despite the freer atmosphere, there was religious controversy enough. Catholicism was associated with the Spanish enemy, and for many the rejecting of Philip II meant the rejecting of the Mass. Most Protestants and Catholics were prepared to live alongside their brethren of the other religion (even while scorning their beliefs), but having taken over Catholic monasteries, convents, and churches, the Calvinist elect made it impossible for members of the old faith to hold responsible offices in state or town; to a less strict degree, the same constraints were placed on Lutherans, Mennonites, and more liberal Protestants. Indeed, there was a bitter long-lasting struggle between the right or Gomarian wing (named after Gomarus, a professor of theology at Leiden University) and the left or Arminian wing (named after Arminius, another professor of theology, also at Leiden) of the Protestant majority of the population. (This was a majority which, given that the Catholics were forced to worship in semi-secrecy and often went uncounted, may not have been large.)

Predestination was the matter of most dispute: did man have free will? Was he from the start marked as doomed or saved? Grotius and Vondel (a Catholic convert) chose the fall of Adam to illustrate this theme, as did John Milton, influenced by Vondel. For many Dutch, the fact that man must die meant an eternal afterlife of either heaven or hell. And yet during life many obviously took plenty of opportunity to work hard, enjoy themselves, and ignore the judgement to come. On the other hand, it was possible for some thoughtful individuals to subscribe to Calvin's doctrine that the individual counted for nothing. Sin and evil excited God's wrath – and brought on such catastrophes as plague, flood, and gunpowder explosions. The Delft Thunderclap was divinely ordained and nothing Cornelis Soetens had done or failed to do could have prevented it. Prayer might induce God to forgive us (only God could change His mind, it seemed). Men, and women, should repent of their corrupt state. On the surface, at least, a class divide was involved in this dispute. The liberal Arminians or Remonstrants (so-called after their 1610 Remonstrance to a Calvinist synod) attracted the more privileged members of society, and the stricter Gomarians recruited the less fortunate. Moreover, the Remonstrants seemed to favour States' rights and regent power, the narrow Calvinists to approve upholding the authority of the stadtholders, the princes of Orange. Consequently Prince Maurice removed certain burghers from the Delft city council because of their Remonstrant sympathies.

Even so, at least a third of the country, rich or poor, talented or hard-working, hung on to the old religion. The Catholics might be forced to hold their Masses in so-called 'hidden' churches, but hold their Masses they did. (As noted, Delft city council allowed Catholics to hold services in the Begijnhof chapel after the 1654 devastation.) The Calvinist elders eventually won the status of a state church for their faith but never achieved overall religious power: jewellery-wearing might be denounced from the pulpit, but women went on wearing pearls. And when Protestant religious disputes got in the way of money-making, those more interested in their livelihoods here-and-now took a firm anti-sectarian line. In 1632, the year Vermeer was born in Delft, the city of Amsterdam, the financial centre of Europe, decided that the Gomarian–Arminian conflict was hurting the conduct of business, and decreed that it should cease.

★

The Nieuwe Kerk – which in 1654 had been a Protestant church for the last eighty-two years – emerged from the aftermath of the explosion with glass restored, the panes now entirely clear and letting in a brighter light, its walls and pillars freshly whitewashed. Within, a pulpit had long replaced the altar as a focus of attention for worshippers; a long, dogmatic sermon provided the backbone of the service. Psalms were sung where the responses of Mass had once been said. Kneeling and genuflection were out, as was incense. Preachers used the Bible's texts to admonish their congregations to live the faith and eschew sin, all the while damning the Papists and other infidels. Churches went on being edifices within which people gathered, not only to worship but to meet and see one another, yet they had become places of instruction rather than sacramental celebration. But if high seriousness and austerity were the Calvinist keynotes, in the Nieuwe Kerk – at any rate on a sunny day – the tall windows let in the light, the white columns paraded in gleaming ranks, the brass candelabra called 'crowns' sparkled, and flags and banners hung in peaceful folds, unstirred by any breeze. The Tomb itself, the princely sarcophagus, furnished a fine object for the eyes as the preacher went on and on. The congregation could look at it as if it were an artistic cornucopia or as a splendid memento mori: we all come to this, though not so grandly.

The year 1648 had brought a sense of tremendous relief. Although there had been little fighting on the watery soil of the northern provinces for two generations, peace – at least with Spain – was now official. On the evening of 5 June bonfires were lit in every Dutch town and village. In Delft, fireworks sprayed light into the air, and a sixteen-year-old would-be artist was probably among the crowds that watched them. It was exactly eighty years since the Counts of Egmont and Hoorn – sent to negotiate Dutch grievances with the Spanish governors in Brussels – had been summarily executed. More recently, Maurice's younger brother, Prince Frederick Henry of Orange, had managed to regain territory in North Brabant and Limburg. In 1647 Frederick Henry's ambitious young son, Prince William II, had succeeded his father as Stadtholder. He wanted to revive William I's ideas of co-operating with France in order to bring the southern Netherlands back under Orange authority. He also hoped to help his Stuart brother-in-law Charles II recover his throne in England. But in Delft as in most of the main trading towns of Holland these policies were not popular. There had been enough fighting and expenses and therefore taxes arising from foreign wars. Those who live in a golden age want to keep it going, and not to rock the boat. William II, travelling around these towns in 1650 to rally supporters to his warlike cause, had got a cheerless reception. It was a filthy summer, with much wind and rain. William locked up six representatives of the States of Holland, including the member for Delft, in Loevestein Castle.* He sent an army of twelve thousand men to besiege Amsterdam and make that wealthy metropolis bow to the stadtholderate. But he was struck down by smallpox, and despite the best medical attention and remedies – clysters, lemon juice and sugar, beer, lard on the pox marks, decoctums and julep – he declined; at the end, on 24 November 1650, he gave a 'gentle hiccough' and died. He was twenty-four; his heir and namesake, William III, was born eight days later.

Three months afterwards William II's coffin was placed in the royal vaults under his grandfather's monument in the Nieuwe Kerk. The foul weather followed him, for his burial, late as it was, had to be put off a day because of downpours. Although all Delft then turned out to bid him farewell, the States had taken the chance to proclaim their power: the infant inheritor to the Orange dynasty was to have few of his ancestors' dignities. It was the beginning of a twenty-one-year period without a stadtholder.

And yet, even with no Orange prince at their head, with provincial rights (particularly those of Holland) paramount once more, many in the United Provinces felt something was missing. In Delft this was evident in the many houses in which portraits of a prince of Orange still hung, and in the number of artists to be found sketching in the

---

*It was at Loevestein Castle that Grotius had been imprisoned thirty-five years before and from which he had made his celebrated escape.

Nieuwe Kerk, the tomb of William I the focus of their attention. Local artists who painted it included Bartolomeus van Bassen, Gerard Houckgeest, Emanuel de Witte, Hendrick van Vliet, and Cornelis de Man, and sometimes their works were very similar. It was a time when painters often reused their own material, and borrowed subjects,

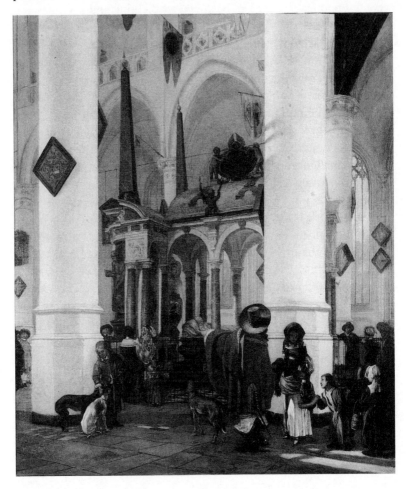

The Tomb of Prince Willem I in the Nieuwe Kerk, Delft, 1656, Emanuel de Witte.

themes, and compositions from their colleagues. No shame was incurred in what we might think of as being a copycat. There was no copyright. Painting was a co-operative as well as a competitive activity. In taverns, at meetings of the Guild of St Luke to which artists belonged, and in each other's studios, painters talked about what sorts of pictures seemed to be finding ready buyers. They sketched parts of each other's paintings. Of course, there was also an element of seeing if it was possible to perform the same theme better than a colleague. And perhaps taking a set subject off the shelf was a way of getting started on a picture if the artist didn't feel inspired before a blank canvas that morning. This was so in other art forms, too: Bredero's rambunctious play *The Spanish Brabanter* was closely based on a picaresque tale from Spain, *The Life of Lazarillo de Tormes*.

Most Dutch painters were prolific producers; to make a living, they had to be. In this respect, as in many others, Johannes Vermeer was an exception. Some thirty-five of his paintings have come down to us. Over the years a small but uncertain number of Vermeers have gone missing: a few recently, several early on. Not long after the gunpowder explosion an art-dealer named Johannes Renialme died in Amsterdam; he had registered with the Delft Guild of St Luke in 1644, no doubt knew Vermeer's father Reynier and his son, and was perhaps part of the movement of artists away from Delft that followed the Thunderclap. In the inventory of Renialme's possessions made after his death, which included paintings by the Delft painters Leonaert Bramer and Hendrick van Vliet, a painting was listed by 'Van der Meer' entitled *The Visit to the Tomb*. One scholar has recently suggested that the subject of this picture was in fact a 'Visit of the Three Holy Women to the Tomb of Christ', as described in St Mark's Gospel (16:1). Certainly by the mid-1650s Vermeer had painted at least one large canvas with a biblical subject and was later to paint one or two more that had religious overtones. But it seems at least a possibility that, in his formative period, Vermeer was drawn into a main current of Delft art and painted a church interior. In that case the Tomb in question might have been that of the Prince, in the Nieuwe Kerk, fifty yards from where the young artist was living.

3. *Calling on Vermeer*

In the summer of 1663, a distinguished fifty-two-year-old Frenchman from Lyons, Balthasar de Monconys, visited Delft on three occasions. Monconys had just come from England where he had met among others Thomas Hobbes, the political philosopher, Mr Reeves, Pepys's acquaintance, who constructed telescopes, and Henry Oldenburg, secretary of the Royal Society. Monconys had attended the society's proceedings with Constantijn Huygens, Dutch diplomat, poet, and scholar, now sixty-seven, who was, even more than Monconys, a man of trained taste and a passionate lover of the arts and sciences. Huygens had been the long-serving secretary to Prince Frederick Henry, a translator of John Donne's poems, an admirer of Rubens and also one of the first to recognise Rembrandt, actually going to call on the young genius and his fellow artist Jan Lievens in their home town of Leiden. Lievens had painted a portrait of Huygens when just over thirty, contemplative and dapper in moustache and goatee beard. Rembrandt had still been on the bottom rung of fame, but Huygens appreciated his ability to convey what he called 'liveliness of emotion'.

Monconys, schooled by the Jesuits, also had an inquiring if somewhat magpie mind. John Evelyn recalled in his diary that 'Monsieur Monconis, (that curious Traveller & a Roman Catholic) was by no means satisfied with the stigmata of those Nunns [whom he had met at 'Loudune' in France] because they were so shie of letting him scrape the letters [on their skin], which were Jesus, Maria, and Joseph.' On reaching Holland, Monconys went by barge from Rotterdam to Delft on 3 August; the canal was higher than the surrounding meadows and allowed the traveller a splendid view. The landscape was like the garden of a pleasure house, he wrote in his journal, the canals bordered by many little woods, the farmhouses solidly built, and many windmills turning, draining the land.

When he got to 'Delphe', as he called it, he was impressed by the regularity and straightness of the streets; the houses were more agreeable than those in Rotterdam because of the canals and trees in front of them. In the Oude Kerk he saw Maarten Tromp's monument and he visited the Nieuwe Kerk to pay his respects to William the Silent's tomb. He then travelled on to The Hague, which was to be his base for several weeks. There he met various dignitaries, including the French ambassador, got to see Huygens in his own home, and attended a service at which the sermon was given by Père Léon, a Brussels-born Carmelite priest, an eloquent preacher and chaplain at the French embassy. On 7 August Monconys went again to Delft by barge – the fare from The Hague was '2 sols par homme' – and visited the Town Hall. Then, on 11 August, after attending Mass at the French ambassador's, Monconys made a third trip to Delft, in company with Père Léon. Was he simply enchanted with the town or was there something or someone he hadn't yet managed to see? Was Père Léon taking advantage of Monconys's plans to visit the Jesuit priest Balthasar der Bekke, who had just been appointed to serve in Delft and was lodging near Vermeer's house in the Oude Langendijk? At any rate, on the evening of the 11th Monconys wrote in his journal:

> At Delft I saw the painter Vermeer, who had none of his works [to show us]. But we saw one of them at a baker's, who had paid six hundred livres for it, although it had only one figure in it – I would have thought it too costly at six pistoles.

This entry is tantalising. It is one of the few records of a meeting between a connoisseur interested in European art and the most elusive master of the time. If only Monconys, after tracking down Vermeer in his own haunts, had asked further questions and recorded the answers. If only he had let us know who had suggested he go to see

Vermeer – was it Huygens? – and why the recommendation had been made. If only Huygens had gone too, and given us his thoughts on Vermeer – though lively emotion was not Vermeer's strong suit. But why didn't someone tell Monconys the names and addresses of other people in Delft who might show him a Vermeer or two? Did Monconys ask the painter Vermeer why, as a professional artist, he had so few pictures to show? Hadn't he painted one recently? Was he hiding some, maybe didn't want to bring them forth for a foreigner, a Frenchman? It didn't seem very business-like. And what was the painting at the baker's with but a single figure? A woman in a blue dress reading a letter? A woman with a water pitcher? As for the alleged value of the picture Monconys saw and about which he got worked up, 600 livres was roughly 600 guilders – a lot of money but similar to what well-known Dutch artists could charge, as Monconys found out a few days later in Leiden, when Gerrit Dou asked that sum for a single-figure painting. Certainly six pistoles or sixty guilders wasn't at all a bad price for a small Vermeer. Hendrick van Buyten, the Delft baker who was probably the man Monconys went to see, later took two paintings by Vermeer as security for a debt of 617 guilders, owed by the Vermeer family for bread delivered. But unlike the painter, the baker van Buyten died wealthy, with a collection of fifty paintings, including one large painting by Vermeer in his front hall and two smaller pictures by him in an adjacent chamber.

As for Monconys, he had now done Delft; it was time to move on, to see other places and other rare objects. In The Hague he visited a Monsieur Vossius to look at his microscope, '*qui n'est q'une petite lentille faite en hémisphère enchaffée dans un petit bois*', and he said goodbye to Constantijn Huygens. In Amsterdam he examined the microscopes – 'tears of glass' – of Monsieur Hudd.

When Monconys finally got home to Lyons, he prepared his journal for publication. The first of its three volumes was brought forth in 1665, the year Monconys died, and it was plentifully illustrated with engravings showing pumping machines, fortifications, microscopes, and Orientals in turbans. It went through four editions in the next thirty years and was also published in a German translation. Fortunately Monconys was not to know the verdict of Larousse's *Grand Dictionnaire* (1874) on his *Voyages*: '*un ouvrage assez faible, rempli de recettes médicales et chimiques bizarres, et écrit dans un style lourd et diffus*'.

Nevertheless, we are grateful to the Frenchman for adding his fragment to what we know about Vermeer. It is a fairly negative fragment – 'no works to be seen' – but that is what we come to expect. We are glad of crumbs that may not show us the shape of the loaf but suggest the texture and taste of the bread. In large areas of Vermeer's life the facts are sparse or altogether missing: for instance, much of his youth, all of his apprenticeship. Absolutely nothing in the way of documents concerning him has turned up between the notice of his baptism in Delft in October 1632 and his betrothal in Delft in April 1653. He seems to have been very much a home town boy – in later years an infrequent traveller – but we don't know whether he left Delft to study with a master elsewhere in the Netherlands or abroad, or got his training in his birthplace. There are no known letters or writings by Johannes Vermeer other than signatures on paintings and a few legal declarations.

Dirck van Bleyswijck not only incorporated in his *Description of Delft* (published eight years before Vermeer's death) the Arnold Bon elegy to Carel Fabritius, that ends by lauding Vermeer, but included Vermeer at the end of a list of living Delft artists: Leonaert Bramer, Pieter van Asch, Adriano van Linschoten, Hans (Johannes) Jordaens, Cornelis de Man, and Johannes Vermeer. Samuel van Hoogstraten, who had known Fabritius and Delft, emphasised that he wasn't going to discuss living artists, and did not mention Vermeer in his *Inleyding* of 1678 although Vermeer had died three years before it was published – but he did discuss Frans van Mieris the Older of Leiden who was still alive. Arnold Houbraken, whose gossipy *Groote Schouburgh* of 1718–21 is the chief source-book for seventeenth-century Dutch painters, merely copies van Bleyswijck's list, drops the last stanza of Bon's poem to Fabritius, and makes no other reference to Vermeer. Renier Boitet, who in 1729 followed van Bleyswijck (sometimes word for word) in chronicling the history of Delft, also failed to print the last stanza of the Bon poem, though like van Bleyswijck he gave Vermeer a brief look-in as one of an even shorter list of Delft artists.

John Evelyn, travelling in Holland in 1641, went to an annual fair or market in Rotterdam and was amazed at the number of paintings for sale there, 'especially Landscips and Drolleries', several of which he bought and sent home to England; one drollery Evelyn acquired was by the Delft-born Christiaen van Couwenbergh, whose artistic execution he called 'excellent'. And Evelyn wrote in his Diary, in a famous passage, 'The reason for this store of pictures, and their cheapnesse[,] proceede[s] from their want of land, to employ their stock, so as 'tis an ordinary thing to find a common farmer to lay out two or three thousand pounds in this commodity, their houses are full of them, and they vend them at their Kermases to very great gains.' Paintings were found not only in Dutch homes but in breweries, lawyers' offices, town halls, guild and militia clubrooms, and almshouses.

The paintings filled a profound need. This had to do with what the twentieth-century historian Johan Huizinga in 1968 called the Hollanders' 'intense enjoyment of shapes and objects, the[ir] unshakeable faith in the reality and importance of all earthly things, a faith that . . . was the direct consequence of a deep love of life and interest in one's environment'. This faith in reality didn't necessarily manifest itself in down-to-earth forms. As Huizinga recognised, Vermeer's paintings, for example, had the reality rather of dreams, with figures whose 'actions are steeped in mystery', in settings 'where words have no sound and thoughts no form'.

The efflorescence of Dutch art at this time (like the great flowering of literature in England a century earlier) happened along with an up-welling of patriotic self-esteem. A nation had been founded and was now being consolidated. Much wealth circulated in a wider sphere than before. As the French painter and writer Eugène Fromentin noted during a tour of the Low Countries in 1875, in the seventeenth century there had been a bursting-forth of painters, even of great painters: 'They were born everywhere and all at once – at Amsterdam, at Dordrecht, at Leyden, at Delft, at Utrecht, at Rotterdam, at Enkhuizen, at Haarlem.' And they had a problem: 'Given a bourgeois people, practical, not inclined to dreams, very busy withal, by no means mystic, of anti-Latin tendency, with broken traditions, a worship without images, parsimonious habits – to find an art to please such a people, an art whose fitness should be apparent to them and which should represent them.' And Fromentin quoted Hippolyte Taine to the effect that such a people could do nothing but paint its own portrait.

The makers of this generally down-to-earth art were for the most part small tradesmen, working at their craft as integral members of a society of artisans and merchants and farmers and seamen; they bought each other's products or produce for need and pleasure. Paintings were to be seen in shops, inns, workshops, and markets; many were bought cheaply; some had been traded for wine, bread, peat, or rent. Among the painters, there were families like the van Mierevelds in Delft and the van Mierises in Leiden where painting ran for several generations, passed on from father to son to grandson as the natural way of making a living; and there were painters who rose from their artisan or petit-bourgeois background to take up a paint-brush instead of a cobbler's last or a miller's flour-sack or an innkeeper's barrel. Rembrandt's father was a miller; his brothers were a baker and a shoemaker. It was exceptional when an artist achieved the fame and fortune that Rembrandt did, early on. Twenty guilders was a good price for a picture at a time when the wages of a Delft cloth-worker were, as noted, less than one guilder a day, and half of that went on bread. An artist had to paint a lot of pictures to stay ahead of the debt collectors. Most painters thought of themselves as craftsmen and the guild they generally belonged to, as in Delft, was one to which artisans and middle-men in other crafts and trades belonged. Church patronage was a thing of the past and really splendid private commissions were most often from abroad; the royal courts, say, in England or Denmark. Gerrit Dou had a retainer of 500 guilders a year from the Danish ambassador to The Hague. Houbraken thought it worth remarking that Michiel van Miereveld, the eminent Delft portraitist, got 150 guilders for some of his paintings; but then Miereveld had notable patrons, including Elizabeth, Queen of Bohemia, and several members of the House of Orange, who liked his matter-of-fact pictures. (The German writer Joachim von Sandrart reported that Miereveld painted over 10,000 portraits, but that was probably a studio or workshop total.) Adriaen Brouwer, the Flemish artist who worked in Holland for part of his short life (1605–38), was thrilled on one occasion to receive 200 guilders for a picture. When he got home, he poured the money on his bed and rolled among the silver pieces. Then, Houbraken said, he spent most of it overnight and felt relieved that he had 'rid himself of all that ballast'.

Some artists like Jan Steen and Gerard Houckgeest had income from breweries. Jan van de Capelle owned a cloth dyeing-works. Philips Koninck bought a canal shipping business. Many painters were happy to take up other better-paying jobs or to marry well. Meyndert Hobbema seems to have become a part-time painter in 1668 when he married the maid of an Amsterdam burgomaster and was given a well-rewarded post as wine-gauger, a sort of weights-and-measures inspector. Ferdinand Bol and Aelbert Cuyp both married wealthy women and could afford to paint less. Yet many artists, even the greatest, found it hard to sell their work for enough money and went through the ordeal of insolvency: among them were Jan van Goyen, who died in 1656; Frans Hals, who died in 1666; and Rembrandt, who died in 1669. Some, like Brouwer, Hals, and de Witte, turned to drink. Hals was usually 'filled up to his neck with drink every night', Houbraken tells us. De Witte, dreadfully poor at the last, was found drowned in an Amsterdam canal, and presumed a suicide.

But it was also possible for a painter to have connections with members of the regents' class or the House of Orange, and to get profitable commissions: to work, say, on decorating Prince Frederick Henry's Huis ten Bosch with biblical canvases, as Gerard Honthorst and the Delft painter Christiaen van Couwenbergh did; to have an aristocratic clientele like Michiel van Miereveld; or to be invited to the Stuart court like van Miereveld and Hals (who both refused to go) and Cornelis Poelenburg and Daniel Mytens (who both accepted). Although the painters were craftsmen, some had begun to think of themselves as something more, as artists, as something special. Rembrandt dressed himself up for a self-portrait as a Venetian nobleman. In some places they eventually weren't satisfied with being in a guild together with other artisans, and set up on their own, the way the painters in Dordrecht did in 1642, forming a separate 'college'. There were now books about painters – Karel van Mander's, for example, published in 1604, or Arnold Houbraken's a century later – that honoured artists by devoting hefty volumes to their lives and achievements.

In Delft, the Guild of St Luke – founded in 1611 – was an association of workers from eight crafts or trades: faience-makers, printers, bookbinders, glassmakers, embroiderers, art-dealers, sculptors, and painters. The first-century evangelist St Luke, their patron saint, was said by St Paul to have been a physician and was therefore patron of doctors and surgeons. At some point in the middle ages St Luke was given credit for painting a portrait of the Virgin Mary, and thus for kick-starting the practice of making religious images, and was adopted by painters as their patron, too. To become a member of the guild an aspiring worker had to satisfy various conditions. He had to serve a long apprenticeship, generally of six years though it could be shorter if he produced a work – a master piece – proving his skills. The would-be artist-member had to be a resident of Delft and pay an *incomstgelt*, 'entrance fee': twelve guilders for those born outside Delft, six guilders for natives, and three guilders for the son of a master who was already a member of the Delft guild. The annual dues were six stuivers. It is unclear whether Delft's guild had any women members, though in Haarlem the painter Judith Leyster was a member of that city's guild, and Anna Maria Schurman – an advocate of women's learning, a glass-engraver and portrait painter – belonged to the guild in Utrecht. In Delft, the six guild members chosen to be headmen for two-year terms had the responsibility of calling monthly meetings, registering new masters and taking note of apprentices, administering the guild's finances, and seeing the rules were obeyed. Roughly a third of the guild's income was devoted to the needs of poor members and their families. Fines could be levied on non-members and outsiders producing art for sale in Delft. A painter wasn't allowed to sign his pictures until he became a master.

It was a time when surnames were not yet general and hadn't absolutely stuck; place-names and nicknames were part of the method of telling people one from another and were becoming part of their identification. Rembrandt had been Rembrandt Harmenszoon before he added the 'van Rijn' after his birthplace, his father's mill, de Rijn, in Leiden, near the River Rhine. Johannes Vermeer's father, Reynier Janszoon ('the son of Jan'), seems to have first acquired the surname Vos, meaning 'fox', through a process that apparently jumped from his *voornaam* in stages: Reynier, Reynard, Vos. Women also had patronymics; for example, Vermeer's paternal grandmother was Cornelia Gregorisdochter, which was often shortened to Neeltge Goris; and such names survived marriages. At any rate, Vermeer's father seems to have used both Vos and Van der Minne, the name of his stepfather Claes, a musician, before settling on Vos and then – by September 1640 – moving on to Vermeer, a surname his younger brother Anthony had adopted fifteen years before and which was used thereafter by Reynier's children Gertruy and Johannes.

Reynier's father – Johannes Vermeer's paternal grandfather – had been a tailor. After the tailor's death Reynier's mother married a second husband, Claes, the musician; her third husband was a ship's carpenter. She made a living as a dealer in second-hand goods, clearing out houses after their occupants died, and also by selling bedding and promoting lotteries. (She died in 1627.) Vermeer's father, Reynier, was sent as a youth to Amsterdam to learn the craft of making caffa, a fairly costly silk-satin damask material. While there, in 1615, he married a young woman called Digna Balthens, who came from Antwerp; the minister who married them was Calvinist. They had their first child, a daughter named Gertruy, in 1620.

Back home in Delft Reynier's career blossomed, although in 1625 there was a slight setback when he took part in a brawl in which a soldier was wounded. Blood-money had to be paid. The soldier – who eventually died – seems to have absolved his fellow brawlers of any blame for his injuries, and there was no prosecution of the participants. (A Dutch saying of the time was 'A hundred Hollanders, a hundred knives'.) Reynier in any event marched on, developing a secondary livelihood as an innkeeper or 'tapster', which at least enabled him to turn a penny from Dutch drinking habits. In February 1629 he, Digna, and Gertruy were living in an inn on the Voldersgracht called *De Vliegende Vos*, 'The Flying Fox'; it seems to have taken its proprietor's name. The Voldersgracht was a little canal, just north of the Market Place, named after the fullers who had used its water in making the whitening material called fuller's earth.

The inn was several doors away from the Old Men's House, an almshouse whose former chapel, afterwards a tanning workshop, some thirty years later was to be converted into the new hall of the St Luke's Guild. In 1631, when he was about forty, Reynier registered with the guild as an art-dealer. With so many painters scurrying to meet the demand for pictures, middle-men came on the scene who could play the market, build up a stock, and advise those who wanted to buy pictures but had uncertain tastes. Running a pub, with plenty of wall-space in need of decoration, and perhaps with many artists among its customers, may have led Reynier into the art trade. It was at the Flying Fox in 1632 that Digna – now thirty-seven – gave birth to their second child, a son named Joannis. In the register of the Nieuwe Kerk, his baptism is recorded as taking place on 31 October.

Vermeer was not an uncommon name. It was sometimes spelled out in documents by notaries and public officials as 'van der Meer', meaning 'from the lake', though neither Reynier nor his son favoured this form. Much later in 1667, witnessing a legal document in which he was referred to as 'Johannes van der Meer, artful painter', the son signed 'Johannes Vermeer'. In 1670, regarding the division of Reynier and Digna's estate, the lawyer Frans Boogert first wrote their son's name as 'Johannes van der Meer' before crossing out 'van der Meer'

and writing above it 'Vermeer'. There were or recently had been quite
a few other van der Meers in Delft including an apothecary, a
physician, and a schoolmaster, and, as we shall see later, several artists
in the United Provinces had that surname, and some of them even had
the same Christian name as Johannes, which would cause confusion.
When signing documents, Vermeer after 1657 switched from using
the old Gothic script to the more modern Roman script. His
preference after his marriage for spelling his first name Johannes
rather than Joannis, as he was baptised, may have been an indication
that he wanted to feel, in that respect, too, in tune with the times.

As far as Johannes Vermeer is concerned, the document-free twenty
years or so between baptism and betrothal might be considered a
blank for biographical research. But is it? We know the boy had a
sister twelve years older, Gertruy, who presumably helped keep an
eye on him while their mother Digna worked in the Flying Fox. All
his grandparents were dead, though his mother's stepmother Beatrix
Gerrits was recorded as applying for the post of town midwife in
Gorinchem, 40 miles to the south-east of Delft, a few months before
Vermeer was born. His mother's brother, Reynier Balthens, a military
contractor, and his father's sister Maertge (one of the three witnesses
at his baptism), sometimes called at the Flying Fox. Growing up in
the Voldersgracht, in a small inn, was to be from the start close to the
heart of Delft. From his early years he was aware of a constant flow of
people, of talk that was genial, humorous, now and then angry, of
tobacco smoke and fireplace smoke, of doors and windows closed
against the winter cold or open in summer when the sun bounced off
the surface of the little canal, and the backs of the houses on the north
side of the Market Place threw long shadows; he had a private world,
one suspects, in which the sun and shadow were his best companions.

Delft was a beer town; few streets lacked an inn or two. Delft beer
was said to be as strong as wine. The process of brewing required
cleanliness and Delft was a notably clean place in a country where
domestic cleanliness was the highest virtue. Yet the great age of Delft
breweries had passed. In the previous century the town had had a

country-wide reputation for its beer but in this period the number of breweries had declined with more competition from other towns and loss of markets in the southern provinces; because of this, the city's tax assessment from the States-General had been reduced in 1612. Even so, in 1617 the English traveller Fynes Moryson claimed that Delft had 300 breweries, certainly enough for its twenty-five thousand people. As we saw, one brewery on the east side of the Pontemarket was that called the World Turned Upside-Down, in which Carel Fabritius painted a mural; the widow who owned the brewery removed the mural when she sold the establishment in 1660. The quantity of beer Delft drinkers put away was said to be 250 litres a year per head of population, and if the city's children were left out of the reckoning, the quantity per head was all the greater: a good deal of Dutch courage. A hangover was the inevitable day-after condition for those attending family parties, weddings, or funerals. A large tankard or *vaan* containing roughly a litre or a quart cost about two stuivers, a tenth of a guilder. Beer was drunk at all times of day, from breakfast on, in inns with such names as the Serpent, the Golden Mill, the Young Prince, the Target, and the Three Hammers. The latter was a pub in the Small Cattle Market where Vermeer's paternal grandmother, Neeltge Goris, had lived with her second husband, Claes Cortiaenszoon van der Minne. Some inns served clienteles drawn mostly from foreign residents who had been attracted by the town's prosperity: for instance, the Delft English House, the French House, or the Scotch Arms. An inn called Mechelen that stood on the corner of the Market Place and the Oudemansteeg, an alley that went through to the Voldersgracht, would have attracted by its name – that of a town in the southern Netherlands – immigrants from those parts. (Many Dutch patriots would recall Mechelen as the place where in 1572 Spanish soldiery had invaded a convent and raped Catholic nuns.)

Some inns were respectable, some were brothels. Visitors were now and then unable to tell which was which. According to the English traveller William Mountague, one party of English on their first trip abroad landed at Den Briel and went to an inn where they 'immediately fell to kissing and feeling the maids, which is not so customary here as at home'. Inns were also establishments where deals were done and business disagreements ironed out to the accompaniment of the shout 'Another round, landlord'.

Legal records tend to deal with financial, civil, and criminal difficulties and therefore can give a warped picture of a person's life if those documents provide the bulk of the evidence about him. Many of the records that have been found concerning Reynier Vos Vermeer have to do with debts but they also indicate that a number of his inn's customers – among them ships' captains, doctors, and military men – were artists. In 1631 a soldier put up at the Flying Fox while waiting for his ship to sail to the East Indies; he was a son of a flower painter from The Hague named Jan Baptista van Fornenburgh. Young Barent van Fornenburgh died abroad, apparently still owing Reynier money. In 1635 Reynier himself owed 202 guilders to Hester van Bleyswijck, a 'breweress', and in 1638 he owed nearly five guilders to the estate of a merchant selling turf – that is, peat; the curator of the estate was the well-known Delft painter Anthony Palamedes, who had married a daughter of the fuel dealer. Some of Reynier's debts were of long duration, including the eighty-two and a half guilders he owed to the brewer Johan Croeser in 1645, a bill still unpaid in 1660. On the other hand, he paid some debts promptly enough, such as money owed for brandy in 1626 and for silk-yarn, no doubt for caffa-weaving, in 1629–30.

Early on Reynier seems to have acquired a stock of paintings, possibly through his wife Digna; the pictures may have been left to her by her father, who died between 1628 and 1632. Digna's father, Balthasar Gerrits, originally from Antwerp, had an enterprising life. He began in Amsterdam as a lighterman or stevedore before becoming a merchant's clerk. He then developed skills as a clockmaker and metal-worker and this expertise led him – and his son Balthens – into deep trouble in the early 1620s in The Hague, where he worked as the diemaker for a group who were arrested for counterfeiting German coins. The senior parties in this scam were beheaded. Balthasar Gerrits and Reynier Balthens were interrogated by the authorities but gave evidence against their employers and were eventually released without charge; whether they were ever free of nightmares after their close brush with the executioner's sword is doubtful. There was another complicated but apparently legal transaction in 1623 between Balthasar Gerrits and his son-in-law Reynier that gave the impression of transferring goods, some of which were pictures, from Reynier to Balthasar and may have masked the repayment by Balthasar of money to Reynier, for the son-in-law's help during the diemaker's recent troubles. The paintings – appraised at the time by an occasional still-life painter named Joris van Lier – were a motley bunch, including still-lifes of flowers and fruit, four portraits of members of the House of Orange, a brothel scene, a night scene, several landscapes, two biblical pictures, and two family portraits, presumably of Reynier Vermeer and his wife Digna. Some of these pictures were still in the possession of their son Johannes Vermeer in 1675.

Like many of his contemporaries, Vermeer therefore grew up in a house with many pictures on the walls. But possibly the pictures were all the more influential for him because the Flying Fox attracted many artists who came to drink, eat, or talk shop there with his father. In early 1641, however, the lease on the Flying Fox ran out, and Reynier Vermeer bought the bigger inn Mechelen, less than a hundred yards away on the Market Place. Johannes was nine and a half when they moved. Mechelen had six fireplaces – a measure of its size – and cost 2,700 guilders; the downpayment was 200 guilders, and the rest was covered by two loans: a Haarlem brewer put up 2,100 guilders and a Delft man 400 guilders. Reynier's annual mortgage payment of 125 guilders was less than the rent he had been paying on the Flying Fox.

At Mechelen, too, artists and art-trade craftsmen such as framers were part of the clientele. Among the painters who dropped in were Evert van Aelst, Egbert van der Poel, and Leonaert Bramer. When Reynier Vermeer couldn't get paid in cash, he bartered: frames were accepted for food and drink consumed at the inn, and pictures may have been taken in trade in the same way for his art-dealing stock. Mechelen also put up lodgers. In 1651 Reynier sued a former guest at Mechelen, a would-be painter named Reynier van Heukelom, who had moved to The Hague but still owed him 126 guilders. Life in the inn or Reynier's art business may also have brought about the meeting of his daughter Gertruy and Antony van der Wiel, a Delft ebony-worker and frame-maker; in 1647, when she was twenty-seven and her brother Johannes was fifteen, Gertruy and Antony were married and went to live in a house called 'De Molen' in the Vlamingstraat, east of the Nieuwe Kerk.

Because of the age gap between him and his sister, Johannes Vermeer was something of an only child, possibly favoured, even spoilt. He may have retreated from the noisy hurly-burly of inn life into a world of his own. Or he may now and then, like a proper Dutch boy, have been sent out to play with the neighbouring children: to hit balls with *kolf* sticks, float bits of wood in the canal, and go fishing. According to his exact contemporary, the draper-turned-scientist Antony van Leeuwenhoek, writing some years later, Delft was 'very well off for water, and in summer we get fresh water into the town . . . from the River Maas; wherefore the water within the town is very good, and river-fish are caught every day by children with fishing rods in the waterways inside the town'. For a boy, it was interesting to watch and even pester boatmen on the canals as they hauled their craft along and loaded or unloaded cargoes. The market place with its stalls and barrows was a close-at-hand source of fascinating activity. There were fairs such as the spring kermess, with side-shows and performers. On St Nicholas Eve, 5 December, the young Vermeer might have gone to the baker's shop to decorate gingerbread, long since restored to favour after a ban on gingerbread-baking in 1607 at the behest of Calvinist ministers; going to bed that night he would leave out a shoe and next morning look to see what the good saint had left for him; a bad child got a cane to be spanked with, a good child got sweets and toys such as a catapult, marbles, or a sort of drum called a *rommelpot*. A month later, on Twelfth Night, 6 January, children paraded through Delft carrying paper stars, knocking on doors for cakes and small coins. In summer there was the River Schie to swim in; in winter, after watching the Voldersgracht and other canals turn pewter-grey and at last gleaming smooth, the people of Delft knew the ice would be hard enough and they could skate freely, though the low bridges in town were closely spaced and the Schie or a flooded meadow was needed for real exhilaration.

And then there was school. At four, the infant school in a nearby house where Vermeer might have got early instruction in the ABCs; on grounds of expense and no real need for it, not all Dutch children were taught how to read and write, but his father could afford it. First with chalk on a slate, then with a quill on paper Vermeer would have copied words from a primer-board. He learned the Ten Commandments and the Lord's Prayer. At seven he probably moved on to a school where arithmetic and the Bible were studied. At twelve, there was the possibility of Latin school: calligraphy, classical studies, sacred history. In the Voldersgracht a portrait painter named Cornelis Daemen Rietwijck ran a small academy that might have served in this way for young Johannes Vermeer, teaching him, among other things, more advanced mathematics and drawing. There he would have been close enough for a fast run home avoiding gangs of bullies who now and then staged battles with cudgels and sticks or pushed smaller boys into a canal. A notable battle took place in 1633 between the boys of Rotterdam and Delfshaven on a dike where they threw 'stones very violently at each other, making holes in the head'.

With an art-dealer for a father and his sister married to a frame-maker, and with artists in and out of Mechelen, Johannes Vermeer's future career may already have seemed ordained. Talent and inclination would have made themselves apparent by his early teens. When he was thirteen or fourteen, and there could have been parental debate about what craft Johannes should be apprenticed to, there was probably no dispute at all: the main question was which master he should serve his time with, and where. Cost may have been a factor here. Rembrandt charged one of his first pupils, Isaak de Jouderville, the fairly high sum of fifty guilders for six months' tuition. But with young Vermeer we are in the dark in this respect. There are no deeds of indenture, no receipts for fees as in de Jouderville's case. The usual thing was to start a boy's training locally, as Rembrandt himself did in Leiden with the architectural painter Jacob van Swanenburgh. In

Delft and its vicinity there were painters enough and Reynier
Vermeer knew many of them. There was Anthony Palamedes, for
example, who in 1640 had taught painting and drawing to the son of
the ebony importer Gillis Verboom; Verboom used to eat and drink at
the Flying Fox. There was the flower painter Jan Baptista van
Fornenburgh, from The Hague, who had come to Delft a few years
before to call at the offices of the East Indies Company and ask about
the back-pay owed his now dead son. The witnesses to a deposition
and receipt on that occasion were the painters Pieter Groenewegen,
Balthasar van der Ast, and Pieter van Steenwijck – and the innkeeper
and art-dealer Reynier Vermeer. Van der Ast and Steenwijck did
still-lifes – van der Ast specialised in groups of flowers or sea-shells –
while Groenewegen, who had studied in Rome and now worked in
The Hague and Delft, was a landscape painter. Another candidate for
the role of teacher might be Evert van Aelst, a Delft painter of
modestly priced still-lifes who happened to owe some money to
Reynier Vermeer and had earlier left a painting with him to sell. Van
Aelst had taught Emanuel de Witte and Adam Pick, and he owed for
food and drink in pubs other than Mechelen. There was also a
borrower–lender relationship between Reynier Vermeer and Cornelis
Saftleven of Rotterdam, whom Reynier owed for some paintings.
Among other putative masters in Delft for young Vermeer was the
renowned Leonaert Bramer, fifty years old in 1646, who had worked
in Italy and was now much in demand for murals, though his agitated
style of drawing and fondness for small figures in dark or torch-lit
surroundings made no evident impact on Vermeer. On the other
hand, Bramer was the most distinguished artist in Delft and had done
a still-life of musical instruments that probably provides a point of
departure for some of Vermeer's later pictures which have similar
instruments in them. Moreover, Bramer – along with van Aelst –
appeared as a witness for a deposition made by Digna Balthens before
a notary in 1653, which speaks for his closeness to the Vermeer family.
And when Vermeer got married in that same year, Bramer, as we shall
see, was a witness to a declaration by his mother-in-law-to-be that she
agreed to the marriage banns being registered.

In the vacuum of evidence, many Delft painters have been mentioned as possible teachers for Vermeer. The list includes both lesser-known and well-known artists. Hendrick van der Burgh has been put forward, a middle-aged member of the Delft Guild of St Luke from 1649 to 1654. Carel Fabritius has also been a popular nominee: his tragic death made necessary an heir to his talent, and the Arnold Bon elegy certainly links him with Vermeer, rising phoenix-like from Fabritius's fire. Arriving in Delft in 1650, Fabritius would have been able to pass on expertise about creating perspective and rendering light, and various bits of knowledge learned in Rembrandt's studio; but Fabritius didn't register with the Delft guild until October 1652, and shouldn't have taken on pupils before then. That he influenced Vermeer and perhaps advised him seems likely if one compares the bare plaster walls of, say, *The Goldfinch* by Fabritius and *The Milkmaid* by Vermeer. Also suggested for the role of master is Paulus Potter, the short-lived landscape and animal painter, mostly connected with The Hague, but a member of the Delft guild for several years after 1646.* In 1647 he painted his famous life-size *Bull*, but a more vibrant expression of a sunny day in the countryside is his *Great Farm* of 1649, which lets the viewer glimpse through the doorway a woman seated inside the farmhouse; de Hooch if not Vermeer has a predecessor here. In a sense all painting is about the handling of light but Potter, like Fabritius, made daylight natural and life-giving and Vermeer could have learned lessons from both men.

The nitty-gritty of apprenticeship was hard work, hard work, hard work. In one indenture agreement of those times, printed by Dr W. Martin, a seventeen-year-old named Adriaen Carmen became a pupil of Isaac Isaaczoon of Amsterdam. Carmen had to live in his master's house, prepare the colours, stretch canvases, provide his own bed and bedding, and be industrious and obedient. For his part, Isaaczoon agreed to provide his apprentice with food, drink, and lessons in painting. Carmen was allowed to paint one picture a year for his own profit. Carmen's father was to give Isaaczoon a barrel of herrings or

---

*Potter died in 1654, aged thirty.

cod every year. The lessons that interspersed the chores were outlined
in Karel van Mander's *Het Schilderboek* of 1604. The master should
be able to teach the pupil how to compose, sketch, shade, and work up
neatly with charcoal, chalk, or pen. Neatness in drawing with stump
or pastels was acquired by copying prints and drawings the master
owned, and by drawing from plaster casts; Samuel van Hoogstraten
recalled that Rembrandt – to whom he was apprenticed in the 1640s –
owned not only heads and limbs taken from antique sculpture but
plaster eyes, noses, mouths, and ears. And then, and always, there was
cleanliness. Van Mander told the aspiring artist: Remember to keep a
clean brush and a clean palette so that you achieve a proper finish. And
above all keep dust off your painting while it is drying. All the while,
until the would-be artist produced a 'master piece' and could become
a guild member, his work belonged to the master, could even be
signed by him and sold as his; an apprentice's best way of getting his
own back – not mentioned by van Mander – was to eat and drink as
much as he could, as did two pupils of the Leiden still-life painter
David Bailly. Bailly complained that young Pieter and Harmen van
Steenwijck ate so heartily and did so little work in his house that he
made no profit out of them.

If young Vermeer served his apprenticeship locally, the cost would
have been about fifty guilders a year, half what Jouderville paid
Rembrandt, but quite enough for those paying it if they were living on
credit, the way Reynier and Digna most often were. The costs would
have risen considerably if, after several years of pupilage in Delft,
living at home, he went away for the last three or four years. When at
the end of 1653 Vermeer came to register with the Delft Guild of St
Luke, he was charged six guilders as an entrance fee instead of the
half-rate of three guilders one would have expected for the son of a
guild member and the possible apprentice for at least two years with
a Delft guild painter. Perhaps the young artist did not get the
concessionary rate because Reynier – albeit a long-serving member of
the guild – wasn't a professional painter, merely a dealer, or because
Reynier at this point had just died. Or was the six guilders due because
Johannes was considered as someone who had studied out-of-town?

In that case, where did he go? Leonaert Bramer may have advised a study trip to Italy and certainly several of Vermeer's early paintings have an Italianate, particularly a Caravaggesque, quality. One that has been ascribed to him is the *St Praxedis* (see p. 64), a near copy of a painting by the Florentine artist Felice Ficherelli (1605–*c*. 1669). Vermeer could have seen the original in the Netherlands, whether in the United Provinces or the southern ones, or even at a Delft art-dealer's such as Johannes Renialme's, or possibly on its home ground in Italy. But there is no hard evidence that Vermeer went to Italy, unlike his Utrecht namesake Johan van der Meer, whose Italian stay is recorded by Houbraken. The Italian influence on our Vermeer may have come second-hand. A local artist – other than Bramer – who could have provided this was Christiaen van Couwenbergh, whose *Woman holding a Basket of Fruit* (1642) depicts a full-breasted woman carrying a fruit basket in one hand while with her other hand she holds back a heavily brocaded curtain.*

The Dutch city in which Italian influence in painting was most evident was Utrecht – some thirty miles (fifty km) from Delft as a crow flies but longer by the waterways on which the *trekschuits* navigated. Couwenbergh, if no one else, might have pointed Vermeer in that direction and in that of his artist-hero, Gerrit van Honthorst, born in Utrecht in 1590. Honthorst had studied with an older Utrecht master, Abraham Bloemaert, who in his long life taught many up-and-coming local artists including Hendrick Terbrugghen and Cornelis Poelenburgh. Bloemaert was still active. Utrecht had been a very Catholic city, the home town of the sixteenth-century pope Adrian VI; and even now, with Roman Catholics and their religious practices semi-suppressed, it remained sympathetic to the old faith. Abraham Bloemaert, eighty-four in 1648, would make a serious if elderly contender for the title of Vermeer's teacher – or one of his

---

*Houckgeest and de Witte were other Delft artists who liked to insert such *trompe-l'oeil* draperies in their pictures, mimicking the curtains that in Dutch households were often pulled across paintings to shield them from direct sunlight. Vermeer also indulged in these deceptive features, which could be useful compositionally; six of his paintings were to have such curtains in them.

teachers – though not a jot of written evidence links them as master and pupil. However, other facts create a network that at least brings them together.

By April 1653, two years after Bloemaert's death and seven months before Vermeer himself registered as a master in the St Luke's Guild in Delft, Vermeer had got to know Catharina Bolnes. Catharina's mother, Maria Thins, was a well-to-do Catholic lady from Gouda, a town a little less than halfway between Delft and Utrecht. She was legally separated from her irascible brick-maker husband Reynier Bolnes and had been living in Delft since 1641, first on the Vlamingstraat and then on the Oude Langendijck in a house bought by her cousin Jan Geenszoon Thins. This cousin was a friend and, through marriage, a relative of Bloemaert's. When J.G. Thins got married for the second time in 1646 at the age of sixty-six, his new bride was Susanna van de Bogaert, already twice a widow, whose first husband's sister was Bloemart's wife. Susanna's former sister-in-law brought the old artist to the wedding, where Bloemaert signed the marriage contract as a family member. At some point J.G. Thins was to give his daughter Lucia a Nativity painting by Bloemaert. As for Maria Thins, she brought to Delft a number of school-of-Utrecht paintings: Dirck van Baburen's *The Procuress* of 1622 was one; another was a 'Roman Charity' painting, showing Cimon, starved in jail, being fed from the breast of his daughter Pero, and was probably by Delft-born Christiaen van Couwenbergh. Both pictures were to appear on several occasions in the backgrounds of paintings by Johannes Vermeer. Moreover, Vermeer's own painting called *The Procuress* of 1656, an original treatment of this traditional subject, has struck many art historians as Bloemaert-influenced.

Other cities have been put forward as places where Vermeer might have served part of his apprenticeship. Montias likes the idea of the young man studying with a master in Amsterdam, one reason being that his father had learned the craft of caffa-weaving there in 1611 and might therefore have suggested to his son that he go to the energetic, commercially and artistically vital metropolis. Perhaps the success seemingly endemic in the golden swamp would rub off on him. Moreover, two large early paintings of Vermeer's, *Diana and her Companions* (see p. 74) and *Christ in the House of Martha and Mary* (see p. 78), show the effect of two painters who at that time were in Amsterdam: Jacob van Loo, who did big mythological and religious scenes, including a very similar *Diana and her Nymphs* of around 1650; and Erasmus Quellinus the Younger, an Antwerp painter who was working on a painted ceiling in the new Town Hall shortly after 1650, and whose own *Christ in the House of Martha and Mary* must have been seen by the young Vermeer – though possibly, as we shall see in a moment, the viewing took place in Antwerp.

Yet two other places should also be considered as likely bases for the apprentice painter. Brussels, in the southern Netherlands, was not at all in the limelight now; in 1650 it was a very provincial capital, the seat of the viceroy for the Habsburg court; after a period of Austrian overlordship, the southern provinces were back under the rule of Philip IV of Spain. But it is worth recalling the southern connections of Vermeer's family. His mother's parents had lived and married (in 1596) in Antwerp. Caffa-weaving had been promoted in Delft by Flemish incomers, and Reynier Vermeer presumably knew many silk- and satin-weavers from the south. Although much of the economic vitality of that region had been sucked out of it by then, the southern provinces were still home for many people of culture and inherited wealth, some of whom were picture collectors. It may be significant that two paintings by the Italian Domenico Fetti, the *Parable of the Labourers in the Vineyard* and the *Parable of the Lost Silver* (both 1618–22), were sold in Antwerp in 1648, and then became part of the collection of the Archduke Leopold William in Brussels. The Christ in the *Parable of the Labourers* lent his pose to Vermeer's *Christ in the House of Martha and Mary*. The Fetti *Lost Silver* provided ideas for Emanuel de Witte's *Jupiter and Mercury* of 1647. One wonders when and where de Witte – who was living in Delft from 1641 to 1652 – and Vermeer saw the Fettis. Did Vermeer serve any of his time in Antwerp or Brussels? Or did he simply travel to those places from wherever he was doing his training in the United Provinces?

★

'Johannis Vermeer' was registered as a master painter in the Delft
Guild of St Luke in 1653. He was twenty-one. He was inscribed as
member no. 78 in the master-book of the Guild and paid only one and
a half guilders of his six guilders entry fee, perhaps planning to pay the
rest when he had begun to make painting pay. His father, a guild
member, had died in October the year before, aged about sixty-one,
and had been buried in the Nieuwe Kerk, and so was not there to help
his son celebrate his mastership. When Reynier died his wife Digna
bought seventeen and a half guilders' worth of material on credit,
perhaps for mourning clothes. The Anglo-Dutch War of 1652–4
caused a considerable slump and the Vermeers, like many families in
trade, may have felt pinched for cash. No contribution was made by
them to the Chamber of Charity on Reynier's death, to the value of the
deceased's best cloak, as would have been customary for those who
could afford it. This sad occasion also prompts the speculation that
Johannes Vermeer – assuming he was away from Delft – would
probably have returned for his father's funeral, and presumably
stayed on to help his mother cope with Mechelen. He was certainly in
Delft and at Mechelen the following spring, in April 1653, when he
got married.

4. *Burdens of the House*

Eight months before his registration in the Guild, Vermeer married Catharina Bolnes, who was roughly a year older. Catharina had had some education, for she wrote in a neat hand which was evident in a document she signed in December 1655. Since Vermeer worked at home and seems often to have taken his models from his own household, immediately at hand, we have a choice of which woman in which painting is Catharina; perhaps, slightly altered, she appears in several. But there is something about the abstracted but fond expression with which the woman in *A Lady writing* looks up and meets the concentrated gaze of the unseen painter that seems to say, This is she.

Where did they meet? Mechelen was on the Market Place, about forty paces from the main door of the Nieuwe Kerk. Catharina lived just off the Market Place, in a house on the Oude Langendijck at the corner of an alley called the Molenpoort, a position – ignoring the intervening canal – that was even closer than Mechelen to the front entrance to the Nieuwe Kerk. They may have met in the Market Place itself, buying produce or attending any of the activities that went on there, or in one of the surrounding shops and businesses. For that matter, if Johannes served some of his apprenticeship in Utrecht, as a result of the Bloemaert connection with the Thinses he may have been introduced to Catharina – 'also from Delft' – while studying away from home. But he was certainly back in Delft and living at Mechelen at the time of his marriage.

The young man and woman had quite a lot in common. The first name of her father, the owner of a brick-making business, was Reynier, too. They were both born late in their mothers' child-bearing years – Catharina's mother Maria was thirty-eight; Johannes Vermeer's mother Digna was thirty-seven. At the time of their marriage both were in different ways fatherless: Catharina by her mother's separation; Johannes by the actual death of his father. Both were the youngest children of their parents, Johannes the younger of two, Catharina the youngest of three. However, there were also a number of differences between them that might have required some overcoming. There was a disparity of status and possessions, for a start. The Thinses of Gouda had patrician connections in various parts of the country; male members of the family became high civic officials such as sheriffs and burgomasters. None of Maria Thins's siblings had married, so that much of her family's property eventually came to Maria and Catharina.

As a young woman Maria had lived for a while in Delft, staying with an upper-class lady friend, before at the age of twenty-nine she married in Gouda in 1622. Her husband Reynier Bolnes was at that point well-to-do from his brick-making business; he brought 4,000 guilders to the match, and when he finally split up with Maria Thins she did well from the settlement. In contrast to this, Vermeer had a now widowed mother who was running a heavily mortgaged inn and whose father, his grandfather, the 'artful master of clockworks', had been in jail for counterfeiting. Yet his immediate family appears to have been happy.

Catharina, on the other hand, had memories of a childhood full of angry altercations and violence, fits of temper and tears. Her father, after thirteen years of being married, had become an ogre. Maria's relatives and neighbours were to testify that they saw him insulting his wife, kicking her, pulling her naked from her bed by her hair when she was sick, attacking her with a stick when she was pregnant, and chasing her out of their house. On one occasion, Catharina, aged nine, ran to some neighbours in fright, yelling that her father was about to kill her sister Cornelia. Bolnes said to the anxious neighbours that, yes, he had dragged Cornelia through the house and hit her, but this was because his wife had wanted to beat their son Willem. Reynier Bolnes declared, 'I'll do it again – whenever she beats Willem, I'll take it out on Cornelia.' He sided with Willem, eating alone with him rather than together with his wife and daughters, and encouraging the boy to treat his mother disrespectfully; in fact he threatened to beat him if he did what his mother told him to do. Reynier took to keeping his money in a garden house. His brick business went downhill; in 1646 he was said to owe some 8,000 guilders. By then Maria had long since moved out. In 1641 she was awarded custody of Cornelia and Catharina and a year later moved with them to Delft, where she received 24 guilders a week alimony from Reynier. Willem stayed on with his father and took his part with vehement loyalty. In early 1648, after a court had ordered the feuding couple to divide their property equitably, Willem met his mother in a Gouda street and – so a witness described Willem's action – 'turned his arse towards her . . . saying, "That's what you get."' (The witness who testified to having seen and heard this felt the need to apologise for the expression he had to use for Willem's insult.) In 1649 Maria collected 15,606 guilders as her share of the couple's joint assets, and this must have given her a sense of victory for the moment, although the interest she would get on this amount would be somewhat less than the alimony she had been receiving. But it was just as well she took the settlement. By the time Catharina married Vermeer, four years later, her father was more or less bankrupt. As for Willem, the relations between him and his mother went on being troublesome.

There was another great difference between Vermeer's family and Catharina's. His people were Reformed Protestants, hers were Catholic. Despite their otherwise privileged background, the Thinses were part of a minority that, if not exactly repressed, was not altogether free to act as it wished. Catholics formed about a quarter of Delft's population; they and their co-religionists in other parts of the United Provinces weren't meant to hold civic office or arrange public religious services. The Catholic faith was sneered at by diehard Protestants as 'Romish superstition'. One aspect of Catholicism that evidently worried the Reformed was its persistence: most skilled craftsmen seemed to stick with the old religion, and a number of distinguished practitioners of various arts did so, too, among them the poet Vondel, the fashionable Amsterdam architect Philips Vingboons, and the artist Jan Steen. And there was also the matter of Catholic expansion: in the States-General in January 1650, a proposal from the province of Zeeland noted the 'infinite number of Jesuits, Priests, Monks, and Friars, who like grasshoppers out of the bottomless pit overspread the land by thousands'. In the early 1600s Rome had set up a *Missio Hollandica* as a counter-attack, to proselytise after the Calvinists' apparent victory in the battle for souls. But Delft had never been a lost cause: it had provided Sasbout Vosmeer, a priest who led the reorganisation of the Catholic Church in Holland, became its vicar-general, and worked tirelessly if often secretly, travelling the country in disguise to recruit candidates for the priesthood, though the number of priests never equalled the number of Reformed ministers. Vosmeer was once arrested during a search of the house he was staying in but allowed to go when the authorities decided they didn't want to make a martyr of him.

In Delft, many Catholic families were prosperous and there was no Catholic ghetto, but the neighbourhood around Maria Thins's house was nicknamed the *Paepenhoek*, 'Papists' Corner'. A so-called 'hidden church', run by the Jesuits, was right next door to her house; it was one of two such Catholic churches in town. But though inconspicuous, most people knew it was there, a few yards from the Nieuwe Kerk, just off the Market Place. Municipal sheriffs had a way of turning a blind eye to Catholic observances, sometimes accepting 'recognition money' for doing so; repression and toleration were often practised hand in hand in a finely balanced *modus vivendi*. Occasionally the Calvinist diehards complained about the growing wickedness of Popery and demanded serious action against the Catholics, and then for a time Catholics had to lie low or change their times of worship. When, in 1643, a bailiff in Rotterdam went to break up a Catholic service, he arrived too late: the congregation had met, heard Mass, and dispersed before five a.m. In Delft on one occasion in the 1650s the sheriff was condemned by vigorous Protestants such as

Petrus de Witte for not enforcing strict measures against the Catholics. The sheriff pointed out that the burgomasters had given the priests a licence to live in the town, but to keep the complainers sweet, he told the priests to be unobtrusive in their behaviour. In 1654, as already noted, special permission was given to Catholics to use the Begijnhof chapel publicly after the Thunderclap; they too were Delft residents, as affected as any by the catastrophe.

So Johannes Vermeer married into a state of dual allegiance: he was apparently loyal to his city and province and newish country but became sympathetic to the religion of Rome and possibly the pre-Alteration arrangement of things, including the old political boundaries. But whether this was clear at once to Catharina's mother is doubtful. When it came to the crunch, it seemed that Maria Thins wasn't happy about her daughter marrying Johannes Vermeer, son of Mechelen. Neither Johannes nor Catharina had presumably told Maria that Johannes had in the family a counterfeiter as maternal grandfather and a bankrupt bedding dealer for paternal grandmother – though Delft being a small enough place in terms of gossip, she may have heard of these relations of his. More to the point, did she want Trijntge (Catharina's nickname) married to a man who had been brought up a Protestant and therefore from a Catholic point of view faced the eventual likelihood of hell-fire? And would there be, with the birth of children, a fight to ensure they would be properly raised as Catholics?

On the evening of 4 April 1653, Vermeer's older colleague Leonaert Bramer and an army captain named Bartolomeus Melling, who had served in Brazil and was now a standard-bearer in the forces of the States-General, called on Maria Thins. They had with them a Delft lawyer named Johannes Ranck. It seems to have been an ecumenical delegation on the young couple's behalf, with Bramer apparently representing the Catholic interest and Melling the Protestant, come to talk Catharina's mother around. Maria's sister Cornelia was also on hand, giving support and sympathy.

The visitors asked Maria Thins whether she would sign a

document permitting the marriage vows or banns to be published and registered. Maria replied that she would not sign such an act of consent. Despite this – a subtle distinction – she would put up with the vows being published; she said several times that she wouldn't stand in the way of this. In other words, she didn't welcome the marriage, but wouldn't block it. Next morning the notary Ranck drew up a deed attesting to Maria Thins's sufferance of the vows being published, and this was witnessed not only by Bramer and Melling but by a man named Gerrit van Oosten and the Delft lawyer Willem de Langue, who had frequent dealings with Bramer and the Vermeer family. De Langue was a serious picture collector, at whose house Vermeer might have seen works by – among others – Rembrandt, Roelandt Savery, and Bramer. He was also acquainted with Johannes Renialme, the Amsterdam art-dealer who had once been registered in the Delft Guild of St Luke, whose stock of pictures might have given young Vermeer the chance to look at works by Italian painters.

The banns were registered by Vermeer and Catharina at the Town Hall on 5 April. And – a surprise! - one of the most talented Dutch artists suddenly showed up in Delft as if to bless the occasion with his presence. Gerard Terborch, fifteen years older than Vermeer, had worked in Haarlem, Amsterdam, and The Hague before settling in Deventer; he painted intimate interiors with figures. His works and Vermeer's later show signs of influencing one another. In any event, on 22 April, two days after the actual wedding ceremony, Terborch and Vermeer were at de Langue's again to witness an 'act of surety' for an army captain. Was Terborch in Delft primarily for the wedding? Should he be added to the list of candidates for Vermeer's master?

The wedding on the 20th was solemnised in the riverside village of Schipluy or Schipluide, now called Schipluiden, a bit less than half the way to Vlaardingen on the Maas and roughly an hour from Delft. The village was the centre of one of the 'sluice districts' that drained the land in the surroundings of Delft and had a nautical coat of arms, a two-masted medieval ship. Schipluy had been heavily damaged by fire in 1616 and exempted from house taxes until 1630. In that year the place saw the birth of Vermeer's near namesake, Johannes van der

Meer, also a painter. Maria Thins briefly owned a house there, as a result of a loan made to a local man for which the house was collateral; she sold it in 1656 after the borrower failed to pay her back. But the place was special in that usually Catholics could be more open about their faith there. Some of the village officials were actually Catholic. Although there are no documents on the matter, it is likely that Vermeer would have received instruction in the Catholic faith in the weeks before the wedding; indeed, this may have been a factor in Maria Thins's acceptance of him as Catharina's fiancé. 'Mixed marriages' weren't common then but nor were they absolutely out of the question. Conversions happened. The renowned seventeenth-century poet Joost van den Vondel converted to Catholicism. The writer Maria Tesselschade, daughter of Roemers Visscher and a friend of Constantijn Huygens, became a Catholic in 1642, causing the good Protestant Huygens much grief. But we have no proof of Vermeer's conversion.

What seems certain was that Vermeer became a willing and active partner in his wife's Catholicism. None of their children was evidently baptised in a Reformed church. The second and third sons were given the Catholic names of Franciscus and Ignatius. Their oldest son Johannes seems to have gone to a school in Catholic Brabant, perhaps to study for the priesthood. Their eldest child, Maria, married a Catholic merchant and her children were baptised as Catholics.

And what do Vermeer's paintings tell us on this score? It would be good if the experts were in agreement as to the authenticity of the *St Praxedis* painting; it has been recently put forward as an early Vermeer, but distinguished art historians are in dispute about this flamboyantly painted work. It is signed and dated 'Meer 1655' – the year after the Thunderclap, two years after Vermeer's marriage. The painting is regarded by those who think it is from Vermeer's brush as a close copy he made of a work – at that point ten years old – by Felice Ficherelli. Those who believe it is not by Vermeer say it could well be by Ficherelli himself, possibly one of two paintings he made on this subject, the other being in Ferrara.

St Praxedis or Prassede was a second-century Christian, daughter of a disciple of St Paul's living in Rome, who prepared the bodies of executed Christians for burial. In the late sixteenth century her fame was revived by the Jesuits. In the two paintings she is shown kneeling next to an ornate twin-handled jug into which she is squeezing a sponge, soaked full with the blood of a decapitated martyr lying

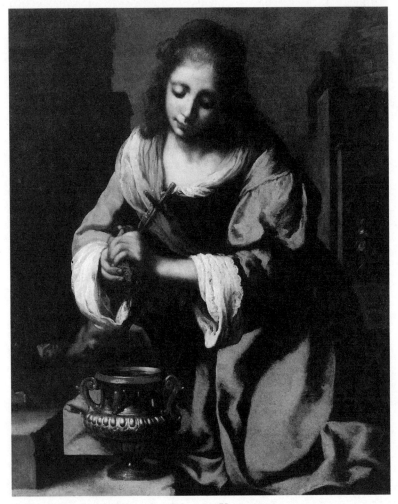

St Praxedis, 1655, attributed to Johannes Vermeer.

behind her. The differences between the paintings are few but important. In the supposed Vermeer, now in the USA, the beautiful saint manages to hold a gold crucifix as well as the bloody sponge, a gesture that might suggest to the Catholic viewer the enaction of a sacrament; to an agnostic eye it seems to overload the picture with Catholic symbolism. This painting seems better lit than the Ferrara picture and the viewer is particularly aware of the saint's lowered eyelids and contemplative melancholy; we feel the element of personal risk has been considered by her, but set aside. The Ferrara picture, certainly a Ficherelli, is by means of light and shade less complicated, a woman simply doing what she is meant to do. The paint of the 'Vermeer' *St Praxedis* is definitely from the seventeenth century, so we are told, thus ruling out the chance that it is a later copy, but the experts differ in their judgement on the brushwork, some saying it is like Vermeer's, some that it is untypical. If he did paint this picture, for a Catholic friend of Maria Thins or for the Jesuits next door in the Oude Langendijk, it would seem to denote his sympathy for the Catholic belief in the power of good works to enable one to achieve salvation, rather than relying on faith and being chosen as the Calvinists required. Moreover, the subject of caring for the dead would have seemed right only a few months after Delft had seen its streets full of the dead and maimed resulting from the gunpowder explosion. We don't know where Vermeer was on 12 October 1654 – perhaps like many in the town, stunned into silence – but perhaps what is being squeezed into the jug is not just the symbolic blood of a martyr but the blood of Carel Fabritius.

St Praxedis doesn't have any immediate kinship with other early works of Vermeer, though Professor Michael Kitson, who first attributed the picture to Vermeer, compared it with the *Christ in the House of Martha and Mary* and saw in it 'a related breadth of form and handling and a similar gravity . . . of mood'. Kitson believed Vermeer could have seen Ficherelli's original in a sale room or with a dealer in Holland; it might have been for a time in his father's stock. The copy looks more like a Vermeer if we leap ahead to the end of his career and compare it with one of his late paintings: the *Allegory of Faith* (see p. 178). This might seem an over-eager, even florid, attempt to depict Catholicism triumphing over heresy. But if Vermeer also painted *St Praxedis*, then the later painting appears less uncharacteristic. It is worth noting that the house he lived in for most of his married life contained among its pictures two Crucifixions, a 'Mother of Christ', a St Veronica, and a picture of the Three Magi, while in at least one room a crucifix was hanging; all in all, a very Catholic assemblage. The art historian P.T.A. Swillens has pointed out that in various legal documents, concerning relatives who were dead, Vermeer and Catharina used the term *zaliger*, meaning 'sainted', which was favoured by Catholics, rather than *wijlen*, meaning 'late', which was the Reformed usage. Vermeer may also have been drawn to Catholicism, as others were at the time, by its traditional aspects. He may have liked the way in which the Roman religion was linked to an ecclesiastical structure of great age and intricate history; it was a religion that allowed its believers to participate in and be loyal to old ceremonies, venerable liturgies, ancient sacraments. Catholicism in the United Provinces required its followers to stand by their faith but to do less declaiming than seemed to be obligatory in the Reformed Church, whether in its hard-nosed or liberal branches. There was less Protestant *unrust* or restlessness. Catholicism provided a more relaxed, more passive allegiance. Moreover, if someone was seeking mystery and beauty in an act of worship, the Latin Mass furnished those qualities in a way that the Protestant service did not.

It may have been a love match where Vermeer was concerned, but Catharina's well-to-do status couldn't have hurt for a young man about to embark on the career of freelance painter. Like Rembrandt, who married a burgomaster's daughter, Vermeer married upwards. In a Delft register of 1674, Maria Thins was one of the 1,300 or so residents of the town recorded as being wealthy enough to be taxed ½ per cent of their assets; she paid 130 guilders in tax, indicating a net worth of 26,000 guilders – though that valuation may have been inaccurately low. She owned land in various places and had an annual income from rents or interest of about 1,500 guilders. And she proceeded to take a practical interest in her son-in-law's circumstances: loans and gifts were forthcoming, and after a while she welcomed Vermeer and Catharina under her own roof.

It isn't known where, after the singing and feasting, the young couple – he twenty, she twenty-one – set up their first home. One suspects that Catharina, if not her mother, wouldn't have been keen for them to reside with Vermeer's mother in her inn, Mechelen. They may have rented a small house. During their first summer of living together, in August 1653, they like other people in the area would have heard the sound of guns from the north, as the Dutch and English fleets fought in the North Sea off Scheveningen. Did they in early August like many Delft citizens attend the funeral – in the Oude Kerk in his home town – of Admiral Maarten Tromp, who died in this battle? The Battle of Scheveningen was a serious Dutch defeat, though in the following year a number of Dutch convoys safely reached their ports, Cromwell assumed the Protectorship in England and wound up the war with the United Provinces, and the Dutch economy was rescued from collapse.

But at some point Vermeer and Catharina did move – perhaps when it became clear that Catharina's mother had more room than she needed in her large house on the Oude Langendijck. This street seems to have been just beyond the circle within which severe damage was caused by the Thunderclap; only one house in that street is found in the list of properties for which repair costs were claimed. We know from several documents, well spaced out in time, that Vermeer and Catharina were living in Delft during their first years of married life. And we know for certain that by 27 December 1660 they were at Maria Thins's house on the Oude Langendijck. On that date a 'child of Johannes Vermeer' of that address was buried in the Oude Kerk.

One set of facts about Vermeer and Catharina is substantial, and though it might now be obscured by the familiarity and fame of his painting, it was probably the big thing in their lives: the number of their children. The couple came from relatively small families. They proceeded to make a very large one. Catharina was fecund, Vermeer had no difficulty with procreation. The statesman and people's poet

Jacob Cats foresaw what marriage meant for many women: 'The burdens of the house, the will of the man, / And nearly every year a child'. Four Vermeer children died in infancy or childhood: the one buried on 27 December 1660, and three others, also buried in the Oude Kerk, in a grave bought by their grandmother Maria Thins in December 1661, on 10 July 1667, 16 July 1669, and 27 June 1673; if newborn or stillborn, all would have been conceived in the previous autumns as the nights turned chilly. The Oude Kerk had been the last of the great Delft churches to be given over to the Protestants, but Catholics continued to be able to bury their dead there – indeed, as more recently a Catholic church than the Nieuwe Kerk, it may have seemed to Maria Thins a more appropriate place to house the remains of her family, although her half-sister Maria Camerling had been buried in the Nieuwe Kerk in 1657. (There was a fee of three guilders to be buried inside the church rather than in an outside graveyard, where burial was free.) It was a time without medical solutions for many serious infections, when perhaps half of all children didn't make it to adulthood, and therefore parental fatalism was called for; but great loss was still felt, and immense sorrow, barely assuaged by hopes of Divine Mercy. John Evelyn wrote after the death of one of his 'deare children' on 26 March 1664, 'Gods will be don', but he felt the blow. Catharina and Vermeer did well in that eleven of their fifteen children lived, and had to be cared for, fed, clothed, and schooled. The house on the Oude Langendijck was a big house but a full one.

It had a semi-basement, a ground floor and an upstairs, with an attic above. We can partly furnish it with the help of an inventory of 1676. The front door gave entry to the *voorhuys*, a vestibule or hall where there was a large cupboard or cabinet containing clothing and linen, among which in the Vermeers' case were 'Twelve bedsheets, good and bad'. Also in this hall was an ebony-framed mirror (one of four mirrors in the house), a wooden 'footbench', some chairs, and many paintings, including a landscape, a seascape, a 'Mars and Apollo', and an unnamed picture by Fabritius. Next, in the *groote zael* or main room were the two portraits of Vermeer's parents, ten of Maria Thins's family, and two small paintings, portrait studies of heads by

Fabritius; another cabinet and chest for clothes and bed linen; a bedstead, probably built-in like a big cupboard that the occupant climbed up into and then drew the curtains to make it snug; and a table with nine Spanish-leather chairs. The ground floor held other smaller rooms for sleeping, eating, cooking, and washing, or for a mixture of these activities. There was also a bed in the basement room. Upstairs at the front of the house the painter had his studio, facing north and looking out, over the Oude Langendijk and its little canal, to the front of the Nieuwe Kerk. (In the attic was a cradle and a stone table on which colours were ground – implements for the two forms of production in which Vermeer was involved.) However, much of the upstairs was Maria Thins's preserve.

In well-to-do residences the floors of downstairs rooms were often tiled, and had a skirting of smaller decorative tiles. Windows were darkened with interior or exterior shutters and curtains. Carpets were used to cover tables rather than floors. Some walls were covered with gold-tooled leather, as in the so-called inner kitchen (in fact the dining-room) in the Thins house, but most had pictures or maps hung on them. Wooden pegs provided hat- and coat-hooks. Warmth came from grates and stoves in fireplaces, where cooking was also conducted on racks over the fire. Ground-floor ceilings were often high and small 'hanging rooms' were sometimes fitted in, mezzanine-fashion, between the ground floor and upper floors. Street- and yard-doors might be divided in two parts, so that the top half could be opened to let in light and air while the bottom was closed, keeping in small children. The brick-paved courtyard to the side or rear generally gave access to a water-cistern or well, perhaps with a pump, and to the 'place' or privy in a separate shed. Water was frequently being carried hither and yon in buckets on cleaning missions, for the Delft housewife, perhaps even more than Dutch women elsewhere, kept her domain spick-and-span. The presence of muddy water on all sides may have been one reason for this Dutch obsession, and the need for cleanliness in making cheese, but Delft had also needed particularly high hygiene standards because of its beer-making. (Foreigners are often amused that the Dutch have one word, *schoon*, for both clean and beautiful.) Brooms stood ready inside most door-ways. A spinning wheel was kept in the washroom of the Oude Langendijk house for spare moments, but judging by the domestic activity in Pieter de Hooch's paintings women were rarely idle, with food to organise, clothes to launder and mend, linen to fold and put away, and children to be taught, amused, and chivvied – and their hair to be fine-combed for lice. People washed less than they do now and men who shaved got away with doing so once a week. Since families provided much of their own entertainment, many musical instruments were on hand; well-brought-up young ladies were taught to sing and perform on the virginal, clavichord, or spinet, so that they could charm male visitors with sweet sounds.

A prosperous household required at least one live-in woman servant.* Though working for pay, she was treated as a member of the family and often ate with them. When she wasn't toiling at house-work, she might now and then help herself to the wine or genever, as shown in a number of paintings of drunken maids asleep while the broom or laundry basket stand waiting; or she might attract the attentions of any unattached men in the house – as Rembrandt's maids, Geertje Dircx and Hendrickje Stoffels, attracted their employer. Geertje was given some of Rembrandt's wife Saskia's jewellery, and sued the great man for breach of promise. Hendrickje became the artist's model, housekeeper, and devoted common-law wife. The soldier and philosopher René Descartes while living in Holland married his servant. Some maids were regarded as fair game, as Samuel Pepys, an English contemporary, regarded his wife's maids, frequently pestering them for hugs and kisses. 'Go and grab the maid, for the wife is in church', recommends one of the characters in Nicolaes Biestken's farce *Claas Kloet*. Tobias Herkenius, a preacher in Zunderdorp, admitted 'with great remorse and many tears' sleeping with his servant-girl; he was unmarried at the time, but when he did marry it was not the girl but a widow he had already proposed to. A woman named Tanneke Everpoel is mentioned in a legal

*Male servants attracted a heavy tax.

deposition regarding the behaviour of Catharina's brother Willem on various occasions in the Oude Langendijk house, where she seems to have been a servant. She remained in the family's service for some time, which might suggest that, despite the upset caused by Willem's visits, she was happy there; she was eventually named as a creditor of Vermeer's estate, perhaps owed for back-pay, and she was most likely the servant who in Maria Thins's will of May 1669 is meant to receive a bequest of twenty guilders after her employer's death, at Catharina's discretion. Tanneke may be depicted in one or other of Vermeer's paintings, holding a water pitcher, delivering a letter, or pouring milk. Professor Montias indeed sees her as the model for *The Milkmaid* – 'a statuesque woman, quite capable by the looks of her of resisting Willem's assaults': a woman with a brawny arm, a strong chin, and a firm bosom, who should not be messed with.

The ne'er-do-well Willem Bolnes lived with his father in Gouda until about 1660. His and Catharina's sister Cornelia had died in 1649 but Willem refused to attend her funeral. His aunt Cornelia, Maria Thins's sister, made a will in 1661 in which she left Catharina a worthwhile annuity but declared that her nephew Willem should not enjoy a penny of her estate because of 'his dissolute, licentious, and useless life, as well as the disobedience, spite, and harm that he had done to his mother'. Willem, who was over thirty in 1660, moved out to a cottage in Schoonhoven on the River Lek, south-east of Gouda; he lived on rents from inherited property and loans, particularly from his long-suffering mother – who also gave him money and paid off some of his debts. In her will, made in 1662, she left him and Catharina equal shares in the residue of her estate. Despite this forbearance on her part, he turned up on several occasions in 1663 at the house on the Oude Langendijck and made trouble. According to one legal document, several witnesses including Tanneke Everpoel testified that Willem created a violent commotion, causing people outside to come to the front door to listen. He swore at his mother and called her an old popish swine, a she-devil, and other words that couldn't decently be repeated. He pulled a knife on his mother and tried to stab her. He threatened Catharina with a stick although she was pregnant 'to the last degree'. The stick, added a neighbour named Willem de Coorde, had an iron spike on one end, which Willem Bolnes thrust at Catharina. The redoutable Tanneke prevented Willem from hitting Catharina with it. (One wonders where Vermeer was. Upstairs quietly painting?) Like his father, who had several times attacked Maria Thins and Catharina, Willem seemed prone to moments of uncontrollable violence. He also had a serious and otherwise unexplained 'accident' soon after this, which left Maria Thins with a seventy-four-guilder fee to pay the two surgeons involved, and the cost of wine – provided by Vermeer's mother at Mechelen – that was meant to help him recover.

The upshot of all this was that Willem was confined in a house of correction, a private institution in the Vlamingstraat run by Hermanus Taerling for 'delinquent and mentally ill persons'. This cost 310 guilders a year. To cover this, Maria Thins proceeded to claim some of Willem's rental income, and in 1665 the aldermen of Delft council gave her custody of her son's property; she then agreed to ease the restrictions on him so that he could go out to church. However, within a year or so he was in trouble again, this time on account of Taerling's maid, Mary Gerrits. She had been sleeping with Willem and seems to have asked him to run away with her and get married. Mary also appears to have been light-fingered; she was accused of stealing a purse and a silver chain. Maria Thins put a stop to the proposed wedding and in a new will ordered that, on her death, Willem was to get only the minimum share of her estate the law entitled him to, one-sixth. The black sheep apparently spent the rest of his years at Hermanus Taerling's, though when he died, still a bachelor, in March 1676, his mother had his body carried from her house on the Oude Langendijck to the Oude Kerk, and he was buried in the grave she had bought for her family.

Just how Vermeer dealt with these interruptions we can only guess. His paintings reflect a turning-away from the messiness of life to a perfected state where there is no discordant clatter, crying, or shouting. (There are no babies, no beggars, in his work, no knife-wielding villains, or knife-grinders.) His live-in mother-in-law wasn't always sweet-tempered, at least according to several of her former neighbours in Gouda, who suggested that sometimes she gave the irascible Reynier Bolnes a piece of her mind. A good deal later, by 1680, when she was eighty-seven, she seems to have quarrelled with Johannes Cramer, the husband of her granddaughter Maria Vermeer, and stipulated that he be excluded from the eventual accounting of her estate. Yet there is no evidence that she ever fell out with Johannes Vermeer. He appears to have done his patient best to handle her affairs when asked to do so. For instance, in 1667 she gave him power of attorney to collect money owed her and her son Willem. Vermeer was empowered to sell her assets if need be. He had already served the family – and his own interests – by going to The Hague in 1661 to register Catharina's ownership of an estate named Bon Repas, near Schoonhoven, left to her by her aunt Cornelia Thins, who had died in Gouda in February of that year. (The church bells were rung at Cornelia Thins's funeral, as she requested.) Before Cornelia died, she and Maria Thins had called in a notary and had sworn before him their ratification and approval of Vermeer and Catharina's marriage; this was apparently necessary for a provision in their brother Jan Thins's will to take effect, so that a bequest of income from him would go to Catharina and her children. The two sisters may have had to testify that certain conditions had been met: Vermeer converting or his children being brought up as Catholics.

The Oude Langendijck household's income from property rents and interest and annuities added up to a fair sum. Aunt Cornelia left Catharina an annuity of 100 guilders. Maria Thins received every year at least 1,500 guilders from various sources. So, even without any money coming in from Vermeer's activities as a master painter and art-dealer, the Thins/Vermeer family was getting an income at least four times that of a skilled carpenter or mason; 850 guilders a year was roughly what the owner of a Delft pottery works earned. However, the cost of raising a child was forty guilders a year or more. Multiply that sum by eleven, and it is clear how much the family's revenues were reduced by the fertility of Vermeer and Catharina.

★

Among their neighbours in the Oude Langendijck was the family of Simon Arienszoon Samuels, a master stonecarver and a Catholic; from his workshop the sound of hammer on chisel and chisel on stone could be heard. The Jesuit church was immediately to the east of the Thins house and a Jesuit school several doors further along. The Jesuits owned several houses in the immediate area. The still-life painter Adam Pick had lived on the Oude Langendijck in his prosperous inn De Toelast, but he had sold up in 1652 and moved to Leiden. Johan de Coorde ran another inn, the reverently named Pater Noster, nearby in the street, and a woman named Margareta Hubrechts was a bookseller. Where the north-south alley called the

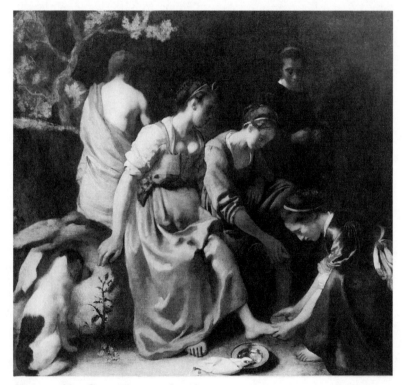

Diana and her Companions, c. 1655–6.

Molenpoort joined the Oude Langendijck alongside the Thins house, a wooden gate closed the alley, perhaps to stop livestock from the Beestenmarket breaking out into the wide world.

What pets did the Vermeer household have? Few cats appear in Dutch paintings of this period but dogs are common, shown in streets, churches, inns, and houses. But compared with the works of his genre-painting contemporaries, the pictures of Vermeer are short of dogs. One was shown in a painting of a sleeping servant-girl, but the artist decided against it and painted it out. Vermeer's sole dog sits confidently next to the principal figure in his *Diana and her Companions* of 1655–6: a docile springer spaniel, by no means the sort of hunting hound the goddess might be expected to have with her; but then, as has been pointed out by experts in iconography, she hasn't got her bow and arrows either, merely a simple metal headband decorated with a crescent moon, her emblem as goddess of the night. Possibly, seeking a model for the animal that traditionally accompanied Diana, Vermeer turned to the family pet. Although it is of a different breed, Vermeer's dog in the *Diana* sits with the same patient attentiveness as the black mutt in Carel Fabritius's painting *The Sentry*, like a canine tribute to his predecessor from the Doelenstraat.

5. *The Way of St Luke*

Vermeer paid the balance of his entrance fee to the St Luke's Guild in July 1656. He was twenty-three and the sum was four and a half guilders. We don't know what brought about this big-spending moment. Had his mother-in-law made him a specific present of the amount he owed the guild, or had he just sold a picture? Maria Thins lent the young couple 300 guilders during 1656; this large advance is mentioned in a will she drew up a year later that also refers to Vermeer's and Catharina's first-born as her godchild, the daughter dutifully or lovingly named Maria. Moreover, in November 1657 Vermeer and his wife borrowed 200 guilders from a wealthy thirty-three-year-old Delft patrician, Pieter Claeszoon van Ruijven, son of a brewer. The loan was for a year, the interest rate a modest 4½ per cent. Van Ruijven seems to have become Vermeer's most stalwart patron and it is likely the loan was meant to be paid off with Vermeer paintings. As we have seen, everyone with a bit of money in Holland bought pictures – a wide-spread middle-class patronage which more than made up for the lack of royal and ecclesiastical buying, but left most Dutch artists dependent on market forces that could be fickle. Wealthy connoisseurs could make the difference between poverty and affluence, buying nudes or battle scenes, still-lifes or history pieces. But for artists who were experimental, idiosyncratic, or unknown, reliance on the taste of private buyers could be very risky.

At the start of his professional career Vermeer generally worked on a larger scale than he did later on. His two chief works of the mid-1650s were in the category called 'history paintings': *Christ in the*

House of Martha and Mary, over 5 feet tall and more than 4½ feet wide, and the *Diana and her Companions*, which was roughly 3 feet by 4 feet. (The less definitely attributed *St Praxedis* is a little smaller than the *Diana*.) They are ambitious works in which, paradoxically, modesty and a sad thoughtfulness set the prevailing mood. The downcast eyes of Martha in one and the shadowed, lowered eyes of Diana and her nymphs in the other, are at the low-key end of a range of gesture, a long way from the rhetorical flourishes many other contemporary painters indulged in. The experts disagree about which painting came first, though most of them seem to think the *Christ in the House of Martha and Mary* is the earlier. The art historian John Nash, on the contrary, believes that 'the *Diana*, which is so satisfactory a piece of juvenilia, is nonetheless a less impressive work than the *Christ in the House of Martha and Mary* . . . It might have been expected that the *Diana* was the earlier of the two pieces.' For a young artist, it was natural enough to want to tackle history painting, then generally regarded (particularly by the Italians) as the loftiest branch of the art. Leonaert Bramer would have pointed him in that direction. Rembrandt and most of his followers trod the same path. The new Town Hall in Amsterdam was at the time being decorated with large scenes whose subjects were taken from biblical or ancient history. As noted, one of the artists honoured with a Town Hall commission was Erasmus Quellinus the Younger, an Antwerp artist who before 1652 had painted an immense *Christ in the House of Martha and Mary*. Vermeer must have seen it.

At this point there was nothing parochial about Vermeer's painting of this subject, nothing even that would now be thought of as 'Delft'. Looking at this work, the one Delft painter who might come to mind is van Couwenbergh whose work was intentionally 'Italian'. Abraham Bloemaert and Hendrick Terbrugghen in Utrecht may have influenced him, too. So did Giovanni Biliverti/Jan Bilivert, who came originally from Maastricht and whose figure of Christ in his *Christ and the Samaritan Woman* of *c*.1640 evidently had an impact on Vermeer's Christ, sitting back in the same way with one hand drooping over the arm of the chair and the other hand outstretched, though Vermeer reversed Bilivert's image. But if the composition, scale, and arrangement of the figures in Vermeer's picture seem to compete with what was going on elsewhere in the Low Countries or Italy, the atmosphere of the picture seems instead a precursor of the unassertiveness, the withdrawal, the domestic silence, the interest in the feminine – the accumulated elements that we come to associate with Johannes Vermeer of Delft.

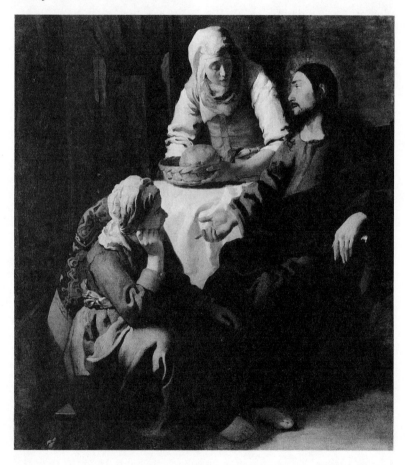

Christ in the House of Martha and Mary, c. 1655.

He had chosen the moment, described by St Luke in his Gospel (10:38–42), where Jesus had stopped at a house in a village and was asked by a woman named Martha, 'cumbered about with much serving', to tell her sister Mary to help get the food instead of just sitting there, in a trance, listening to him. Jesus replied, 'Martha, Martha, thou art care-full and troubled about many things: but one thing is needful: and Mary hath chosen that good part, which shall not be taken away from her.' And yet, though Vermeer seems thus to be recommending a passive stance rather than an active one, the picture itself puts the two elements in a fine balance. Mary's contemplative attitude is beautifully rendered, with her face in profile against the vivid triangle of cream table-cloth at the very centre of the picture. But leaning in from above, Martha gently lowers the basket with its loaf of brown bread. Her *action* is submissive, caring, and as right and necessary as Mary's motionless, reverent attention to Christ and what he is saying. While it may be safe to believe, as some commentators do, that Vermeer here is taking a catholic, all-inclusive approach to the requirements for salvation – i.e. faith plus good works, and not a fundamentalist Protestant view of election simply by God's grace – it is worth pointing out that Vermeer's subject-matter comes from the Gospel of St Luke, the patron of painters, and therefore patron, co-opted at a distance, of the Delft guild in which Vermeer was a new member. Perhaps the painting was in a way his 'master piece', though the guild rules may not have required one.

In his early twenties Vermeer was seeking his own voice, as young artists will. He was spending time looking at pictures by other artists that took his fancy. And just as his *Diana* took its theme from Jacob van Loo's *Diana and her Nymphs* of around 1650, and maybe something of its mood from Rembrandt's *Bathsheba* of 1654, and his *Christ in the House of Martha and Mary* borrowed from Quellinus's picture of the same name, so his *Procuress* of 1656 owed a lot to a painting that was close at hand, belonging to his mother-in-law and hanging in her house. The inventory of November 1641, at the time of Maria Thins's separation from her husband, mentions a painting of a procuress, evidently that painted by Dirck van Baburen and later used as part of the decor in two of Vermeer's own pictures.

By way of Utrecht, Caravaggio was making an impact. But so, too, was the local confraternity of painters, exchanging ideas and freely lifting subjects from one another. One such was Jan Steen, who worked in Delft around 1655. His father had rented for him a brewery named 'In the Snake', on the Oude Delft, perhaps to give young Jan a steady income, and though Steen remained registered with the guild in Leiden and didn't join the guild in Delft, he seemed to get a boost from the artistic ferment in Vermeer's town. He, too, did a *Christ in the House of Martha and Mary,* in which Mary also sits at Christ's feet with her head in profile against a table-cloth, though Steen's composition is otherwise much more diffuse than Vermeer's. Intensity was, early on, one of the qualities Vermeer had to offer. Which of the two pictures – Steen's or Vermeer's – was painted first is not known.

Another artist making his influence felt in Delft was also an immigrant there. Pieter de Hooch had arrived in town in 1652, aged about twenty-three. He had signed a contract for pictures with a linen merchant named Justus de la Grange, probably handing over work in return for board and lodging; de la Grange owned eleven de Hooch paintings by 1655 and also had in his collection a Fabritius (whether by Carel or his brother Barent isn't known) worth forty guilders. On 20 September 1655 Pieter de Hooch registered as a member of the Delft Guild of St Luke. He and Vermeer were to share subjects, perhaps trading them, and to influence each other greatly. It is often hard to say when looking at their paintings who had the common idea first, but it seems to be de Hooch who leads Vermeer from his early gloom into the daylight. It may be de Hooch who brought Vermeer to see the possibilities of a smaller scale.

De Hooch, several years before, had painted *A Soldier with an Empty Glass.* In this a military man wearing a broad-brimmed hat is grappling amorously with a servant-girl who is leaning over him as she recharges his wine-glass. Drinking in slightly erotic circumstances, 'merry companies', and love-for-sale were favourite themes with

Dutch painters, but de Hooch was renovating them; Vermeer may have accepted the challenge to do so, too, and *The Procuress* may have been a result.

The Procuress (see colour section) was another big painting – after this Vermeer generally began to think small – and in it some have seen the impact of the United Provinces' 'biggest' painter. Rembrandt may have reached out to Vermeer by way of his pupil, Carel Fabritius. This was to be seen not so much in the manner in which Rembrandt and Fabritius put paint on canvas as in their presentation of character. John Nash has pointed out that 'mental activity' – or should one say, being in a reverie? – is often a Rembrandt subject, witness his *Titus at his Desk* and the *Bathsheba*; and so it is with Vermeer's letter-reading women. *The Procuress* has also been taken for a painting showing the Prodigal Son – and that was another subject Rembrandt tackled. In Vermeer's painting, the young woman holds a wine-goblet in one hand while the other is stretched forth, palm open, for the coin which the young full-faced cavalier – the Bad Boy – is giving her; his other hand lies across her left breast, as if, once the money side of the transaction has been made, he will give it a squeeze. Her eyelids are lowered but her half-smile is not so much demure as self-satisfied, like that of a child accepting a piece of birthday cake. The young man seems to be suggesting, without saying so aloud, that there are more coins like this to follow.

Alongside this pair of venal lovers stand two of the most curious characters Vermeer ever painted. One is a middle-aged woman, the presumed manager of this little market, her rather gnome-like face ringed by a black hood, looking at the couple and smiling thoughtfully (the thoughts are carnal and mischievous, we feel). The other, on her right, is a youngish man holding out a glass in salutation. He also holds, in his other hand, a stringed instrument, a sort of cittern or lute. This brothel musician (as we may suppose him to be) wears an ornate black-slashed-with-white jacket and, tilted on his head, a large black beret, a badge of the artist familiar to us from numerous Rembrandt self-portraits etched, drawn, and painted. His curly hair is shoulder-length reddish-brown. A painting by Frans van Mieris, *The Charlatan* of 1650–5, contains as part of the quack doctor's audience a similarly posed, beret-wearing young man, known to be a self-portrait of the artist and looking out at the viewer with a wondering sort of grin. Vermeer seems to have taken note of this. His musician is smiling in a slightly inebriated way that also suggests a complicity with the artist who is painting him; the musician's gaze is directed straight at the artist/viewer. 'I know you and you think you know me', he seems to be thinking; and yet he has other, deeper thoughts he isn't sharing with anyone.

Male characters are not so common in Vermeer's paintings; there are twelve in all, compared with at least thirty-eight women. We will see clothes similar to this man's costume again, in ten years' time, in a picture called *The Art of Painting*. There the man will be seen from the rear, faceless. But one wonders if his features are those of the musician in *The Procuress* or the similar features of one of the two men in the *Girl being offered Wine* of 1659–60, he who is sitting disconsolately at a table in the background with his head resting against his hand while his companion courts the young woman. Or is it the man who is seen in *The Astronomer* of 1668 and *The Geographer* of a year later? The long straggly hair, the prominent nose, the large chin? Certainly many viewers have looked at the musician in *The Procuress* and felt that here is a self-portrait. We will never know; but not long ago John Nash put it well when he said that this figure's role 'may perhaps be likened to that of the first-person narrator in a novel who speaks directly to the reader yet is a fiction embedded in the events of the narrative and not the actual voice of the author'. So we feel bound to give the 'I', the narrator of Marcel Proust's novel *À la Recherche du Temps Perdu*, the name 'Marcel'. Making only a slightly greater leap, we may call this lute-player 'Johannes Vermeer'.

What experience of brothels did our painter have, in Amsterdam, Utrecht, or Delft? The brothels or 'music-houses' in Delft were to be found in alleys such as the Donckersteeg, Hopsteeg, and Harmenkokslaan, and the women to be met in them might after a few drinks and dances go to bed with the clients for roughly a guilder, more than a day's wages for an ordinary craftsman. The refinement of

Vermeer's works would lead us to suppose that he wasn't a brothel-visiting type, but who is to say that as a young bachelor he didn't, like many, have his first sexual experience with a woman in a music-house?* Yet in *The Procuress* there is a suggestion of theatre rather than reality, or is it that for the first time Vermeer presents us with a dream vision rather than a waking one? – the curious line-up of the cast in line-abreast; the strange barrier between cast and audience that is created by the coat and carpet thrown over what appears to be a balustrade; and the one section of balustrade that is visible, below the young woman, painted in bizarre perspective. And what is the wine jug doing in that precarious place on the very edge of the table? If the carpet is ever so lightly tugged, the jug will fall off, dumping its contents. And what does that suggest to the iconographers about the duration of earthly pleasures? Rather like Rembrandt's *Polish Rider*, the *Procuress* has a superficial purpose and a surface meaning which, the longer one looks at its overlapping, almost life-sized, stage-lit figures, dissolve into mystery.

Some of the props are the same in his next picture, a painting of a young woman also with tilted head and lowered eyelids and also a wine jug, a glass, a colourful carpet. She may indeed have been the same model as the girl in *The Procuress*, but much else has changed. *Girl asleep at a Table* is the work of a painter whose ambitions have altered greatly. The painting is much smaller than the *Diana and her Companions, Christ in the House of Martha and Mary*, or *The Procuress*. The light is subdued daylight. Utrecht and Caravaggio drop away and we are now in a recognisable, realistic Dutch interior. Rather than being confronted with a piece of action, we are given a picture of inaction. Nothing much is happening. Can we just about hear the girl's faint breathing? What is she dreaming about? And a slight air of suspense has been introduced by the door left half-open, for someone may come in from the hall or the room beyond and find her here, very

*The French travel-writer René Le Pays seems to have encountered Dutch prostitutes in such places; he complained that in the middle of love-making, a Dutch woman was liable to start eating an apple or breaking nuts with her teeth.

much off-duty, with one of the two wine-glasses on the table knocked over. Probably this is the picture given the title in a 1696 Amsterdam sale catalogue '*A Drunken, Sleeping Maid at a Table*'. Sleeping maids were a subject Dutch artists liked painting. Nicolaes Maes in Dordrecht, two years younger than Vermeer, had studied with Rembrandt and probably knew Carel Fabritius, if not Vermeer himself, and was now busy turning out domestic scenes of women and

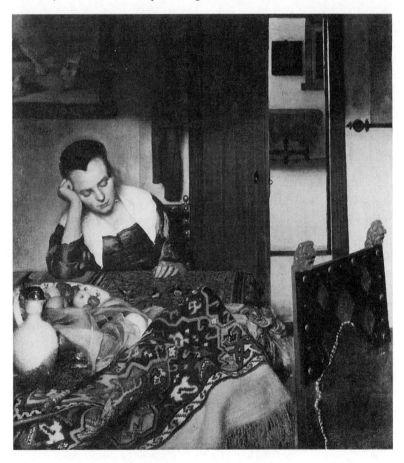

Girl asleep at a Table, c. 1657.

children. *A Young Girl leaning on a Window-sill* was one, while *The Idle Servant* of 1655 was his contribution to the sleeping maid category; her slothfulness is forcefully brought to our attention not just by the closed eyes and head resting on her hand but by the parade of pots and pans awaiting washing and scouring.

But it is Delft, not Utrecht or Dordrecht, that makes itself primarily felt with Vermeer's sleeping girl. The half-open door and the view beyond create what was then called a *doorkijkje*. The now local painter who was particularly interested in such interior views was Pieter de Hooch. This could indeed be the inside of a house painted by de Hooch: the back wall parallel to the plane of the picture; the mellow light. Vermeer, Delft-born, had apparently been looking at de Hooch's work and learning from the recent arrival, whose style was being transformed by his adopted town. De Hooch's people are placed realistically in real rooms and courtyards; they have their feet on the ground or the floor in a definite space – we know what they are doing.

This was what in the following century came to be called 'genre painting', pictures of daily domestic life, sometimes with allegorical or emblematic overtones, but often with an underlying commitment to the accepted idea that running a well-ordered household was next to godliness, or even made for godliness, in the hierarchy of human endeavour. Gerard Terborch, the possible guest at Vermeer's wedding, was another skilled practitioner in the genre, painting young women writing letters or prettying themselves before mirrors. In de Hooch's pictures, the women were often caught doing housewifely jobs, with open doors and windows letting in the sun. With Vermeer, however, the subject-matter and the 'meaning' of the picture were never straightforward. There are more questions than answers. Is it a matter for moral judgement that his sleeping girl's dress is indelicately open at the neck? The picture hanging on the wall behind her allows a sharp observer to note a detail of a painting of Cupid – more visible in one of his later paintings, *Young Woman standing at a Virginal* – with a discarded mask near the Cupid's foot. To Michael Montias 'the mask signifies dissimulation or deceit. Is the girl feigning to be asleep?' Montias wants to know whether she pretends to look as though she is sleeping when her apparently impending lover appears. But perhaps, equally credibly, we may suppose she got drunk because her lover has already been here and has now abandoned her. John Nash has pointed to the overturned second glass or *roemer* and wondered whether 'the strong light that reflects off the jambs of both doors be entering the corridor from a street door left open when the girl's companion left after overturning the *roemer*'. Vermeer has successfully set up the possibility of this unseen man but left us in the dark as to whether he is expected or has departed.

The observer will have had to be more than sharp-eyed to detect some of the secrets of this painting. Modern X-ray and infra-red equipment reveal that Vermeer first painted a dog in the doorway; a dog might be usefully, emblematically, standing in for Diana's hound, the dog who accompanies the goddess of love. But he painted out the dog and replaced it with a high-backed chair, neutral in portent. He had also shown a man entering the room, and this intruder too he eventually painted out, replacing his hat, head, and shoulders with a mirror on the wall in the back room. And he got rid of a bunch of grapes he had originally painted in the bowl on the table, grapes being (we are told by the scholars) a symbol of maidenly virtue. Vermeer enlarged in their place the painting of Cupid, who is said to be throwing down his mask 'in contempt for deceit or duplicity in love', though the painter himself doesn't quite come out and say this. Indeed, Vermeer's alterations and corrections can be seen as moves away from the 'this is what it's all about' toward the less explicit.

In his mid-twenties, Vermeer was an active if unprolific artist. For his early pictures he seems to have stood at his easel; later he sat before it, the way the artist does in *The Art of Painting*, and consequently the eye-level in his paintings drops lower. By now his studio space had probably become a permanent one, with daylight entering through two or three north-facing windows. The inventory of his moveable goods of 29 February 1676 lists in the front room upstairs two painter's easels, three palettes, six panels, ten painter's canvases, three bundles with all sorts of prints, and a reading desk, as well as an oak table, a small wooden cupboard with drawers, two 'Spanish chairs', and what was probably a painter's maulstick. In his attic room above he may have made some of his pigments, grinding them on the stone table there and mixing them with linseed oil; but he probably also bought some from art-supplies shops and apothecary shops. In 1664 Vermeer owed Dirck de Cocq, a Delft apothecary, money for medicines, but de Cocq also stocked natural white lead, massicot (a pale yellow), booklets of gold leaf, Venetian turpentine, and linseed oil. (The apothecary shop also sold wine and spirits for drinking, including gin.) Art-supplies dealers in Delft or Rotterdam could have provided his prepared canvases and colours, including ochre, smalt (a blue), and ultramarine, the most expensive pigment of all, made from lapis lazuli from Afghanistan, which he used extensively. He seems to have designed a picture directly with brushes on the coloured ground of the canvas, often with the help of optical aids, but without preliminary drawings – at least no such drawings have been found.

Although the small number of his paintings that exist suggests that he was a costive artist, this doesn't mean he was a slow worker. Experts in examining painting technique have read his broad brush-strokes as often applied wet-in-wet, that is, painted quickly, putting paint on top of paint before it had dried. But one may still suspect that there were considerable periods when he didn't paint anything. One gets the impression of a man who changed details, added and deleted things, who left a canvas on an easel and went away for a while and allowed it to germinate, coming back with new thoughts and a renewed desire to achieve perfection. Perhaps he didn't feel he had to make lots of pictures. Possibly, the perfectionist was subject to depression – 'What's the point of painting if you can't get it absolutely right?' – and this led to periods when he felt blocked, unable to paint. At any rate, where most Dutch painters produced nearly fifty paintings a year, Vermeer created two or – at the most – three. He may have become a diligent dilettante, as it were, a Sunday painter who worked now and then any day of the week, when he felt like it. As time goes on, his paintings are almost always of rooms into which sunlight falls, and if this means he waited for sunny weather before picking up his brush, the usual number of grey and rainy Dutch days would have ruled out the act of painting on many of them. With up to eleven children in the same house with him and Catharina, and his mother-in-law, and a servant trying to keep the place clean, it is perhaps amazing that he got anything done at all.

Certain motifs, like trademarks, are found in many of his pictures: the white wine jug, quite likely made in a Delft pottery; the bowl of fruit on a carpeted table; a girl's downcast eyes; finials in the form of a lion's head at the back of a chair. But apart from these, he often enjoyed making his own mark to identify his work, and he soon worked out a neat way of signing his paintings. The signature in *Diana and her Companions* was 'I V Meer', but this was replaced by 'I VMeer', with the V and M joined together as one letter, and later with slight variations such as 'VMeer', 'Meer', or 'M'.

Out of the house, it was a very short walk across the market place to Mechelen to call on his mother, where she was still running the family inn. From there it was only another few yards through the Oudemansteeg to the Voldersgracht and the headquarters of the Guild of St Luke. In the mid-sixteenth century Maerten van Heemskerk gave the St Luke's Guild of Haarlem a picture he had done of the good saint at work on his legendary portrait of Mary and the infant Christ. In 1611 the Delft guild listed all its craftsmen: 'All those earning their living here with the art of painting, be it with fine brushes or otherwise in oil or water-colours, glassmakers, glass-sellers, faienciers, tapestry-makers, embroiderers, sculptors working in wood or stone, scabbard-makers, art printers, booksellers, [and] sellers of prints or paintings.' In 1661 St Luke's was the biggest of the Delft guilds and moved to the former chapel of the Old Men's Home, empty after its previous occupants, the Cloth- and Serge-makers' Guild, had moved to accommodation in the Prinsenhof. The chapel was rebuilt, the façade decorated with masonry garlands for each of the crafts in the guild, and with coats of arms of the guild and the town; the interior of the meeting hall was redone with a painting over the fireplace by Cornelis de Man and ceiling frescoes by Leonaert Bramer. Bramer had been one of the six headmen of the guild in 1660 and a few years earlier had done paintings for the new Doelen buildings, including one of a target that the civic guard archers could use for shooting practice.

The guild's governing board was made up of two faience-makers, two stained-glass-makers, and two painters, who each served for two years in overlapping terms – i.e. three of the six resigned each year. Their chairman or dean belonged to the *vroedeschap*, the forty-strong town council. The guild's big day was 15 October, St Luke's Day, when six candidates were nominated by its members for the three posts of headmen that became available every year, the final selection being made by Delft's burgomasters and aldermen. Vermeer was appointed to the board in 1662, when he was just thirty and young for the job. Although the guild's new, restored quarters might suggest that it was flourishing, the balance of prosperity among its member-crafts was shifting. Professor Montias, who has examined the guild's records, reckons the number of master painters in Delft to have been forty-seven in 1613, fifty-eight in 1640 (the peak for painters), fifty-one in 1660, and thirty-one in 1680. Printers, not painters, generally formed the wealthiest profession. But as the century passed the faience-makers were those who showed the greatest increase in numbers: in 1650 there were thirteen of them, when there were fifty-two painters; in 1680 there were fifty-seven faience-makers and, as noted, thirty-one painters. New potteries were being set up, many in former breweries.

In the Guild of St Luke, Vermeer obviously knew, and even knew well, most of his painter colleagues, including Bramer and de Man. Evert van Aelst, Pieter de Hooch, Hendrick van den Burch (a genre painter like de Hooch, who was his brother-in-law), and the portraitist Anthony Palamedes were among the painters he would have met at guild get-togethers. There are no documents – other than the guild register – linking Vermeer and de Hooch, but Montias tells us that 'de Hooch's name frequently crops up in the records of Frans Boogert, who was Maria Thins's and Vermeer's family notary'. Vermeer's brother-in-law Antony van der Wiel, a successful ebony frame-maker,

had registered with the guild as an art-dealer in February 1657, and at
the Guild Hall Vermeer would also have run into the representatives
of other crafts, such as the printer and poet Arnold Bon. Although we
don't know what shop-talk and art gossip passed between Vermeer
and, say, de Hooch or Bramer, such trends as a decreasing demand for
history paintings in general and the decline in sales of House of
Orange portraits in particular could have been discussed. Following
the death of Fabritius and the move away from Delft of de Witte,
Potter, van der Poel, and Couwenburgh, there may well have been
discussion about where to turn next. William II's death and the
Thunderclap seemed to signal the end of a phase and to some degree
a liberation from past ideas. In the last years of the 1650s, a bright new
dawn in Delft art became manifest.

Here de Hooch was in the vanguard. He had served part of his
apprenticeship with the Haarlem landscape painter Nicolaes
Berchem. De Hooch had been painting men and women carousing in
cheap taverns and soldiers drinking and gambling in inns and stables
where they were billeted. Now he turned to the houses of Delft,
especially their ground-floor rooms and courtyards, and to the women
and children to be seen in them. There are about fifty pictures from
this period of de Hooch's career, a good deal more than in Vermeer's
entire *oeuvre*. De Hooch recycled his subjects, as did other thrifty
Dutch painters, reusing figures of card players, army officers, women,
and children, and moving them from one interior or backyard scene to
relocate them in another. Sometimes he used different figures but
kept the same space. Sometimes he copied a previous picture and
added, or removed, a single figure to make the painting new. Sometimes he simply copied a whole picture – and later copied it again. The
interiors usually show a way through or a way out, an open door, an
open window, a passage – leading to a yard or street – in which a
woman stands or a man is striding towards his family. The women,
housewives and servants, are generally at work on domestic tasks:
nursing babies, combing lice out of hair, getting water from wells,
spreading laundry on the grass or rearranging the contents of the linen
cabinet, sweeping the floor, preparing vegetables, making beds. The

children hold *kolf* sticks or pet dogs. The figures are often a bit gawky and roughly rendered; the paint seems transparent, rather penuriously laid on as if this was all that de Hooch (son of a bricklayer) could afford, though time and restorers may also have taken their toll.

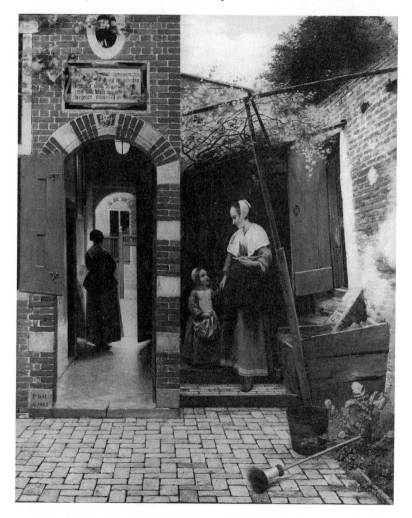

Courtyard of a House in Delft, 1658, Pieter de Hooch.

The family of his wife Annetge, the van den Burchs, lived on the Binnenwatersloot, which ran into the town from the Watersloot-sepoort, Delft's major gateway on the west, and joined the canal of the Oude Delft. Van den Burch senior was a candle-maker; his son Hendrick, a fellow painter, had been a member of the St Luke's Guild since 1649. The van den Burch home may have provided the *mise-en-scène* for some of de Hooch's paintings. So, too, did his own house, which seems to have been close by, off the Oude Delft; the tower of the Oude Kerk appears on the near skyline in several of his pictures, not always accurately but in such a way that the viewer feels the painter was making use of his own neighbourhood. In two de Hooch paintings a stone plaque or tablet of 1614 is shown, fixed over the entrance to a passageway leading to the former Hieronymusdael Cloister, a monastery dissolved in 1536 after the great Delft fire. This entrance, the St Hieronymuspoort, was on the west side of the Oude Delft, less than a hundred yards from the Oude Kerk. The inscription on the plaque says: 'This is St Jerome's vale, where you may go to find patience and meekness. For we must first descend if we wish to be uplifted.' In one of the two paintings three people are shown in a courtyard under a trellis: a man holds a beer tankard, a woman stands with a glass of wine, and a skimpily bearded man smokes a clay pipe. We might see here de Hooch and Vermeer having a chat, while Catharina, a brick-maker's daughter, stands by.

The influences of one Dutch artist of this time upon another can be part of a circular pattern as much as a linear one. Gerard Terborch was a courtyard painter who appears to have had an effect on de Hooch. And de Hooch, humbly enough, seems to have made Vermeer conscious of the fact that subjects for paintings were right under his nose. But where de Hooch was evidently portraying motherhood and 'good house-keeping', and parading their associated straightforward virtues, the slightly younger Vermeer decided to go in for apparently simpler compositions, seen at closer range, that resulted in altogether more complex pictures, such as the sleeping servant-girl, the maid pouring milk, and the young woman having a drink with an officer. The latter – *Officer and Laughing Girl* of 1658 (see p. 139) – is a small and intimate picture, almost a view through a keyhole into a nearby room; the room, albeit on a larger scale, is very like that in the de Hooch work called *A Woman drinking with Two Men, and a Serving Woman*, now in London's National Gallery. There is a similar table under high windows on the left-hand wall and a similar map of the Low Countries hanging on the back wall. However, where de Hooch places a woman – possibly singing – standing with a glass, her back turned to the viewer, Vermeer has his officer with a black broad-brimmed hat seated and silhouetted against the light streaming in. And where de Hooch has his two soldiers sitting at the table with fairly silly expressions on their faces, Vermeer puts his girl, sitting in one of the chairs with the lion's-head finials we get to know so well, facing the light and the officer, at whom she is smiling. Where de Hooch keeps us at a decorous distance, Vermeer zooms in and takes the viewer with him. De Hooch's people are head-to-toe figures posed in an interior which they by no means dominate. Vermeer's couple, though portrayed only in part, *are* the picture. Vermeer lights his scene from the left, a method he seems to have borrowed from de Hooch but which is evident in more subdued form in the early religious paintings, and which he stuck with, mostly, to the end. But when it comes to saying what the pictures are about, the de Hooch seems to present no trouble and the Vermeer presents a lot. Some critics have insisted that his painting shows a mercenary encounter. If so, how fresh and innocent the girl is, how openly she smiles. How little do we know of what will happen next.

Until the *Officer and Laughing Girl*, Vermeer's indoor pictures have a somewhat murky light. Now – perhaps thanks to de Hooch – the light floods in. So it does in Vermeer's *Girl reading a Letter at an Open Window*, now in Dresden, where a crimson curtain is draped up and over the open casement allowing the girl and her precious letter to be bathed gently in light. Although de Hooch often favoured the light-from-the-left treatment, he sometimes painted sunlight entering from the right, and on at least one occasion superbly also from the rear, coming in through the glazed transom and open top-half of the Dutch door in the *Mother and Child with its Head in her Lap* of around 1658.

In this the outside light bounces off the swung-back door and falls in
a bright rhomboid on the tiled floor. But Vermeer, as if going one

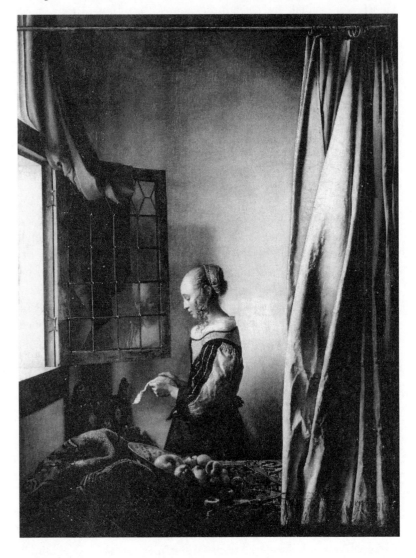

Girl reading a Letter at an Open Window, c. 1657.

better, has his light not only illuminate the letter-reading girl but strike the folds of the other curtain, a green one, that he has painted hanging from a rod across the top of the picture. De Hooch never played with the viewer in this way, giving us the illusion that we are looking at a real curtain drawn across a painting on the wall, although of course the church interior painters – Houckgeest, de Witte, and van Vliet – had done so and continued to do so. (Gerrit Dou painted a self-portrait in the 1640s with a similar *trompe-l'oeil* curtain, and Rembrandt, Nicolaes Maes, and Jan Steen used the same device.) Vermeer obviously enjoyed dissembling with this effect, though he must have known that few viewers would have been truly deceived and thought the curtain real; it was more of an aid to link the artificial creation which was the picture with the surrounding reality of wall, room, house, daily life. And did the curtain also, drawn back and therefore not fulfilling its potential to keep things dark, emphasise what it allowed to be shown – the sunlight entering the window? It is a light that never hardens but slowly moves, shadows moving with it, and indicates both time passing and warmth of life: the power of creation making itself felt in humdrum human circumstances. This life-giving light was beyond de Hooch, and yet one feels that Vermeer got to it via de Hooch; indeed, one feels that in the late 1650s Vermeer learned more from de Hooch than de Hooch learned from him.

We know from Balthasar de Monconys who visited in 1663 that at least one of Vermeer's paintings belonged to a local baker, presumably Hendrick van Buyten, who eventually owned at least three Vermeers, one large and two small. His supposed *Visit to the Tomb* had been sold, as mentioned earlier, to the dealer Johannes Renialme, whose stock at one point also included paintings by Rembrandt and Poelenburgh. A Vermeer painting of unknown subject-matter belonged to the Delft innkeeper Corneliszoon de Helt, whose death inventory listed 'a painting in a black frame, by Jan van der Meer', as hanging in the front hall of the Young Prince Inn. 'A face by Vermeer' is known to have been owned by the sculptor (of The Hague and London) Johan – or Jean – Larson. But his most stalwart patron, and therefore a major influence in his life, was most likely Pieter Claeszoon van Ruijven. His father had owned a brewery, 'The Ox', on the Voorstraat, which closed down in the mid-1650s, one of the many Delft breweries to succumb to out-of-town competition. Although one of Delft's upper class, Pieter Claeszoon van Ruijven was disqualified from high civic office because of his liberal Remonstrant Protestantism; even so he served for four years as a master of the Chamber of Charity, a post his father had held. But he married well in 1653, his wife Maria de Knuijt bringing with her a good deal of wealth, and they eventually owned at least three Delft houses: two were in the Voorstraat and one on the Oude Delft. One of the Voorstraat houses was damaged in the Thunderclap, and van Ruijven claimed compensation for this. We don't know if this was the 'Gouden Anker', which he bought for 2,100 guilders in 1660, or in which house he and Maria de Knuijt then lived. Later they moved to the Oude Delft house and though they were living in The Hague in July 1674, they apparently moved back to Delft, to the Voorstraat, shortly before his death, aged forty-nine, in 1674.

In 1669 Van Ruijven had also bought land near Schiedam that brought with it the title of Lord of Spalant. Twelve years earlier, as noted, he had loaned Vermeer and Catharina 200 guilders for a year, no doubt expecting to receive paintings in return. In 1665 Maria de Knuijt mentioned Vermeer in her will, leaving him a legacy of 500 guilders, though this was to lapse if the artist died before her death (as in fact he did). It has been argued that by this qualification to her bequest, the only legacy to someone not a member of her family, Maria de Knuijt ensured that only Vermeer and not his Catholic wife would benefit from it, if Catharina survived him. But it may be too much to read any anti-Papist or anti-Jesuit feeling into this, particularly if Vermeer himself was regarded as just-about-a-Catholic; Maria may simply have wanted to help a living artist while he could put paint on canvas, and not provide funds for his relatives after his death. But the friendship her husband Pieter felt for the Vermeer family seems evident in the fact that, in 1670, he witnessed the last testament of Vermeer's sister Gertruy and her husband, the picture-framer Antony van der Wiel, who were described as 'well-known to the notary and the witnesses'.

Most of the pictures in the cherished van Ruijven collection – the *Schilderkonst* mentioned especially in their joint will, with dispositions made clear in a record book they had put aside for that purpose – seem to have gone to their daughter Magdalena. In 1680 she married Jacob Dissius, who was registered in the Guild of St Luke as a bookbinder and seems to have been given by his father a printing shop, the Golden ABC, in the Market Place, at the time of his marriage. Two years later Magdalena died, aged twenty-seven, and Jacob, her 'beloved husband' as she calls him in her will, became the owner of the van Ruijven pictures; they included at least twenty Vermeers. (For a time, he shared their ownership with his father, Abraham Dissius, who was named by Magdalena as a joint heir to her estate, perhaps as some sort of compensation for the printing shop gift, but the father predeceased the son.) Van Ruijven had apparently favoured small cabinet-sized paintings. In the catalogue of the sale in Amsterdam in May 1696, seven months after Jacob Dissius's death, twenty-one paintings by Vermeer were listed, one more than before, and from their descriptions it is possible to determine which of them van Ruijven chose for his collection. Among them are the *Girl asleep at a Table*, which the sale catalogue calls 'A drunken sleeping maid at a table'; the *Officer and Laughing Girl* – 'a soldier with a laughing girl, very beautiful'; the *Little Street* – 'a view of some houses'; the *Milkmaid* – 'A Girl pouring milk, extremely well done'; the *Girl being offered Wine* – 'a merry company in a Room, powerful and good'; and the *View of Delft* – 'The Town of Delft in perspective, to be seen from the South'. We don't know who proposed or disposed – whether van Ruijven steered Vermeer towards themes that he knew the artist would handle well, whether Vermeer detected sympathies for certain subjects in his patrician patron, or whether Vermeer said simply 'What about this?' or 'What about that?' and van Ruijven answered 'Yes' or 'No'. But with a few exceptions, Vermeer's pictures that ended up in the van Ruijven/Dissius collection reflected the painter's move upmarket, towards more *burgerlijk* subject-matter. Many of the leisured young women in these pictures look more Oude Delft than Voldersgracht. The Lord of Spalant's wife Maria and daughter Magdalena may have set the tone and even modelled for Vermeer.

Certainly no artist paints pictures over twenty years against the grain of his own inclinations. No matter how tortoise-like his process seemed, Vermeer was devoted to perfection; and the pictures speak for his ambitions, for his day-dreams, for what he liked his gaze to rest on, and for the problems of composition and construction he made for himself and dealt with, with brush and paint. The most evident thing is that he liked painting young women. When the Amsterdam municipal surgeon Jan Sysmus made a list of contemporary artists between 1669 and 1678 he characterised Vermeer's subjects as *jonkertjes*, 'little gallants', with the 'little' applying to the size of the pictures, but as the art historian Albert Blankert has pointed out, a more apt term would have been that which Sysmus used for the subjects of Metsu and Terborch: *juffertjes*, 'little damsels'. Conversation pieces of fancy young men and young women were fashionable at mid-century, shown in interiors where they are to be seen drinking, eating, playing music, writing and reading letters, and flirting. Owners of such pictures could vicariously enjoy these pleasures.

After the *Procuress*, Vermeer's young people – mostly young ladies – know how to behave. Not all his young women are involved in pleasure or the arts: a maid pours milk, a young woman makes lace. A few servants have walk-on parts. But generally infants and children, middle-aged and old people have no interest for him. He stands firmly in the tradition of Netherlandish art of painting demure young women – following, for example, *The Magdalen Reading* by Rogier van der Weyden two centuries earlier. And if one seeks a precursor from a wider field, though of a similar date, there is Ghirlandaio's lovely portrait of Giovanna Tornabuoni, painted in profile, facing left, whose hair-do of ringlets and bun is curiously similar to that of Vermeer's *Girl reading a Letter at an Open Window*. Vermeer's young women have in common serenity, prosperity, and a touch of secrecy. They evidently found acceptance in the van Ruijven household and later with several other Delft patrician families including the van Berckels and van Assendelfts.

Although we can't say for sure whether Vermeer himself had social ambitions, there are hints of it. Lawyers' documents following 1655 refer to him most often as 'Seigneur' – a title given to wealthy merchants, naval commanders, and higher-ranking officials. The Thins ladies were called *juffrouws*, as befitted their position. Somewhere along the way a Vermeer coat of arms was acquired and was displayed, in a black frame, in the great hall of the Oude Langendijk house. Vermeer definitely didn't consider himself to be an artisan. Although his annual income from painting, say, three pictures a year was probably around 200 guilders, roughly what was earned by a common sailor, that wouldn't have been enough. He needed the Thins money and the free accommodation Maria Thins apparently allowed him and his large family. His total income including these subsidies has been estimated at between 850 and 1,500 guilders. Another source of income is rarely given deep consideration. Vermeer had taken over his father's art-dealing business, and like many other artists – Rembrandt, Aelbert Cuyp, and Jan van Goyen among them – he used that trade to support his painting. In his later years, Rembrandt lived by dealing in works of art with the help of Hendrickje Stoffels and his son Titus. Vermeer's art-dealing may have involved more, in time and profit, than has been generally assumed. Ludwig Goldscheider is one of the few art historians to stress this and suggest that it may have been Vermeer's 'chief source of income'. After Vermeer's death, Catharina blamed their impoverished condition on the fact that during the French war her husband 'was forced to sell at a great loss works of art he had purchased and intended to sell'. This may have been why his stock of pictures in 1675 seemed low, at twenty-six, and worth not quite twenty guilders each, valued at a total of 500 guilders. There were probably times in earlier years when stock and takings had been higher.

6. *Little Castles*

Interiors. Inside. Indoors. These are words that suggest the subjects of much of Vermeer's art, even while out-of-doors the sun shines and daylight enters the rooms within. But at least twice he looked *out* of an upstairs window and painted the subject he saw outside, leaving little sign in the work itself of his viewing post. In the late 1650s, when he was in his mid- to late twenties, he painted a bit of streetscape: an adjacent pair of houses, one more fully shown than the other. He did this from close range, possibly looking across a small inner-city canal as well as the narrow roadway that is just visible in the picture. And in 1660 or 1661, he went to the south end of Delft, outside the walls, and to the far side of the harbour called the Kolk where the River Schie joined the town's canal network. There he apparently climbed the stairs in a house on the Schieweg and from a room overlooking the quay gazed north across the water to the Delft skyline: rooftops, church towers, city gates, battlements, and drawbridges; and closer to hand, fishing boats and passenger barges. The first picture, the streetscape, was small, almost a private view. The second was large; not as big as the *Christ in the House of Martha and Mary* and *The Procuress*, but larger than the *Diana and her Companions*.

Het Straatje – 'The Little Street' – is in fact a little painting of a small section of street. There is nothing to indicate how wide the street is, though we get the impression that the painter's view (which is our view) is from a house opposite, from an upstairs room, at no great distance. Topographical experts and local historians in Delft have spent much time trying to pin down where this was. The Oude

Langendijk, the Nieuwe Langendijk, the Trompetstraat, the Spieringstraat, Achterom, the Vlamingstraat, and the Voldersgracht are among the numerous streets put forward for the honour. The Voldersgracht has been a consistent candidate, for the back of Mechelen overlooked the little canal of the Voldersgracht and its narrow carriageway, on to which faced the Old Men's Home and – a few doors further east – the Flying Fox inn. In a few years the Old Men's Home was going to be partly rebuilt, with its chapel converted in 1661 into the hall of the St Luke's Guild; drawings of the hall show a small house and archway similar to the part of the left-hand house and archway depicted in *The Little Street*. But the house on the right in that picture has its gable-end facing the street, while the building which housed the chapel of the Old Men's Home stood side-on to the street. The two arched outside doorways in the painting – one with a closed door, the other with door open revealing a brick-paved passage in which a servant-woman is leaning over a barrel used as a washtub or cistern, and waste water runs towards us along a gulley – form the heart of the picture. What is behind the dark closed door? Its shut state, the openness and light of its companion, bring to mind those weather-predicting devices styled as miniature cottages out of which figures swing to declare that it is going to be fine or rainy.

There must have been many hundred such passageways in Delft then. However, an adjacent pair, with twin gates like those in the picture, is now not to be found in any of the favoured streets. But given the artist's close relationship with van Ruijven, it seems a possibility that the house on the right belonged to that gentleman. *The Little Street* was painted around the time Vermeer and his wife borrowed 200 guilders from van Ruijven. The house on the right has signs of a good deal of hasty repointing and patching of cracks, as if it was shaken severely by the Thunderclap, and we know that van Ruijven owned a house on the east side of the Voorstraat that was damaged in the explosion. The picture was in his collection.

For all that, it also seems probable that here, as in many other paintings, Vermeer picked and mixed his details. He took some elements of 'reality' and put them together in an 'invented' scene; he may have observed some details and remembered or imagined others. When we look closely at it, the main house in *The Little Street* is a strange mish-mash of architectural features, to which an air of plausibility is given by the wonderful painting of brick, wood, and glass, of the trees and sky, and of the figures of the two women and two children. The front doorway, in which one of the women sits sewing, is not quite in the centre of the façade, as might be expected, but is offset to the left. Did Vermeer place it there to accommodate the swung-open shutter on the right with its vivid rectangle of red? And what about its partners, the closed green shutters on the left of the doorway? The right-hand one of those would be impossible to open, at least with abandon, all the way, without partly obstructing the front doorway. A further impracticality in terms of sound building practice is to be seen in the position of this left-hand ground-floor window. It immediately abuts the side wall of the house. The shallow arch of bricks above its wooden lintel presses against the very edge of this wall, and few Dutch builders would have risked their reputations – or the lives of the children playing under the wall-hung bench – with such a construction. The house wouldn't stand up to a good push, let alone a gunpowder explosion.

For Vermeer, form clearly preceded function. He has apparently taken various details from various houses (maybe more from one than from others) and stuck them together, as if with the tie-rods and mortar that make us believe we are looking at an 'actual' streetscape. The leaves of the vine that is growing up the wall of the cottage on the left, the rough bricks, the places where ridge-tiles are missing over the passage entries, and the weathered in-need-of-attention framing of the windows are painted with such a light, almost pointillist touch that we are seduced into feeling that all this has been rendered with utter verisimilitude. The liberties he has taken include theft, or at least major borrowing, from fellow artists. The vine, passageway, and servant-woman are more than somewhat de Hooch, while the beautifully observed children crouching on their knees are extremely similar to the children in a 1650 Houckgeest painting of the interior of the Nieuwe Kerk and William the Silent's tomb. And yet! – and yet the ultimate effect is original. The painting is an elegy for a moment which – unless Vermeer had captured it – would have slipped away for ever: the women busy with their chores, the children entranced by their game, the clouds filtering the sunlight, two doors and one window open, and air wafting through the house.

Time, halted for this instant and therefore in a sense for eternity, seems to be his essential subject. Its wear and tear is visible in the bricks and mortar, the fabric of fact that bluntly underpins our tenuous and temporary hold on existence with its many unanswerable questions, such as 'What are we doing here?' And yet according to some art historians the picture is also about the ideals of domestic virtue: the grape-vine symbolises love and marital fidelity. Psalm 128 says: 'Thy wife shall be as a fruitful vine by the sides of thine house.' Catharina was often 'full and sweet', as the Dutch described the state of pregnancy. And Vermeer allows for this sense of development in his painting. Unlike de Hooch, who freezes his figures for once and for all, he gives us the feeling that at any moment the woman in the doorway will put her sewing or embroidery away and call to the children; time for some food. And the servant will come in from the passageway and help in the kitchen.

Dr Sysmus in Amsterdam, making his list of artists and their subjects, added another exotic term to *jonkertjes* in reference to Vermeer: this was *casteeltjes*, 'little castles'. Perhaps he had in mind the crenellated appearance of the sixteenth-century gable in *The Little Street*, the stepped brick 'merlons' with slits between, like battlements from which arrows could be shot. Or was it the pedantic doctor's response to the atmosphere of the picture that seems – to adapt the English adage – to embody the idea that 'a Dutchman's home is his castle'? Not that Vermeer felt the need to put a man in the painting, as de Hooch might have done. Here, the man of the house is off at work, in his shop, his office, his studio or workshop, but this house, these household duties, this childhood play are all underwritten by him.

At the rate of almost one birth a year, the Vermeers had five or six children by 1661, three or four of whom survived. We know that one child was buried in the Oude Kerk on 27 December 1660. The first five children who apparently lived into adulthood were all girls – Maria, Elisabeth, Cornelia, Aleydis, and Beatrix. With an eventual eleven living children, Vermeer may well have pondered how to divide his energies; his slow production of paintings meant he completed only some three pictures for every child. The poet Yeats later put the dilemma as which to choose, perfection of the life or of the work? A ruthless genius may plump for the latter. A more difficult task faces the home-loving artist who tries for both.

We haven't much to go on for daily details. We assume the children were got safely to and from school, taken to Mass on Sundays and holy days, made to say their prayers at night, and taken to city events such as fairs. They will have played the childhood games shown on Delft tiles of the time. In the winter of 1660 Vermeer apparently bought an ice-boat for the large sum of eighty guilders. Michael Montias has found a record of a debt for that amount owed by 'Johan van der Meer' for such a craft in the estate accounts of a sailmaker, Daniel Gilliszoon de Bergh; that it was owed by our Vermeer seems probable given that those who witnessed the accounts were both painters, de Bergh's sons, Gillis and Mattheus. Many of the winters of the early 1660s were extremely cold in northern Europe, with rivers, lakes, and canals hard frozen, and Holland a white landscape of a sort the paintings of Avercamp and Cuyp have made us familiar with. Among the skaters and the stalls on the ice selling hot food and drink, a sled-like boat whizzes along under sail, a man and some children its happy crew.

On 25 May 1660 King Charles II of England came to Delft. He had been waiting in Breda for the summons to return to England where his crown had just been restored to him, and he entered Delft on a yacht the city of Amsterdam had presented him with. He was to have been given a tour of the new States-General gunpowder magazine, built on the banks of the Schie River at a spot called the Vaert, outside the town, but he arrived too early, at five a.m., and finding no one there sailed on to the Rotterdam Gate. There the burghers of Delft rushed to greet him. But he didn't stay long, his yacht going round to the north end of town to pick him up from The Hague Gate and take him on to that city.

Among the Englishmen who were in Holland on Restoration duty was Samuel Pepys, aged twenty-seven, soon to be an influential Clerk of the Acts in the new Navy Board but at that point secretary to Sir Edward Montagu, later Earl of Sandwich. Pepys came to Delft a week before Charles and described it as 'a most sweet town, with bridges, and a river in every street. Observing that in every house of entertainment there hangs in every room a poor-man's box . . . it was told me that it is their custom to confirm all bargains by putting something into the poor people's box, and that that binds as fast as anything.' Pepys showed his current nautical predilections by writing in his diary not about William the Silent's tomb in the Nieuwe Kerk but the memorial in the Oude Kerk of Admiral Maarten Tromp, who had died in battle with the English: 'a seafight the best cut in marble, with the smoke the best expressed that ever I saw in my life'. His guide in Delft, a blacksmith's boy, could speak no English. Later that year Pepys had his first cup of tea in London but tea-drinking had been fashionable in Holland since 1650.

There was a long-standing English connection with Delft. English actors had often played there; for example, as members of the Earl of Leicester's drama company before the turn of the century and with a group of *camer speelders*, or travelling players, around 1616. In 1609 two Englishmen were tried in the town for counterfeiting coinage and sentenced to long terms in the galleys. The English House tavern did good business. Merchants of the English East India Company stationed in Delft gave a banquet in August 1623 for the King and Queen of Bohemia (she being Charles II's aunt). English cloth merchants formed a 'staple' or branch of the Merchant Adventurers Company there for a number of years, selling their wares from a brokerage by the Boterbrug, before moving to Rotterdam in 1635. However, many English weavers went on living and working in Delft, as did English carpenters, brewers, and lawyers. A number of English soldiers and sailors also lived in the town, for even during the Anglo-Dutch wars some preferred to serve the United Provinces; the sailors liked being paid in cash rather than with the sometimes valueless IOUs or 'tickets' they got for crewing their own ships; and there were specifically English and Scottish companies in the States armies, whose soldiers sometimes married local girls. English printers in Delft did a steady trade producing Calvinist Bibles, which they exported to England as part of a Puritan campaign against the Established Church. Some had Dutch apprentices, some got into disputes with Dutch competitors, though none joined the Guild of St Luke.

The English enclave in Delft had its own small church, and some of its records are still in Delft's archives. In most years two or three children were baptised in the church, with names such as William, Edward, Moses, Ezekiel, Mary, Abigail, and Judith. Among the new members 'received' in the church under the long pastorship of Alexander Petrie was Lieutenant-Colonel Dolman, an English officer who commanded the troops accompanying the Dutch naval expedition of 1667 that created havoc in the English fleet moored in the River Medway and then carried off the English flagship the *Royal Charles*. (Dolman's forces stormed and destroyed fortifications at Sheerness.) Mr Petrie was an acquaintance of Antony van Leeuwenhoek, the Delft draper, civic official, and amateur scientist who became an executor of Vermeer's estate, and on one occasion Petrie acted as a witness for his microscope experiments.

It was in this seemingly hospitable town that three Englishmen, who had been involved with the capture and execution of Charles I in 1649, took refuge in 1661. When the Cromwellian protectorate came to an end, some of the so-called regicides – Colonel John Barkstead, Colonel John Okey, and Mr Miles Corbet – fled to the Continent, and after wandering here and there arrived in Holland. They thought they had assurances from the States-General that they would be unmolested. They thought they had the word of Sir George Downing, the English Resident, that he had no orders from Charles II to seize them.

Downing, one of Harvard University's earliest students, had been a soldier before becoming a public official and managed to traverse the change of regimes while remaining the English ambassador to a country which he disliked and which he enjoyed harassing as a commercial competitor. He once boasted to Pepys that he had had the Dutch statesman Johan de Witt's pockets picked so that he could read important state papers. Downing soon heard that the regicides were in Delft and arranged for them to be arrested in their lodgings. They were put in shackles and imprisoned, despite the professed reluctance of the Delft authorities to go along with the proceedings. Assurances from the States-General that they wouldn't be shipped to England without a public hearing proved equally untrustworthy. Downing had them sent off to an English frigate which carried them home. After a short sojourn in the Tower, they were executed at Tyburn on 19 April 1662 – hanged (for fifteen minutes) and then quartered. Pepys had written of Downing a month before, 'All the world takes notice of him for a most ungrateful villain.' Colonel Okey, who some years before had helped Downing find employment on his return from New England, must have felt the same.

Vermeer, like all his fellow citizens, would have heard of these English tragedies. Perhaps he gave only a sympathetic shudder at old hatreds still at work and a grateful thought that for Dutchmen things were now better. In 1662, when he became for two years one of the headmen of the Guild of St Luke, his close ties with Catholics and Catholicism were evidently no hindrance. In his first year, his fellow-painter in the post was Cornelis de Man; in his second year, Anthony Palamedes. To be appointed headman at thirty was an acknowledgement by his comrades that he was one of Delft's best artists. In several documents of this time, Vermeer – guaranteeing a loan, witnessing a will – is referred to as 'master painter' or 'artful painter'. Whether or not it was a conscious return of the compliments, Vermeer's affection for his city seems evident in his second and largest cityscape, which he painted around 1660 and 1661.

For the *View of Delft*, his viewpoint was – as noted – across the triangular canal and river harbour outside the twin Schiedam and Rotterdam gates, which were joined by the Capels Bridge. Delft's

gates were still locked at night, though latecomers could call a guard
to let them in. The fortifications had last been brought up to scratch
in 1573, but some outer bastions were demolished when the Kolk was
extended in 1614. This basin was Delft's access point, not to the
north, to The Hague, the seat of government, but to the south, to
Delfshaven and the two ports after which the gates were named; the
Kolk thus connected the trade of Delft to the Maas River, the North
Sea, and the world beyond. (Delfshaven had been Delft's primary
port since 1389 and was controlled by Delft town council.) Vermeer
presumably had some connection with the owner of the house on the
Schieweg (now the Hooikade) that he worked from – perhaps a friend
of a friend and possibly the owner of a *trekschuit* or passenger barge
firm – and didn't just knock on the door and say 'I'd like to do a
painting from your upstairs window.' He would have known of
previous city portraits. Hendrick Vroom had painted Delft twice, in
1615 and 1617, from a westerly or north-westerly standpoint, and
showing the entire extent of the walled town from north to south. Jan
van Goyen working in the same tradition had done a panoramic view
of The Hague around 1650, showing sunlight slanting down from
beneath clouds on to a mostly shadowed city, with farmworkers and
cattle in the foreground countryside. Vermeer did not try for such
comprehensiveness. He limited his scope to what could be seen from
the Schieweg window: a hundred metres or so of quaysides, city walls,
fortified gates and drawbridges, houses, roofs, and towers. There is an
effect of battlements – once again Dr Sysmus's *casteeltjes* – that may
remind readers of Constantijn Huygens's poem 'Hofwijk' and his
evocation there of 'Delft's strong circling walls'. Vermeer saw his
town end-on, without the mills Huygens had also remarked.
Compared with the ways in which Vroom and van Goyen viewed the
town, he zoomed in on Delft as through a lens, and the result was not
so much inclusive as intense.

It is summer; trees are in leaf. Early morning, with the sun striking
the buildings from the south-east, and the clock on the Schiedam
gatehouse showing the time for the benefit of barge passengers: it has
just gone seven o'clock. The pervasive brightness under the overhead

cloud allows the painter to show without shadows the figures standing on the quay in the foreground. A very light breeze – the clouds are barely moving – makes catspaws on the water of the harbour. Three women (one holding a baby) and two men apparently waiting for their tow boat are talking quietly. There is a Sunday calm: no frenetic activity on the boats fitted out for herring fishing and the *trekschuits* tied up alongside the Schie quays near the gates; no other boats sailing by or being poled or towed to their terminus here at a waterway junction usually thronged with craft. Perhaps Vermeer saw the scene, or made the scene, quieter than it most often was. Nothing is here to make us think of anything but peace: no sign of war, of gunpowder explosions, of sudden death. What serenity pervades this little world. How he must have loved the place. And yet what professional sleight-of-hand has been involved here, rearranging the facts to produce this magical mood, making it seem this picture was painted out-of-doors, in *plein-air*.

For those of us who have come to the *View of Delft* after the invention of the photographic camera there is a disadvantage: the picture at first appears 'too photographic'. It must have seemed an even greater miracle of realism before Niepce and Daguerre led the way to Kodaks and Leicas. Some viewers have indeed criticised Vermeer for as it were turning himself into a camera for the occasion. Jozef Israëls and Philip Wilson Steer were among several twentieth-century artists for whom Vermeer's painting seemed to be trying too hard to cross every 't' and dot every 'i'. For others, Vermeer's 'precision' provides much of the painting's power to enchant. Albert Blankert hails the *View of Delft*'s 'topographical accuracy'. However, as Arthur K. Wheelock Jr and C.J. Kaldenbach have more recently pointed out, some of this accepted accuracy is illusive.* 'The Town of Delft in Perspective', as it was called when sold at the Dissius sale in 1696, far from confronting us with reality in a brutal, photographic way, reorganises reality for the sake of artistic simplification; it deceives us brilliantly. Wheelock and Kaldenbach have shown that

*Their article appeared in *Artibus et Historiae* in 1982.

the actual buildings in this scene were sited in a less regular pattern than as presented by Vermeer. The buildings of the Rotterdam Gate, on the right, protruded more towards the Schieweg and therefore towards the viewer; the bridge on the viewer's side of that gate in reality stuck out at right-angles to the line of the city wall rather than at the wider angle at which Vermeer has shown it, swinging it away from us. Moreover, various structures in fact stood up higher in the skyline than they do in Vermeer's *View*. The roadway over the Capels Bridge, which spanned the canal entrance between the Schiedam and Rotterdam gates with a goodly arch, was flattened by our artist for motives of his own. (Hump-backed bridges were a factor that led many goods to be carried on sleds rather than wheeled carts, which tended to slide back down their steep slopes.)

Behind the Capels Bridge can be seen, accurately rendered, the red roof of the Armentarium, an arms depot of the States of Holland and West Friesland. A small amount of gunpowder was kept here for the province's emergency needs; a fire in the building in January 1660 was quickly put out, but not before people were reminded of 1654. To the left of this in the painting, behind the city wall and sundry houses, is a long-roofed building with a small tower, Vermeer's interpretation of the Parrot brewery's rear quarters, and painted in such a way as to emphasise the horizontal impact he wanted to make. The Parrot reminds us that sixty years earlier a third of Delft's craftsmen had been brewers; beer, though still the national and local drink (water was drunk only when beer was in short supply), was suffering from the inroads of tea and coffee; and now the Parrot was one of fifteen Delft breweries where there had been more than a hundred establishments making beer. It also reminds us of Vermeer's family connection with beer through the two inns his father and mother ran – Mechelen was still his mother's – and with 'beer-money' via the van Ruijvens.

As usual, Vermeer created a reality whose bits and pieces can be disputed in terms of factual 'truth' but whose artistic rightness is overwhelming. Here on the Schieweg he looked across the Kolk, where at any moment a *trekschuit* might arrive, and he gave Delft the special status of an island. The city, surrounded by water and air, floats peacefully: dramatically lit cloud and sky above, quiet quayside and pewter-like water below. A broad band of red roofs extends leftwards from the centre of the painting, a less continuous band of light strikes the roofs that stretch out to the right, and the tower of the Nieuwe Kerk at the heart of the town gleams like an oriflamme for the House of Orange. For whatever reason, political, clerical, topographic, or artistic, Vermeer pays less attention to the Oude Kerk, the tip of whose tower is only just visible in his picture. But his chiaroscuro – the contrast between the shadowed and sunlit areas – draws us into the city. We feel we can go in through one of the gates and walk around and call on people.

Vermeer's linen canvas measured roughly 3 feet by 4. He painted, so the experts tell us, on a light-brown ground containing chalk, lead white, ochre, umber, and black, bound with oil. The lighter parts of the picture were underpainted with lead white, the darker areas with black. Vermeer produced something of the texture of the stone walls and roof-tiles by mixing sand with lumps of white lead in his under-layer. In the darker roofs he gave the impression of separate tiles by putting on the red, brown, and blue paint in hundreds of little dabs. For the lighter roofs he used a thick and bumpy band of pale yellow or salmon colour. One of his most original elements (at this pre-Impressionist time) was what, at a glance, appear to be pinpoints of light on the slate roofs of the Rotterdam Gate and the dark topsides of the nearest fishing boat, a herring *buss*, which is being outfitted at the shipyard on the viewer's side of the gate's drawbridge. These highlights, like so many pearls, were made up of globules of ochre, grey, and white paint laid on 'wet-in-wet', and represented light reflected off the water. They were probably an effect Vermeer saw with the aid of a camera obscura – a device that captured a reflection of a scene and took it through a lens on to a surface inside a darkened chamber, where the artist could ponder it and trace it. A camera obscura would also have helped Vermeer focus his view, foreshorten it, and cut out extraneous detail, making for a more intensely observed composition.

Did someone ask Vermeer to paint this view or did he paint it for himself? There is no evidence of a municipal commission or a private one from, say, the family which owned the Parrot brewery. As we have seen, civic loyalty and pride were strong at this time, with the new Doelen and St Luke's Guild hall being rebuilt and redecorated and Dirck van Bleyswijck's *Description* of Delft soon to be published. Delft's city council was to sponsor the splendidly detailed *Kaart Figuratif* in 1675, also under van Bleyswijck's guidance; this was a map as aerial picture or bird's-eye view, with the buildings shown in an isometric perspective. But we know that the *View of Delft* was among the pictures at the auction of the Dissius collection in 1696, where it fetched 200 guilders, the highest price at the sale. It was therefore, like *The Little Street*, probably one of the paintings Pieter Claeszoon van Ruijven bought from Vermeer. It doesn't seem to have been on hand when Monconys called to see the artist in August 1663, though possibly Vermeer didn't want to show it or have it considered as for sale. It was the warmest picture he had painted so far. (Although Lawrence Gowing suggested in 1952 that some of this warmth derived from old varnish, the painting has been cleaned since he made that comment, and it still glows.) The light that is reflected forth from within the town is the light of fulfilled creation – the mild light that we might be lucky to find in heaven, the perfect place, should we ever get there.

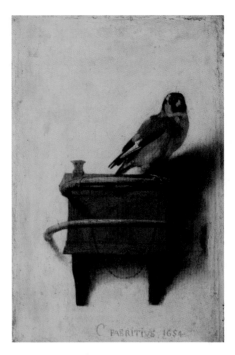

Carel Fabritius,
The Goldfinch, 1654

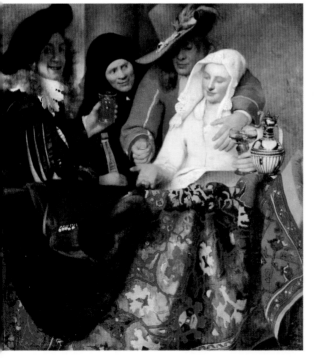

Johannes Vermeer,
The Procuress, 1656

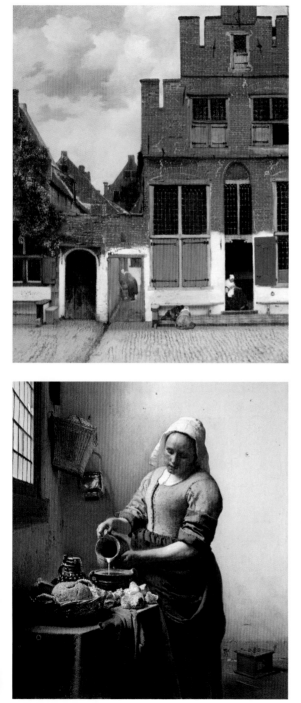

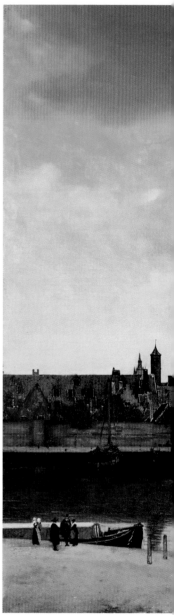

The Little Street, c. 1657–58

The Milkmaid, c. 1658–60

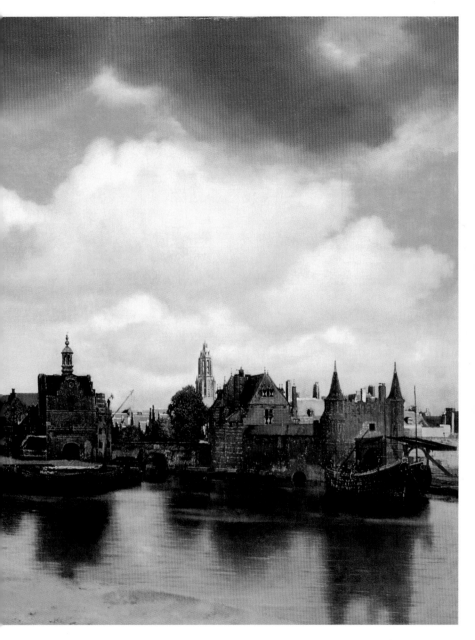

View of Delft, c. 1660-61

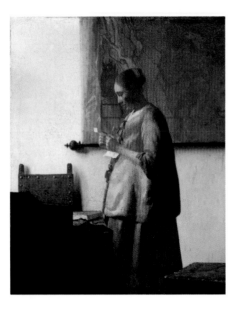

Woman in Blue reading a Letter, c. 1663-64

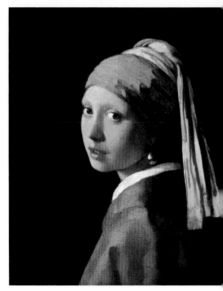

Girl with a Pearl Earring, c. 1665-66

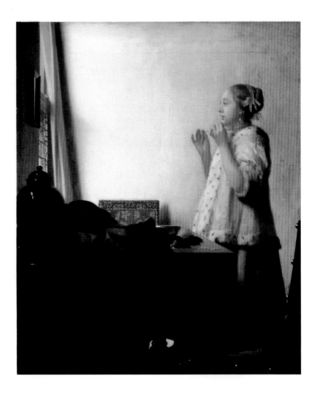

Woman with a Pearl Necklace,
c. 1664

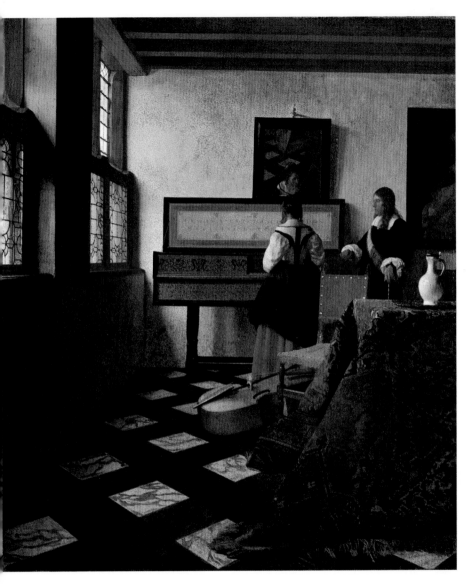

The Music Lesson, c. 1662-64

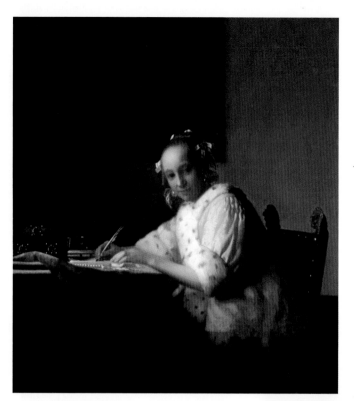

A Lady writing, c.166

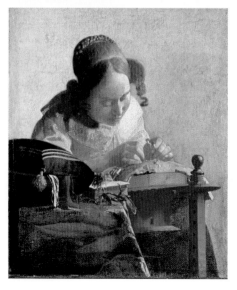

The Lacemaker, c.1669-70

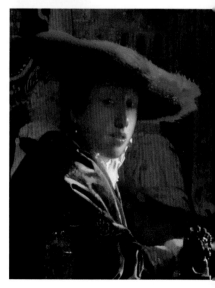

Girl with a Red Hat, c.1665

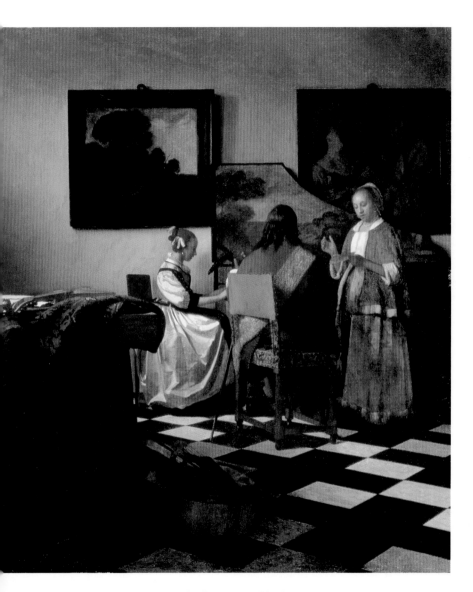

The Concert, c. 1665-66

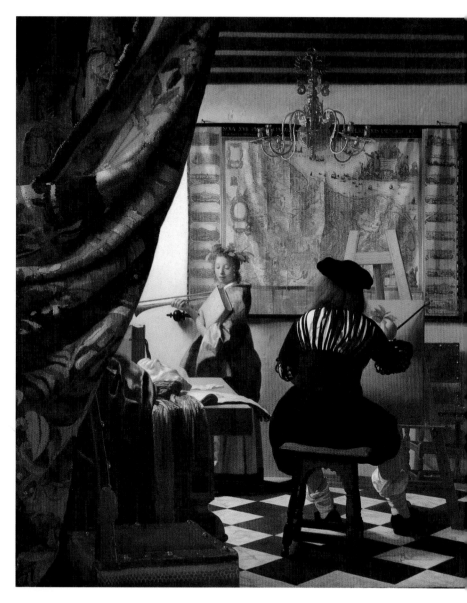

The Art of Painting, c. 1666–67

7. A Houseful of Women

Between the years 1664 and 1667 a second war was being fought between the United Provinces and England, but there is little sign of that maritime, mercantile, and totally male conflict in the paintings of Johannes Vermeer. Even more than in the novels of Jane Austen a century and a half later, set during a long war between Britain and France, the concerns of his work are pacific and close to home. What is most evident is women. In the rooms in which women preside, maps are sometimes shown hanging on the walls – maps of the United Provinces, of the entire Low Countries, of Europe – and these may prompt thoughts of historic frontiers and geo-political problems and the tensions between states that lead to bloodshed. But it is obviously the women who matter.

With one or two exceptions they are not conventionally 'beautiful'. In most of the paintings they are alone, preoccupied with simple tasks. In several they have company: a female servant, a male admirer, a military officer, or a music teacher – who might also be a lover. Musical instruments are often to be seen, whether being played or just lying around. In some of the pictures wine is on hand in white ceramic jugs or fine glasses, in which white wine seems to be preferred. Letters are written, delivered, and read. Jewellery is carefully considered and put on. And all the while the pellucid Dutch light pours in, making things as yellow as pollen. Who are these women? Vermeer seems to have known a good deal about the work of his European predecessors, and in many ways his young women follow patiently in the steps of thoughtful saints and demure angels depicted in paintings from previous centuries while being very much of their own time.

His life was dominated by women. In 1665 his mother was about seventy and still lived near at hand across the Market Place. His sister Gertruy, in her mid-forties, resided not far away in the Vlamingstraat. Here in the Oude Langendijk he lived with his mother-in-law Maria

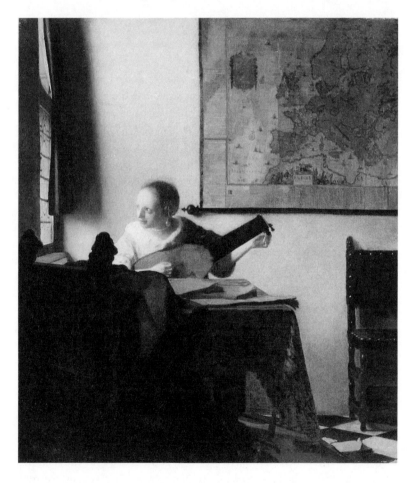

Woman tuning a Lute, c. 1664.

Thins (about seventy-three), his wife Catharina (about thirty-four), and by now five or six daughters and two sons. And there was at least one woman servant, for some years Tanneke Everpoel – as we have seen, probably a maid of all work, who helped with the cooking and may have modelled for him, pouring milk.

Many Dutch artists celebrated in still-lifes and kitchen scenes the abundance of food that could occur in season: cheese, bread, prawns, crabs, lobsters, oysters, all sorts of fish, lemons, oranges, apples, pomegranates, grapes, nuts, melons, quinces, squash, artichokes, cabbages, peaches, plums, pears, turnips, cherries, raspberries, sugar, ham, chickens, pheasants, ducks, mutton, and hare. But Vermeer's only painting to touch on these necessities of life is *The Milkmaid*. He seems (as Gowing noted) to have taken the idea from Gerrit Dou; in Dou's painting in the Louvre, the cook is also pouring from a jug into a basin, with her left arm bare below the elbow; but how much less fussy is Vermeer's treatment of the subject. Bread sits on the table and in the wicker basket, rough-shaped, the grain in it evident on the freshly baked surfaces. The milk that his earth-goddess servant pours unendingly is a perpetual blessing but the picture is also remarkable for its movement; more often his paintings are notable for the stasis within them.

Until the late 1660s Vermeer's daughters would have been too young to be models for any of his paintings (except the children who play bit-parts in *The Little Street*), but Catharina, as we have seen, may have appeared in some. 'A yellow satin jacket with white fur' is listed in the 1676 inventory of the painter's possessions. (The fur trimming is dark-spotted, and probably came from a white squirrel or cat.) This jacket is worn in six paintings: by the *Woman with a Pearl Necklace,* the lady in *The Love-letter*, the mistress in *Mistress and Maid*, and the women in *Woman tuning a Lute* and *The Guitar Player*; and the woman who looks so familiarly and with such wifely devotion at the viewer, just as she looked up at the artist painting her, in *A Lady writing*, wears this jacket too. Catharina may also have been the model for the Dresden *Girl reading a Letter at an Open Window* – who certainly appears to be the same woman as the one writing a letter.

Catharina must have been pregnant much of the time, and though some scholars dispute the incipient maternity of several of Vermeer's women – fashions of the time give them a bulky look, so they say – it is hard not to go along in this matter with Vincent van Gogh, who wrote to Emile Bernard in 1888 of what he took to be the pregnancy of the *Woman in Blue reading a Letter*. The *Woman holding a Balance* also appears to be with child, and *The Lacemaker* is probably in the same fecund condition. Childbirth was such a normal event, but Vermeer may have had in mind a sense of the connections, bloodlines, inheritances and such that could be handed on as pieces of fine lace were, as heirlooms.

Vermeer's older daughters may be the models in *Girl with a Pearl Earring*, *Girl with a Red Hat*, and the *Portrait of a Young Woman* (*c.* 1666–7) who is broad and rather plain of face but smiles so sweetly. Modelling without payment, they also perhaps posed as the young women who perform in *The Concert* and the girl who acts as the Muse of History in *The Art of Painting*. Some of the women in the later paintings particularly may have come from outside his immediate household. In these pictures the rooms are expensively furnished and decorated – ornate fireplaces, marble floors, costly musical instruments – and we sense that his models are in their own homes; at the van Ruijvens' house, for instance, in which case one of them may be Magdalena who married young Dissius. (Pieter Claeszoon van Ruijven had a number of musical instruments, including a viola da gamba, a violin, and two flutes.) These later pictures reflect Vermeer's gradual move towards more ostentatious interiors, which took place as his country felt the impact of French fashions and the growing popularity among art-buyers of 'fine painting'. De Hooch's later figures are similarly more fashionably dressed and housed.

With Vermeer, however, there is less feeling of masculine intrusion than there is in de Hooch's work. Even in the paintings where Vermeer shows men courting women, the women generally seem to have the situation under control. The men are in supporting roles; they don't attract the same interest from the painter. Dutch married women were traditionally just about equal in law; unlike women in

England and France, they could inherit and bequeath their own property and their marriage portion could be recovered on the deaths of their husbands. Indeed, foreigners assumed that women ruled the roost in Holland, taking as a benign instance the resourceful wife of Hugo Grotius, who had organised her husband's escape from Loevestein Castle in a book-chest. The Spanish writer Antonio Carnero in 1625 reckoned that Dutch women managed most of the business in the United Provinces because many Dutchmen were incapacitated by drink. In John Fletcher's play *The Little French Lawyer*, one character says: 'Nor would I be a Dutchman / To have my wife, my sovereign, to command me.' But there are, despite Maria Thins's marital history, no signs in Vermeer's work of the 'raging wife' whom Jacob Cats portrays in one of his verses and who, when a

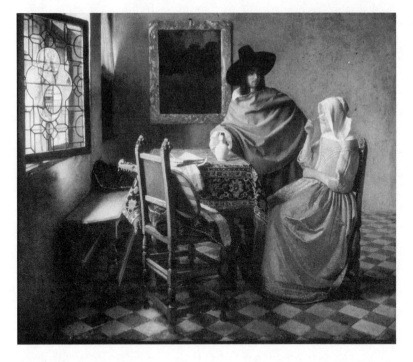

The Glass of Wine, c. 1658–60.

piece of pottery is broken, wants to go into battle, thrash the maid or her own children, 'whomever she finds first, / And, in between, the man / Will certainly get his share'. On such occasions no house would be big enough, no studio far enough removed from the domestic battlefield.

Vermeer hadn't got these concerns; or if he had, he didn't show them. His young women rule in silence, receiving the attention of their admirers – present or unseen – with gentle looks and quiet composure as male lips are lowered over the backs of their hands or a wine jug is held ready to refill their glasses. They may be playing a short passage on a guitar but this – we are led to understand – is what they were doing before they were interrupted and will go on doing afterwards. Passion is left in the next room. In two paintings, a tangential reference is made to restraint of feelings: the same leaded glass window in the *Girl being offered Wine* and *The Glass of Wine* displays an allegorical female figure who represents Temperance, holding a square and a bridle.

Whatever the rights of wives, daughters were expected to follow their parents' wishes: Agatha Welhoek, daughter of a Delft regent, had to wait from 1653, when she was sixteen, to 1670, when she was thirty-three, to marry an older man her father didn't think right for her. Emblem books were popular, illustrated collections of sayings and proverbs that according to Jacob Cats showed 'mute pictures which speak . . . , humorous things that are not without wisdom; things that men can point to with their fingers and grasp with their hands'. In one such book, this figure of Temperance is shown with an accompanying motto, *Serva Modum*, meaning 'observe moderation'. Of course Vermeer doesn't display the motto; he doesn't underline the point; and the young girl with a wine-glass may or may not heed the moral – indeed, from the funny way she holds her glass and her slightly tipsy smile, she might be going to say Yes, not No. It was also a bridle or bit by which the southern provinces were often seen to be mastered; the French ambassador to The Hague noted on one occasion that chances of a revolt in these provinces were small, given 'the gripping bit by which they are held'. The same motif occurs in the one extant painting (now in the Rijksmuseum) by Jan Simon van de Beeck, known as Johannes Torrentius, who had the reputation of being a brilliant still-life painter. In 1628 Torrentius was sent to prison in Haarlem for twenty years for debauchery and atheism; satanic activities were mentioned; but he was let out after two years, was given sanctuary for a while by Charles I in England, and died in

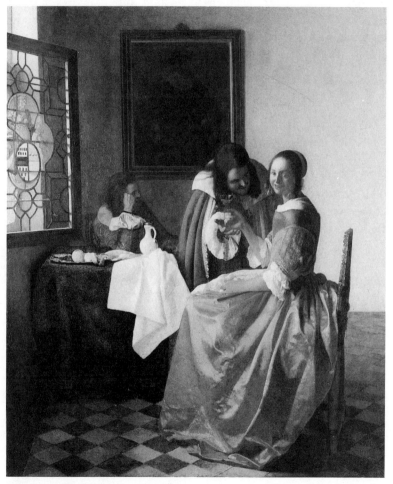

Girl being offered Wine, c. 1659–60.

Amsterdam in 1644. His one surviving picture is round in shape and the still-life objects in it seem to float mysteriously beneath a bridle. This implement symbolised the constraint of passion, and in Torrentius's case was perhaps painted by him as an ironic gesture.

But Vermeer introduces these notions in a characteristically diffident way. The background music is refined. A young English lawyer, Joseph Taylor, met a girl at a ball in Rotterdam in 1707, and next day visited her at her home; he found her playing the harpsichord. He wrote to a friend:

> It is impossible to tell you how I was delighted with her genteel reception, which was mixed with such an air of modesty and freedom that she appeared inexpressibly charming. After I had heard her sing several Latin, Italian, French, and English songs and enjoyed the pleasure of a most engaging conversation, I retired home, melancholy at the thoughts of being so soon deprived of it.

The melody that haunts Vermeer's pictures is also melancholy much of the time; but despite a Calvinist glum distaste for church music, a synod in Delft in 1638 had declared that each congregation should determine whether or not to have organ music, and this effectively meant no sweeping prohibitions. Dutch families frequently entertained themselves with small musical parties, as in *The Concert*, and young women received private music tuition, as in *The Music Lesson*, though the young man attentively listening to the young woman play in this picture may be a suitor rather than a tutor: the bass viol on the floor and the white wine jug are objects that viewers at the time would have understood as underlining a theme of the solace provided by love and art – here, the art of music.

Vermeer once again showed no originality in his subject-matter. Music lessons and private recitals were painted by Jan Steen, Gerrit Dou, and Gerard Terborch, among others. The proximity of the male teacher to the female pupil – hand to hand, breeches to skirt – might arouse faintly lascivious thoughts. Even when no music-making is going on, Vermeer sprinkles his pictures with the possibility of its sounds, with citterns, zithers, lutes, guitars, and trombones ready to hand. In the rather murky still-life of musical instruments that hangs on the back wall in *A Lady writing* one can make out a bass viol as well. Andrew Marvell wrote anti-Dutch political verse in his day but seems to strike the right note for his music-making Dutch contemporaries in his poem 'Music's Empire':

> Some to the lute, some to the viol went,
> And others chose the cornet eloquent;
> These practising the wind, and those the wire,
> To sing man's triumphs, or in heaven's choir.

Music teachers and musicians were seen as free spirits who could cross class boundaries, as did Mark Smeaton, one of the men accused of adultery with Anne Boleyn. A member of Henry VIII's household, he was a virginal player. The virginals in Vermeer's paintings are believed to have been made by the firm of Ruckers in Antwerp. Constantijn Huygens senior ordered a Ruckers virginal in 1648 with the help of Diego Duarte, the Antwerp banker, jeweller, and art collector, and either Huygens senior or his son of the same name may have prompted Duarte to buy one of Vermeer's paintings showing a young woman at such an instrument. We don't know who owned the Ruckers in the Vermeer pictures but he had to have been wealthy to afford the 300 guilders that it cost. A so-called 'pair of virginals' – a single spinet-like instrument that is now generally called a virginal, and perhaps took its name from being played by young women – had strings that were plucked and needed frequent retuning. The presence of these instruments in Vermeer's work emphasises the distance that had been put between his young people and earlier 'merry companies'. Here we see comfort and calm, the byproducts of inherited wealth. The fighting and the strife are over and done with, and these young women have a life of harmonious advantages won by their parents' hard work – as, in a way, Vermeer did, too.

Rather than feeling the need to rebel against the women in his house, Vermeer seems rather to have been absorbed by them. The feminine enveloped him and he was a willing and happy victim. Although not all the women he painted are conventionally good-looking, he apparently liked painting women's skin and their clothes and accoutrements. Did he say to them, 'Please wear such-and-such a dress', 'Those pearl earrings today', or 'Do your hair with those blue ribbons – they make you look so pretty'? Or did he take them as they came, perhaps already dressed for the occasion, dressed for him? He enjoyed catching the self-regard of a young woman looking in a mirror as she put on a necklace. The challenge of portraying the folds in the

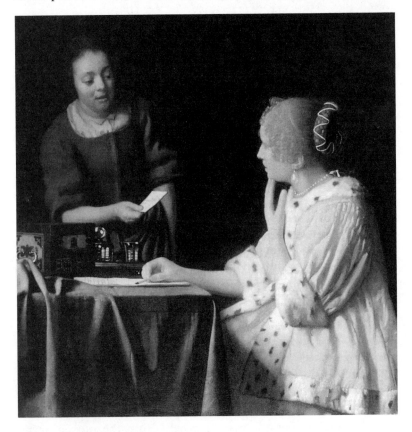

Mistress and Maid, c. 1667.

much seen yellow jacket or the sheen, shadows, and creases of the red dress worn by the *Girl being offered Wine* clearly excited him. (The result was art, otherwise one might have said it sexually excited him.) His repertoire included many of the means women employ to hold on to male interest, from the devoted care, both practical and spiritual, that Martha and Mary had shown, to more enticing types of attraction, such as subtleties of hair-do. Hair is pulled straight back from the forehead, held in place with bows, tied in a bun or braided in a chignon – these are the ways of arrangement in *A Lady writing*; in the young woman playing the keyboard instrument, a clavecin, in *The Concert*; of the mistress in the *Mistress and Maid*; and in the *Woman with a Pearl Necklace*. Ringlets are the favoured style in *The Lacemaker*, in the *Girl reading a Letter at an Open Window* (who also has a chignon), and in *The Guitar Player*. Other women have their heads modestly covered with scarves or hoods, or wrapped in a silk turban, like the *Girl with a Pearl Earring*.

He liked painting pearls, using various techniques. In the mid-1660s he counterfeited their likeness with two layers of paint, so Arthur Wheelock tells us: 'a thin greyish one beneath a white highlight – a technique that permits him to depict both their spectacular highlights and their translucence'. Pearls could be understood in various ways, which suited him, too, as someone who enjoyed beclouding the obvious rather than presenting open-and-shut indications of his meaning. Pearls were linked with vanity but also virginity – a wide enough iconographic spectrum. They could be attributes of elegance or symbols of purity and faith. Constantijn Huygens senior wrote in his poem 'The Day's Work' of his wife under the name of Stella, 'star and pearl together'; the woman one loved was indeed a pearl; and Huygens would have known the parable (Matthew 13:45) in which we are told: 'The kingdom of heaven is like unto a merchant man, seeking goodly pearls: who, when he had found one pearl of great price, went and sold all that he had, and bought it.'

The most beautiful pearl in Vermeer's work is undoubtedly that worn by the *Girl with a Pearl Earring* (see colour section) – a massive creation of highlights and shadows and obscure edges. The largest known natural pearl with a perfect skin or 'orient' had a circumference of 4½ inches. Artificial pearls were invented by M. Jacquin in France around this time, thin spheres of glass filled with *l'essence d'orient*, a preparation made from white wax and the silvery scales of a river fish called *ablette*, or bleak, but cultured pearls were also coming in from Venice. This girl of Vermeer's seems to be wearing a glass 'drop earring' which has been varnished to look like an immense pearl; such earrings were currently fashionable in Holland, as we see in paintings of women by van Mieris, Metsu, and Terborch. But Vermeer's pearl is probably doubly artificial, having been enlarged to such a size by the painter's imagination and desire to adorn the girl with something spectacular.* One wonders if the model's name was Margriet, since that is the Dutch form of the Latin *margarita*, meaning 'pearl'. Her colleague who modelled for his *Girl with a Red Hat* is wearing tear-drop earrings of slightly different shape and finish, as is the *Young Girl with a Flute* (see p. 182)– a painting Vermeer probably started but may have left to be completed by another artist. There is another object of attention in the *Girl with a Pearl Earring*: her moist lips, probably reddened with one of the crayons that women used before lipstick was invented. And one wonders if those limpid eyes shone from belladonna and if those cheeks were flushed with the help of cochineal.

In six of these women-only pictures letters are being written or read, delivered or readied for sending. In *A Lady writing*, of about 1665, the woman we may imagine to be Catharina holds a quill pen in her right hand; her pearl necklace with ribbons to join its ends lies next to the writing-paper on the blue velvet table-cloth; and beyond the paper is the ink-well. After the letter has been written, she will fold it to make its own envelope and then seal it with wax or lacquer. If the letter is for someone in Delft, the servant may deliver it, but for an out-of-town destination – Gouda, say, or Utrecht – one of the by now well-organised postal services may be used. The delivery charge, fixed by the burgomasters, may be paid when the letter is handed in at

---

*Van Dyck also painted imaginary oversize pearls, as in his portrait of Maria Ruten.

the post office, but more commonly is marked in red crayon on the outside, with the charge to be paid by the person it is addressed to. Some senders cheated by writing the gist of their message on the outside of the letter; there the recipient could read it as he or she looked to see what the cost was going to be, and then refuse to pay for the now unnecessary message within. A letter from Delft to Utrecht cost about three stuivers in postage, more than an hour's wages for a skilled worker, so the service was a luxury. The letter could go in one of two ways: fast, carried with other letters in a leather mail-case by a postillion (employed by the town) riding on horseback and blowing a posthorn to announce his coming; or, more slowly, on a privately run *trekschuit*, whose skipper – with the help of his wife – delivered the letters at their destinations.

More people were becoming literate, more letters were being written. And would-be letter-writers could now buy aids to correspondence, like the books of The Hague poet Jacob Westerbaen (author of a well-known ode in praise of the pickled herring) that adapted Ovid's *Art of Love* or translated Ovid's imaginary love-letters from women to their absent husbands or lovers – the latter published in 1657 as *Eenige brieven van doorluchtige vrouwen*. Another letter-writing manual of this time was *Le Secrétaire à la Mode*, by Jean Puget de la Serre, published in Amsterdam and reprinted nineteen times by mid-century. This guide – which also appeared in Dutch in 1651 – provided models for polite and amorous correspondence, both for men and women, and showed them how to concoct confessions that hinted at love and suggest the desolation of being apart from a loved one.

Steen, de Hooch, Metsu, and particularly Terborch took up the theme of letters in their paintings. In his 1654 painting *Bathsheba*, Rembrandt shows his bemused and naked heroine having her feet washed. She is holding the letter by means of which King David intends to seduce her while her husband is away fighting. We know what will happen to Bathsheba and David. But as is usual with Vermeer, the 'stories' behind his letter-pictures are obscure. What does the writer say in the letter that the seemingly very pregnant woman in the blue jacket holds so tightly in her two hands? What words are inscribed on the sheet of paper being read so intently by the girl at the open window? What unsatisfactory message is on the scrunched-up page with its seal broken, clearly just received, that lies on the floor in front of the *Lady writing a Letter with her Maid*, where the lady has bad-temperedly thrown it?

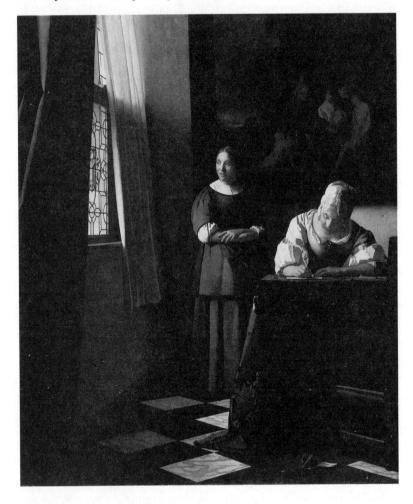

Lady writing a Letter with her Maid, c. 1670.

If we assume love is involved, we may be right but Vermeer doesn't always want us to jump to that conclusion. The look the *Lady writing* gives the viewer incorporates some reticence as she looks up and wonders what to write next; we get the impression that she doesn't want to be asked, 'Whom are you writing to?' The total absorption of the *Woman in Blue* and the reading-each-word-at-a-time concentration of the *Girl reading a Letter at an Open Window* (see p. 94) may have their causes in family matters. But modern investigations have shown that in the latter painting Vermeer had painted a picture of Cupid on the wall behind the girl, but then painted it out, making the wall bare again, as though not wanting to tip his hand so obviously. The painting called *The Love-letter* (see p. 224) is also one that begs questions: the somehow strange open doorway through which we see the well-to-do young woman, holding a lute in one hand and in the other a letter she is handing to (or is it receiving from?) a servant, seems less like a regular doorway than a tall mirror in a narrow wooden frame; and so we feel like voyeurs twice over, as if glimpsing this painted scene in reflected form. Yet the traditional title has a basis in the inquiring look the lady gives her maid and in the servant's faint and knowing smile. With *Mistress and Maid*, the unheard conversation between the two women about the letter in the maid's hand *is* the subject and we are dragged bodily into the heart of the speculation.

There is another way in which some of these paintings of Vermeer's women can be seen: as annunciations. Back beyond Metsu, van Mieris, and Terborch, an older tradition is in evidence, that of earlier Netherlandish and German artists in whose pictures the Virgin is depicted being informed by a celestial messenger of what is to come. The Calvinists had got rid of all the paintings of the Madonna with the Christ-child in the churches they had taken over, but a need obviously remained. Ludwig Goldscheider pointed out some years ago the similarities between the figure in Matthias Grünewald's *Virgin of the Annunciation* and that in Vermeer's *Girl reading a Letter at an Open Window*, and the nearly identical curtains that hang from rings on rods across the spaces they inhabit. Of course the

Annunciation is meant to happen only to a maiden. Vermeer's young women are not always immaculate in the sense of undefiled; some of them have a touch of erotic complicity in their eyes; but there is no hint of the complications and exasperations of married life – no babies, small children, toys or pets; no burnt pots in the kitchen or unmade beds; no spills or messes. It is all immensely tidy and dust-free. If Delft was Holland's cleanest city, where good citizens like Antony van Leeuwenhoek had their house-gutters scoured twice a year so that they looked like new, Vermeer was its cleanest painter. Life in his paintings has been poured through a filter. That crumpled letter, a few rumpled table-carpets, are the only signs of disturbance. Probably the most alarming feature in these house-proud pictures is the fancy wine jug teetering on the very edge of the table in *The Procuress*, or else its nervous-making fellow, the pristine white jug in the *Girl being offered Wine*. There would seem to be a message here, even if not shouted at us: that nothing in life is as secure as it looks. Perhaps when Vermeer indicates the possibility of the Jug Turned Upside-Down he is alerting us to this. But the white jug appears in another three of his paintings, so it evidently survived that precarious placement while being used as a prop by the painter.

We begin to cherish some of these domestic objects that furnish his understated dramas of correspondence, courtship, and music being made or interrupted. Among the objects which become familiar are the white Delft tiles with blue drawings glazed on them that skirt the foot of the walls; several massive-legged tables; and a number of straight chairs with the fabric of their seats and backs held in place by large round-headed brass studs – he changed the material and the colour of the fabric on these from time to time, but the upright back supports were topped by characteristic finials, each shaped as a lion's head, with a brass ring under its chin. Vermeer had an enjoyable, impressionistic, shorthand way of painting these finials. Whether, as he did so, he thought of the Netherlands lion, the symbolic figure of unity for the United Provinces that Rembrandt paraded in his *Concord of the State*, is not known. (Such chairs were not uncommon in prosperous households: Pieter de Hooch shows one with similar finials in his *Boy bringing Bread* of 1660–3 and Cornelis de Man has lion's-head finials on the chairs in his paintings *The Chess Players* and *The Card Players*.)

Pictures that belonged to his mother-in-law also recur in Vermeer's paintings. We get used to seeing the Dirck van Baburen *Procuress*, the 'Roman Charity' that was probably by Couwenbergh, and the painting (which no longer exists) of a Cupid by Caesar van Everdingen, all presenting moral messages we may or may not read aright. The most conspicuous Cupid is that which hangs behind the *Young Woman standing at a Virginal* (see p. 198), holding a bow in one hand and in the other hand, upraised, a blank playing-card. Love is evidently in the air. But what else? In a contemporary emblem book, a very similar Cupid holds up a card showing the number one to suggest that a true lover has only one object of affection. Did Vermeer paint the Cupid's card as blank or is it just the result of severe cleaning? If the artist painted it so, we might take it that his young woman (no longer a girl) was still waiting for Mr Right. It's worth noting the other background picture in this Vermeer, a little landscape in a gold-painted frame, hung to the left of the Cupid and seemingly without moral baggage of any kind – simply a lovely piece of painting which one would like to abstract from the *Young Woman standing at a Virginal* and hang on its own.

Then there are the maps. These hang on the walls in half a dozen of Vermeer's paintings and as emblems of a larger territory – whether provinces, country, or continent – make another window out of his withdrawn interiors. Samuel van Hoogstraten expressed his enthusiasm for maps in his *Inleyding*: 'How wonderful a good map is in which one views the world as from another world thanks to the art of drawing.' Metsu, de Hooch, Steen, and Terborch – many of the usual suspects – also decorated their interiors with maps. At the time, maps were popular with well-to-do householders, being good to look at as well as educational and useful for showing off their owners' interest in geography and politics and even their patriotism. Most of Vermeer's maps have been identified. One, of Holland and West Friesland, shown almost totally in *Officer and Laughing Girl* and partly in *Woman in Blue reading a Letter*, was made by the cartographer Balthasar Floriszoon van Berckenrode and published by Willem Janszoon Blaeu; in 1661 it was about forty years old. The band of text running across the bottom of the map praises the steadfast Dutch and the land they have successfully held. In the first of those two paintings, Vermeer may have been suggesting by way of the map that the army officer had something to do with the preservation from the enemy of the provinces displayed; in the second, he might have meant to hint that the young woman's letter was written by someone 'out there'. The map of the entire Seventeen Provinces in *The Art of Painting* was by Nicolaes Janszoon Visscher and was published in 1636, when the northern and southern provinces were still theoretically if not actually together (the formal separation took place in 1648), and like the map of Europe in the *Woman tuning a Lute* helps create the impression of a room which was a real, lived-in space.

It is possible that Vermeer traded in maps as he did in pictures. He obviously enjoyed painting the shape and texture of maps, sometimes changing their colours and the colours of their support rods to suit different schemes, to contrast with or relate to the figures in his paintings, but sometimes sticking closely to the maps as they were. The patterns and tones made by the cartographers in their depictions of land and sea are those of a picture within a picture. Some of Vermeer's maps are more in focus than others and thus seem more prominent. The horizontal rods with turned knobs at each end could serve for visual emphasis, though they occasionally seem to have been used by him like tie-rods in buildings to hold parts of the picture together. Where he eventually decided such a binding device was unnecessary, he got rid of it, as in the *Woman with a Pearl Necklace*, in which we now know from autoradiography that he first painted and then removed a map of the seventeen provinces. (As a result, there is a daring amount of blank wall – which gave him room to show how well he could emulate Fabritius and simulate bare plaster.) Professor Montias has pointed out that the vertical crease in the map in *The Art of Painting* runs more or less along the dividing line between the northern and the southern provinces, though whether this was a political allusion by our painter or just happened to be there in his copy of the map, remains uncertain. Perhaps Vermeer meant to make us think of a crease as something that could be ironed out, just as the sundered provinces could one day, despite the present tide of events, be brought back together. Perhaps he simply liked the way the crease looked and enjoyed painting it. The fact that he shows only the southern provinces of the map in the *Woman with a Water Jug* is probably due to his compositional intentions rather than to an expression of Catholic sympathies.

As we have seen, Vermeer's debts to his contemporaries for his themes were great – so much so that Steen, de Hooch, van Mieris, Dou, and Terborch might each have said to him good-humouredly, even admiringly, 'I liked what you did with my idea.' But there would have been no sourness in the remark; such ideas were in a common domain, and what Vermeer made of them was in the end quite different. Vermeer's *Woman holding a Balance* of (it is thought) 1664 is – to put it neutrally – closely related to de Hooch's *A Woman weighing Gold* of the same year. But the scholars believe that even though de Hooch was then in Amsterdam, Vermeer saw his painting and was influenced by it, rather than de Hooch seeing and adapting Vermeer's picture. Similarly, Vermeer's *Love-letter* of 1669–70 owes a good deal to de Hooch's 1668 *Couple with a Parrot*: there is the same dark foreground with a view through what in the de Hooch is definitely a doorway, and a similar curtain partly obscuring the view of the room beyond; and there, in both pictures, two figures are to be seen – although they are two women in the Vermeer and a man and a woman in the de Hooch. Vermeer's *Woman with a Pearl Necklace* of about 1664, the painting that shows a young lady admiring herself in a mirror as she deliberates whether or not to don a necklace, is – in positioning and composition – very like Frans van Mieris's *Young Woman before a Mirror* painted a few years earlier. Between Vermeer and Terborch, Vermeer and Metsu, there were also obligations. And Vermeer, when borrowing, jumped with ease out of his home town and even out of Holland to – once again – Italy: his *Milkmaid* not only has colleagues in emblematic illustrations to poems by Jacob Cats and in paintings by Dou, Metsu, and de Hooch (and a strapping farmyard ancestress in a picture of 1510 by Lucas van Leyden), but also a royal precursor in the *Queen Artemesia* painted by the Italian artist Domenico Fiasella around 1645; this shows the queen pouring what appears to be wine from a similar earthenware jug and leaning over in much the way that Vermeer's servant-woman will.

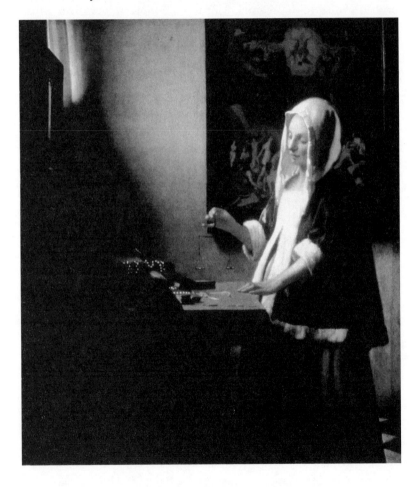

Woman holding a Balance, c. 1664.

Yet, for all these debts, Vermeer's women are individuals who can't be mistaken for anyone else's; once seen, they can't be forgotten. The painter thwarts our incessant demands for a story-line by freezing the action, by bringing time to a stop for an instant or two while contemplation exercises its power. The passivity or stillness he creates, reflecting his own nature, is in its way more dramatic, more *active*, than any action. So the young woman with a metal water jug pauses, one hand on the jug, one hand on the frame of the casement window which she seems about to open further, and the earth for a moment ceases to spin on its axis. So the woman in blue's downcast gaze travels along the lines of the letter she has received, word by word by word, over and over. Vermeer seizes the moment and it repeats itself indefinitely. And in the same way his milkmaid, his figure of Fortitude, tips her jug and the milk falls from it in a silent stream for ever.

8. *The Art of Painting*

The Art of Painting was a picture specifically mentioned in a document of February 1676 concerning a debt Catharina owed her mother. Catharina declared that in part-payment of her obligation she was handing over to Maria Thins 'in full and free property' rights to the picture 'wherein is depicted "The Art of Painting"'. Painted in the mid-1660s, it had obviously remained in the Oude Langendijk house, treasured as Vermeer's masterwork, and the family did not want to let it go.

The picture shows a painter in action, possibly Vermeer though in improbably pristine circumstances. Assuming that this is the picture listed as number 3 at the 1696 Dissius sale, one of the first to make this identification was the writer of the auction catalogue who called it a 'Portrait of Vermeer in a room, with various accessories, uncommonly handsome'. The elements of self-portrait in it were characteristically cautious. The artist's back is turned towards us. We see only his straggly hair and beret – as noted before, very like the hair and beret of the musician in *The Procuress* – and his exotic-looking but fashionable clothing, slashed doublet and pantaloons. We seem to be present at a symbolic event, a *tableau vivant* or little play by means of which the art of painting is being celebrated, albeit a performance in which, rather as in an opera – Mozart's *Magic Flute*, for instance – the absurd contrivances of the plot don't prevent the work from being appreciated as 'a work of art' and regarded as wonderful.

Paintings of artists in their studios were *à la mode*, created by Vermeer's contemporaries from Rembrandt down. Sometimes the artist was portrayed directly, sometimes shown in a subsidiary role, and occasionally the reflection of the painter at work was seen in a glass or mirror. But in *The Art of Painting* a greater ambition is evident than Gerrit Dou or Adriaen van Ostade manifested in their studio pictures. Leonaert Bramer a few years before this had made an allegorical representation of the art of painting for the ceiling of the new St Luke's guild-hall in the Voldersgracht. And Vermeer presented his painter as an emblematic figure who reaches for the heights of his art by way of the creation of a history painting. Vermeer's artist is not an impoverished-looking, isolated type, like Rembrandt's gawky young painter in his lonely and threadbare studio. In rather splendid surroundings he paints not the Madonna or a commissioned portrait but Clio, the Muse of History.

The scholars tell us that the pretty girl who was his model is posed in a way that recalls the figure of Fame in Cesare Ripa's symbol book *Iconologia*, first published in Rome in 1593 and in Dutch in 1644 when its translator recommended it as 'useful to all orators, poets, painters, sculptors, draughtsmen, and all other art lovers'. Vermeer's Clio holds a trombone in her right hand and wears a laurel wreath on her head, both attributes of Ripa's Clio. We recall too Hendrick de Keyser's bronze statue of Fame who still blew her trumpet for the dead but immortal Prince of Orange in the Nieuwe Kerk, less than a hundred yards away from where Vermeer was painting. In her left hand, hugged to her breast, Vermeer's young woman holds a heavy book which is perhaps Karel van Mander's *Schilderboek*, a compendium of the lives of Netherlands painters that van Mander wrote 'to elevate and ennoble the art of painting'. The plaster mask on the table in front of the girl model in Vermeer's picture is no doubt placed there to make us think of what Ripa calls 'the imitation of human activities', and the art of painting was one such activity. This is therefore an allegory in which Vermeer could pay tribute to his profession and his colleagues, and let us know what his ultimate aims were as a painter. But it rises above the pedantry and fussiness of allegorical art and what could be the ponderousness of historical painting. Moreover, Vermeer's brilliant rendering of Visscher's map, as we have just seen, reminds us of the larger country from which Netherlands artists hailed, northern and southern alike.

Vermeer made *The Art of Painting* in or about 1667, the year Dirck van Bleyswijck – with Arnold Bon's versifying assistance – hailed him as artistic successor to Carel Fabritius. If there was a time for publicly unfolding his full talent, this was it. Indeed, the high moment of his own fame was prolonged by this painting. Two years later, and six years after Balthasar de Monconys had made his not very successful visit to Delft to see Vermeer's work, another visitor called on the Delft master painter; in fact he came twice in May 1669. On this occasion the inquisitive caller was Dutch. His name was Pieter Teding van Berckhout and he was twenty-six years old. Van Berckhout was the well-connected scion of a prominent Hague regent family, but he preferred life in Delft, with which his family had ties; one of his aunts had been the wife of Admiral Maarten Tromp, his mother was from Delft's van Beresteyn brewing family, and his father Adriaen, a member of the Council of State of the province of Holland, was commemorated by an ornate plaque in the Nieuwe Kerk in Delft. Van Berckhout moved there the following year, becoming an active member of the town council and naturally an acquaintance of van Bleyswijck. He served as harbourmaster of Delfshaven in 1676 and as a Delft alderman and burgomaster in a number of the following years.

Van Berckhout was also well acquainted with that great man and all-round impresario of the age Constantijn Huygens and with Huygens's family in The Hague. (Pieter's sister was to marry Huygens's son Lodewijk.) As it happened, Huygens senior was on hand in Delft, with two other friends, when young van Berckhout came by boat on Tuesday 14 May 1669, and may have accompanied him on his visit to facilitate an introduction; no other reason is given for Huygens being in Delft, but it is tempting to think that the secretary to a Prince of Orange, a man who knew Rubens and Rembrandt, was also there that day to see Vermeer. Van Berckhout doesn't enlighten us on that score but writes in his diary, in French:

'having arrived, I saw an excellent painter named Vermeer, who showed me some curiosities by his hand.'

A week later, apparently taken with what he had seen, he returned to Delft and called again on Vermeer. This time Vermeer was described in van Berckhout's diary as 'a celebrated painter'. He showed van Berckhout examples of his art, which made the diarist think that 'the most extraordinary and most curious part consisted in the *perspective*'. A fuller analysis would have been welcome, but that was all; at least, unlike Monconys, van Berckhout didn't go away disappointed. One of the pictures he saw would have been *The Art of Painting*, which never left Vermeer's family during his lifetime.

Among the first things we notice today in *The Art of Painting* is not the perspective – that seems to be perfect and draws no attention to itself – but the way the light enters the room in an almost tangible thrust from behind the room-dividing curtain. This beautifully painted tapestry is pulled up and back over a chair in the left foreground and helps to delimit the inner space; it makes us feel we have a privileged view of the painter's studio. The light falls directly on the girl who is modelling, keeping as still as she can, her eyes intently downcast; she is framed on the left by the tapestry curtain and on the right by the painter at his easel, with his back to us. A line of white floor tiles takes our eye slightly to the left of centre towards the brightest patch of wall, above the girl's trombone. There are black tiles among them, which aren't arranged chess-board fashion but instead form crosses, five tiles to a cross. The painter's legs are stretched forward under his easel; his bright orange-red hose – de Witte's favourite colour – show up between his knee-length pantaloons and the turned-down tops of his white over-stockings, which were called 'canons'. His feet are planted with what appears to be natural happenstance, the left shoe tilted sideways on a cross of black tiles, the right one flatter to the floor and with its heel partly covering a white tile. He leans slightly forward, so that the light draws attention to the white shirt beneath his slashed black 'pourpoint' doublet, a fashionable revival of earlier styles. The artist holds in his right hand both his brush and the scarlet-tipped maulstick which he uses to steady his hand. He is glancing at the model as he considers his next brush-stroke. Above, an ornate brass candelabrum of the sort that was called a crown, with eight branches bearing candle-holders (without candles), hangs from the exposed dark ceiling beams. It is crowned with a twin-headed eagle, symbol of the Habsburg Empire. This, like the map of all the provinces that covers most of the back wall, may indicate nostalgia for the old Netherlands and the pre-Alteration way of things, or may simply be a Thins possession, hung for its beauty and utility. The painter is at work on a smaller canvas than that of *The Art of Painting*. It has room for little more than a portrait of Clio. He is starting at the top, painting her laurel wreath.

One imagines Pieter Teding van Berckhout in the house on the Oude Langendijk, looking at *The Art of Painting* and thinking 'most extraordinary' and 'most curious'. Here was a canvas a little more than 4 feet high and 3 feet wide and – the least noticeable dimension – a fraction of an inch thick: to all intents, a two-dimensional object. And on this structure of almost entirely surface the painter had created an all-encompassing effect of three dimensions. Van Berckhout would have found it difficult not to exclaim, How do you do it?

Vermeer is unlikely to have told him precisely, though he may well have had the words to do so. But he probably felt it was chancing fate to over-analyse or explicate his craft to a layman – there were devices, almost mysteries, that might slip from one's grasp if dwelt on too publicly – and the language he preferred to speak was that of brush and paint. However, by the time of his second visit Berckhout was able to put his finger on one word that might unlock the artful magic and that was 'perspective'. There was a great deal of expertise in Delft on this subject. Dirck van Bleyswijck had written in his *Description* that Carel Fabritius 'was so quick and sure in the use of perspective'. The architectural paintings many Delft artists specialised in were called 'perspectives'. Berckhout would have been able to pick up some background information on this from Vermeer or his colleagues without going into too much technical detail.

For a start, perspective was a skill that made objects depicted on a flat surface look deep and substantial, by the artist's drawing or painting distant things as smaller and closer things as bigger, and with a logical progression between the two. The theory of perspective had been worked out in Italy two hundred years earlier by Brunelleschi and Alberti, and described in the French mathematician Jean Pélerin's *De Artificiali Perspectiva* of 1505 and Leonardo's *Trattato della Pittura*, written about 1510 but first published in Paris in 1651. A Dutch manual on the subject by Hans Vredeman de Vries appeared

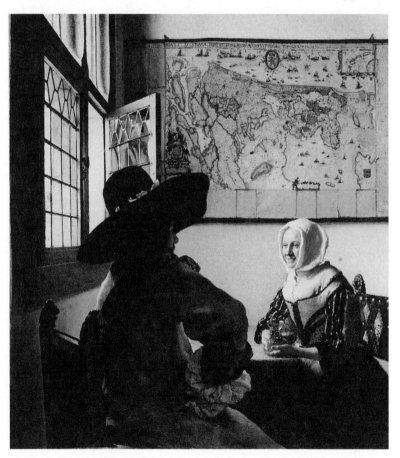

Officer and Laughing Girl, c. 1658.

in 1604. The theory of it was studied by young artists who learned how to make a convincing illusion of three-dimensional space with methods that involved using a vanishing point and one or two distance points. Houckgeest, de Witte, and de Hooch followed a technique in which a piece of string was attached to a pin placed at the vanishing point on the canvas or panel they were going to work on. The string would be rubbed with chalk and then pulled taut and snapped, leaving on the working surface one of the straight lines (known as orthagonals) needed for creating a correct perspective. Vermeer did this too, using a straightforward system Pélerin had called *tiers point*, with a central vanishing point halfway between two distance points on a horizon line. Thirteen Vermeer paintings have a small hole at the vanishing point where the pin pierced his canvas. The pin-hole is usually not hard to discover, because one can use the lines of tiles or the edges of tables, maps, and picture frames to determine the orthagonals and find out where the hole, at the vanishing point, should be. The pin-hole in *The Art of Painting* is on the wall just below Clio's right hand and the knob at the end of the map rod. Other aids Vermeer used to establish a sense of depth were curtains, chairs, tables, and figures 'up front' – as in *The Art of Painting* and *Officer and Laughing Girl*.

Judging by the vanishing point in Vermeer's mature works, only a seated position would account for the lowered level of his viewpoint; he painted them sitting down, as the artist does here. And this may have had other effects: Philip Hale, an American artist and writer of the first half of the twentieth century, thought that sitting down instead of standing to paint produced a mood of 'quietude' rather than restlessness. The easel at which Vermeer sat is visible in the mirror he painted hanging over the young woman in *The Music Lesson*. His low viewpoint is particularly emphasised in that picture by the way the carpet-covered table looms high in the foreground, only just below the painter's (and viewer's) line of sight. And we can probably assume that Vermeer did the foundation work on canvas in the way the artist in *The Art of Painting* did, without any preliminary 'rubbing-in' of his design with paint and only a slight sketch of his subject in white chalk. He started painting at the top, with Clio's laurel wreath, and then moved on down to her face. As for his materials, in the inventory made of his possessions in 1676 are listed two easels and three palettes, ten canvases and six panels, ready to hand in his upstairs studio. He probably bought some of his pigments, including the rare natural ultramarine he so much liked, from Dirck de Cocq's apothecary shop; but he could have prepared some paints himself in his attic, grinding the pigments and mixing them with linseed oil. The brushes he used were both large square-tipped ones and smaller ones with round tips.

Although Vermeer was a painter who produced a relatively small number of finished pictures, he doesn't seem to have been particularly slow when he was actually at work. As stated earlier, his brush-strokes indicate that he often painted 'wet-in-wet', in other words applying new paint before the underlying paint was dry. It has been noted, moreover, that he was skilful at simplifying shapes and patterns, using a pictorial shorthand to render reflections and the materials of carpets and curtains, and this would speed the process of painting. Although some parts of the earlier pictures have a separateness and solidity that result from the way he applied his paints – like the letter in the *Girl reading a Letter at an Open Window* (see p. 94), where the white impasto accentuates the effects of the folds and creases in the paper – in *The Art of Painting* his technique was more seamless. Philip Hale calls it 'perfect' and John Nash, who also trained as a painter, writes that, though the application of the paint seems various, the paint 'is applied with effortless control [and] overall, applied as if invisibly'. Vermeer had an uncanny ability to create the effects of sunlight playing on different textures and surfaces or passing through glass and hair.

The 'technical description' in the catalogue of the 1997 Vermeer exhibition, seen in Washington DC and The Hague, details the materials he used to achieve the softness and delicacy and life in his painting *Girl with a Pearl Earring*:

The composition was laid in with light and dark areas. The ground is a thick, yellowish-white layer containing lead-white, chalk, and possibly umber.

The dark background and the deeper shadows of the girl's face, turban, and bodice were established with a mixture of black and earth pigments, and further modelled with a paler, ocher color. The shadow of her nose was underpainted with red lake while the highlights on her nose, right cheek, and forehead have a thick, cream-colored underpaint. The turban was painted with varying shades of an ultramarine and lead-white mixture, wet-in-wet, over which a blue glaze was applied, except in the highlights. A thin, off-white scumble of paint over the brown shadow of the girl's neck defines the pearl, and is painted more opaquely at the bottom where the pearl reflects the white collar. Small hairs from Vermeer's brush are found in the half-tones of the flesh areas.

From this we may understand that the art of painting was hard and thoughtful work, though no doubt accompanied by moments of happiness when things went right. But it didn't always result in perfection. Like other great painters – Rembrandt was one – Vermeer had bad days which may have run into later sessions when he tried to improve matters and failed. At this date we have to be careful not to blame him for errors that may be the result of restoration and retouching since a painting left his studio, but in the *Girl interrupted at her Music* the young woman's hands and clothes are clumsily done, and in the *Portrait of a Young Woman* (also known as the 'Wrightsman portrait') the stunted left hand also fails to convince anatomically. Not being able to get it right must have been depressing, and may have left him feeling disgusted with his inability – so much so that he might have given up painting for a time.

Van Gogh, writing to his friend Emile Bernard in 1888 about the *Woman in Blue reading a Letter,* remarked: 'The palette of this strange artist comprises blue, lemon-yellow, pearl-grey, black and white. It is true that in the few pictures he painted one can find the whole gamut of colours. But the combination of lemon-yellow, a dull blue and a light grey is as characteristic of him as the harmony of black, white and pink is of Velasquez.' There are bold yellows in the dresses of Diana and one of her companions; in the tight jacket, with one button provocatively open at the top, of the young woman in *The Procuress*;

in the equally well-filled rough blouse worn by *The Milkmaid*; and in the famous satin jacket trimmed with fur that his models wore so often. *The Lacemaker* wears a yellow jacket, too, but one collared with lace. Yellow served well for highlights where fabrics were creased: big impressionistic dabs of yellow and smaller raindrop-like touches of it are so employed in the *Girl with a Red Hat*. But if Vermeer were asked

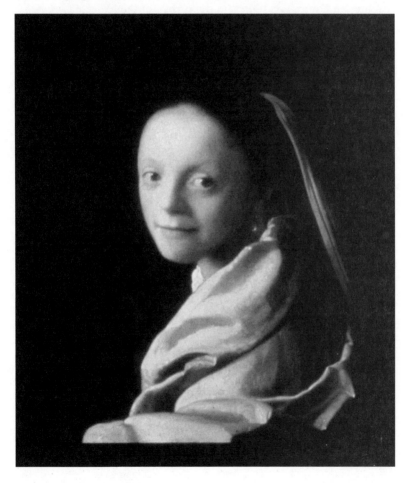

Portrait of a Young Woman, c. 1666–7.

which was his favourite colour, surely he would have replied, with a charitable grin at the naiveté of the question, 'Blue'.

The skirts worn by Mary in *Christ in the House of Martha and Mary* and by the maiden sitting next to the goddess in *Diana and her Companions* are blue. There is the soft, maternal shade of the jacket of the *Woman in Blue reading a Letter*, a faded Delft blue. There are the brighter and more vivid blues in the turban of the teenage *Girl with a Pearl Earring* and the apron of *The Milkmaid*. There is a lot of blue in *The Music Lesson*: blue tiles, blue back and seat of the chair, and the young woman's blue overskirt. In the *Girl being offered Wine* the table-cloth and many of the floor tiles are light and dark blue respectively. The *Mistress and Maid* has its blue table-cloth and the model being

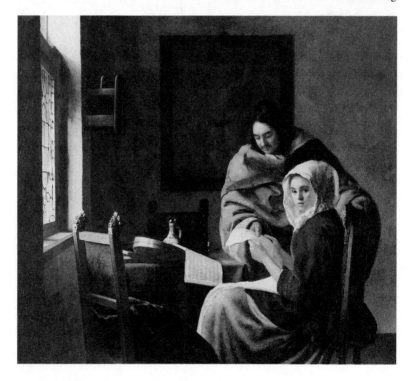

Girl interrupted at her Music, c. 1660–1.

Clio in *The Art of Painting* wears a blue jacket. There are silkier dark blues elsewhere in dresses and dressing gowns, like the robe worn by the *Girl with a Red Hat*. Blue is generally considered a cool colour, but with Vermeer it doesn't necessarily have that effect. Some of its comparative warmth in the *Red Hat* picture may have to do with the fact that the ground paint he applied underneath the blue robe was reddish-brown. Being a lover of blue, he perhaps wouldn't have

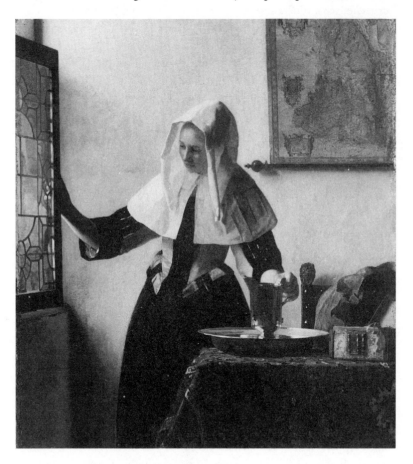

Woman with a Water Jug, c. 1664–5.

worried that the greens in the *View of Delft* would turn blue with time, so that the leaves of the trees are now blue – indeed, he may have known that this would happen; greens were fugitive. The *Woman with a Water Jug* is very much a study in blue: the open window at her side has bluish glass; there is blue in the shadow that runs down the wall beneath the window; an underlayer of the off-white wall behind her contains not just grey but ultramarine; her skirt is dark blue and her jacket dark blue and yellow, with its blue visible also through her white collar and headdress; a length of lighter blue material is draped over the chair with lion's-head finials and a dark blue back whose colour is reflected in the metal ewer; the carpet on the table has blue flowers woven into its red background; the rod that holds down the bottom edge of the familiar map on the wall is now blue; and, in a final miniature gesture, the ribbons – possibly those used to tie her pearl necklace – that poke out of her jewellery box on the table are light blue. I think his model here was once again the ever-at-hand Catharina; she has the same aquiline nose and slightly compressed lips as the *Lady writing*.

Vermeer had an intuitive understanding of 'colour values' – the separate power of each colour and the relationships between one colour and another – and he took a much less formulaic attitude to this than other painters. This knowledge enabled him to make very subtle, local adjustments to light and shade, mingling and contrasting warm colours and cool ones; each shadow resulted from a slightly different combination of colours from his palette; and hence his interiors seem filled by real light, real air. He had different methods for applying paint, but as John Nash notes in relation to the *Girl reading a Letter at an Open Window*, 'the dominant is a series of small dabs like crumbs of light adhering to and defining the surfaces of things. Already, there is the first development of that technique of minimal definition that is the basic characteristic of his mature style.' For the creation of light as it struck or brushed the surfaces of objects his weapon was the small round-tipped brush with which he produced little points of light – what's called *pointillé* – on the topsides of the herring boats in the *View of Delft*, on the handles of the bread basket and the bread itself in *The*

Milkmaid, on the lion's-head finials in a number of pictures, and on the fabric of ruffs and cuffs, as with the collar of *The Lacemaker* and the lace she is working on. This patter of paint has immediacy. Small pearls of light make a luminous lustre and this, despite the silence and seeming stasis of the pictures, stirs the air in them, counterfeiting the breath of life.

In this task – the greatest forgery of all – Vermeer had going for him, along with the arts of his craft, a number of scientific aids and appliances. Devices used by artists at the time included a frame with glass in it that could be looked through and traced on, and an eyepiece or tube for viewing an object and screening out extraneous matter. Gerrit Dou employed a convex mirror that limited his field of vision and condensed the scene he wanted to paint. As we've seen with Carel Fabritius, a good deal of inventive energy was then being applied by several Dutch artists to the making of perspective boxes or 'peep-shows', as they were called. These applied the principles of perspective and used as the walls, ceiling, and floor of the box separate paintings, each distorted-looking on its own, to create an illusion of a single realistic space, the ground floor of a house, say, when looked at through a peep-hole – a voyeuristic activity that obviously appealed to many viewers. (A small outside lamp lit the interior through a painted glass panel.)

The indispensable John Evelyn saw one of these peepshows, an import from Holland, in London on 5 February 1656: 'Was shew'd me a prety Perspective & well represented in a triangular box, the great church at *Harlem* in Holland, to be seene thro a small hole at one of the Corners, & contrived into an handsome cabinet: it was so rarely done, that all the Artists and Painters in Towne, came flocking to see & admire it.'* The perspective box most accessible to viewers today is that painted by Samuel van Hoogstraten, celebrated for his *trompe-*

---

*Walter Liedtke suggests that the church in this box was in fact not St Bavo's in Haarlem but the Nieuwe Kerk in Delft, and this could have been a peepshow Fabritius made, of which his brilliant but warped-looking little *View in Delft* is a surviving part.

l'oeil and doorway views, and Fabritius's fellow-student in Rembrandt's studio. The box, now in the National Gallery, London, is the size of a small cabin-trunk or Flemish *kist* and has a peep-hole at each end, at the level of the horizon line of the construction painted within. And the view through these 'keyholes' is of a series of adjoining rooms and spaces – hallways, passages – in which various figures are to be seen, not all at once but one by one, as in life, in a house: a woman in bed lying on three plump pillows; a woman sitting with her sewing; a woman sitting by the front door while through the nearby window the shadowy shape of a man appears outside, maybe just about to come in; and sitting patiently, a springer spaniel, whose plaintive eyes catch the viewer's.

Hoogstraten in his *Inleyding* described such a box as a *wonderlijke perspectyfkas* and in the same text he wrote: 'The Art of Painting is a science for representing all the ideas or notions which the whole of visible nature is able to produce and for deceiving the eye with drawing and colour.' On the outside of his London box he painted emblematic figures to represent the motives of painting: desire for fame; desire for money; and love of art. Hoogstraten lived in Dordrecht, and would probably have gone through Delft on his way to and from Amsterdam. There's no evidence of any meetings between him and Vermeer, but the Delft master had two small heads painted by Hoogstraten in his collection, and we can imagine Vermeer reading with approval these words in the *Inleyding*: 'I say that a painter whose work it is to fool the sense of sight, also must have so much understanding of the nature of things that he thoroughly understands by what means the eyes are fooled.'

Did Vermeer borrow such a perspective box or attempt to make one? In the study needed for its construction he would have had to come to grips with complicated figurings and trial-and-error conjunctions of different planes in order 'to fool' the viewer. His possession of a peepshow might provide one answer to the questions that have arisen about the box-like object glimpsed in the one other painting of his in which we are given a hint or two of the artist at work, *The Music Lesson*. In this picture, the mirror that hangs at a fairly steep angle above the virginal reveals not just the face of the young woman who is playing the instrument but, behind and over her head and shoulders, the edge of the carpet-covered table that fills the right foreground of the painting. And then – quite a shock! – we notice in the mirror several objects that aren't in the main part of the painting at all. We glimpse the artist's easel: one foot and the cross-bar and part of the canvas that sits on it. We see two feet of his stool, a section of tiled floor, and a tiny bit of the wall behind him. And we see a curiously shaped (not quite rectangular) box, placed between stool and easel. There is no sign of Vermeer himself. He shows us the position he painted the picture from and some of his equipment, which is self-explanatory, and he shows us the box, which begs several questions. What is the purpose of the box? Is it simply some sort of storage container for brushes and pigments, kept close to hand and useful for resting the feet on while painting? Is it a *perspectyfkas* he had been examining, restoring, or even making? Or is it a device he has been using to help him compose the picture and so – although he didn't want to confront the viewer with it – he has left this clue in the mirror's reflection for his brother artists to find and say knowingly, 'Ah, look what Vermeer has been using!'

For at least a century artists had known about an apparatus called the camera obscura – literally, a darkened room. It could be a chamber from which the light was kept out and within which the viewer sat, or it could be a box into which the viewer peered. It made use of a phenomenon long noted in Mediterranean countries, where shutters screened the windows against the midday heat and glare, and where a small chink in the shutter might let in a concentrated shaft of bright light which in turn formed on an inside wall an inverted image of objects outside. Euclid in 300 BC had realised that light travelled in straight lines. The eleventh-century Arabian philosopher Alhazen in Cairo studied the effect that the light coming in through a pin-hole made on a white surface inside a dark space. Roger Bacon, the thirteenth-century English scholar, and Alberti, architect and philosopher in fifteenth-century Italy, made further experiments with cameras obscura. Leonardo mentioned the device in his *Trattato della*

Pittura as 'a means of studying colour and coloured shadows'. The playwright and amateur experimenter Giovanni della Porta in 1558 suggested using a mirror to correct the image, and the scholarly Venetian nobleman Daniel Barbaro eleven years later seems to have been the first to use not only a mirror but a convex lens or 'old man's spectacle glass' in the aperture to condense and focus the image which would otherwise appear, inverted and reversed – a little world turned upside-down – on the screen inside the viewing device. Others, including Johannes Kepler, worked out that a second lens could be used instead of a mirror to right the image. Kepler soon after 1600 made a portable darkened tent with a telescope lens and used it as an aid in sketching landscapes. His pupil, René Descartes, experimented with a camera obscura after he retired from serving in the army of the United Provinces and was living in Leiden. The Dutch of course were used to living in a world of reflections, constantly seeing their houses, trees, and sky mirrored in canals and lakes.

Closer links with Johannes Vermeer now appear. Constantijn Huygens, later related by marriage to van Berckhout, friend of Duarte, and eventually the sponsor of the Delft microbiologist Leeuwenhoek as a member of the Royal Society in London, bought a camera obscura in that city in the early 1620s from his fellow-countryman Cornelis Drebbel, an alchemist, engineer, and inventor of clocks, water systems, oar-powered submarines, and microscopes, who was at that point being made much of at the English royal court.* In 1622 Huygens wrote to his parents from London that the camera obscura

certainly produces admirable effects in reflection-painting in a dark room. It is not possible to describe to you the beauty of it in words: all painting is dead by comparison, for here is life itself, or something more noble, if only there were words for it. Figure, contour, and movement come together naturally therein, in a way that is altogether pleasing.

---

*Drebbel's new method for dyeing wool was seen to have practical advantages and was taken up in London.

Huygens brought his camera back to Holland and demonstrated it. He thought artists were negligent if they did not make use of 'so pleasant and useful an aid'. One artist who heard and apparently heeded this was Johannes Torrentius – he of the bridle, the man accused of heresy and much else – though Huygens suspected that Torrentius already knew of the device and had used it to achieve some of the realistic effects in his still-lifes. Huygens also lauded the camera obscura in his poem 'The Day's Work':

> . . . These are things reflected to you,
> Secrets told within our fortress,
> Mirrors of the world without:
> As the *camera obscura*
> Topsy-turvy through its lenses
> Draws the sunlit world inside.
> Topsy-turvy, Stella, mark this:
> Not the real thing, but reflection,
> Just as lies may work upon
> Truth that's tender and new-born,
> Transparent as the noonday sun.

'Stella' was Huygens's wife Susanna van Baerle, who had died in May 1637, about a year before he wrote this. It was thirty-two years later that Huygens probably accompanied young van Berckhout on his first visit to Delft to look at Vermeer's 'perspectives'. Huygens was in his late seventies then but still, according to John Evelyn, 'a vigorous brisk man'. He would have been qualified and delighted to discuss the ins-and-outs of the camera obscura with Johannes Vermeer.

If the box beneath the easel in *The Music Lesson* isn't a perspective box or a curiously shaped trunk for paints and brushes, then it may be a portable camera obscura. These weren't uncommon at this point. In England Robert Hooke, assistant to the president of the Royal Society, had made one, a long box into which the viewer thrust his head and arms and traced the view on a small screen; Hooke just happened to be a correspondent of Leeuwenhoek in Delft. John

Evelyn saw such a device in June 1670 – though we don't know whether or not it was Hooke's – 'a dark large box [which could] take the profile of ones face as big as the life; which it did performe very accurately'. A late seventeenth-century Dutch writer on perspective, Willem Jacob s'Gravesande, described a larger portable device which he called 'A Sedan Chair Camera Obscura' and wrote that 'several Dutch painters [presumably of the previous generation] are said to have studied and imitated, in their paintings, the effect of the camera obscura'.

A century later, Sir Joshua Reynolds owned such a device in somewhat smaller, portable form and used it for his portraits. It was constructed like an immense leather-bound book. Lift the front cover or lid and, like a jack-in-the-box, a sort of bellows opened upwards, with a periscope on top and within it a mirror that reflected the image downward on the paper placed on the floor of the box. The viewer put his head and shoulders into an opening and drew a curtain tight round himself to keep out the light as he traced what he wanted of the view. (The darker the space within, the brighter the image.) Not surprisingly Reynolds, travelling in Holland in 1781 and impressed by the fidelity of its artists' vision, wrote (to Edmund Burke) that 'Dutch pictures are a representation of nature just as it is seen in a camera obscura'. Vermeer's *Milkmaid* was one work Reynolds saw while in the Dutch Republic and both Vermeer and Samuel van Hoogstraten may have been among the painters W.J. s'Gravesande had in mind. Hoogstraten was certainly knowledgeable about all sorts of mirrors and lenses, spherical, angular, and cylindrical, and of the effects of the camera obscura he wrote in his *Inleyding*: 'I am sure that the sight of these reflections in the dark can give no small light to the vision of young artists; since besides gaining knowledge of nature, one sees here what main or general [characteristics] should belong to a truly natural painting.'

A camera obscura does not figure in Vermeer's inventory – perhaps he shared or borrowed one – but evidence that he used such a camera is there in his pictures. A number of the details in them obviously resemble those of the images seen in a camera obscura: note, for instance, the fluid way the red and white threads in *The Lacemaker* are painted and that some parts of the same picture are in sharper focus than others; observe the highlights on the brass lion's-head finials and the extravagantly contrasted colours of the *Girl with a Red Hat*; and look at the diffused rings of light, or 'circles of confusion' as they have been called, not seen by the human eye on its own but visible with the help of a camera obscura, which were rendered by Vermeer on the topsides of the fishing boats in the *View of Delft*. For that matter, the way the light falls on the *Girl with a Pearl Earring* has been taken (by Gowing) as 'very possibly . . . a direct transcription of the incidence of light on the screen of a camera obscura', while the tapestry curtain in the immediate foreground of *The Art of Painting*, like the hat of the military man in the *Officer and Laughing Girl*, has a feature we recognise as familiar from modern photographs, where the foreground is brought into unreal prominence by the camera lens. The emphatic contrast in scale between the artist and Clio – the disparity in size between two figures who were in fact close together – has also been seen as a sign of Vermeer's use of a camera obscura.

None of this is to say that we are absolutely certain that Vermeer actually traced the outlines of a picture with the help of a camera obscura. Some art historians are loath to entertain the notion that Vermeer used any optical aid, perhaps because it seems to detract from the idea of him as an impeccable, consummate artist who worked entirely from direct observation. But we know from two of his later pictures that he was interested in scientists and, like many artists, may well have been keen on any labour-saving device that contemporary science brought into being. Moreover, he seems to have enjoyed studying the effects of a camera obscura image and both mimicking and transforming them in his paintings. He saw and painted things in a way that none of his colleagues did, and the camera obscura would have helped him do so.

Beyond this, the camera obscura seems to have been the tool that permitted Vermeer to compose his very partial, contained, and withdrawn interiors. As well as circles of confusion, he made rectangles of utter calm. A number of people, including P.T.A. Swillens and

Lawrence Gowing, have tried to re-create the room or rooms Vermeer used. (Swillens did not believe Vermeer used a camera obscura; Gowing did.) In 1966 two French photographers, Michel Gall and Tony Saulier, made a three-dimensional replica of *The Milkmaid* and her kitchen corner, working on the basis that seventeenth-century Dutch tiles, used as a skirting in the picture, were 13 centimetres square; and they concluded that Vermeer used a camera obscura to obtain his almost perfect perspective and fall of light. More recently, Philip Steadman, a professor at the Bartlett School of Architecture and Design of the University of London, has re-created the room shown in six Vermeer paintings, using the 'perspective geometry' in them to establish vanishing points, distance points, and horizon lines, and employing the known size of items such as wall maps or floor tiles or the Ruckers virginals or the Dirck van Baburen *Procuress*. (The six pictures are the *Girl being offered Wine*, *The Glass of Wine*, *Lady writing a Letter with her Maid*, *The Music Lesson*, *The Concert*, and the *Young Woman standing at a Virginal*.) Steadman worked out from these objects the size of the room. The angles of view allowed him to determine the viewpoint for the pictures. Steadman then discovered that 'if the angle of view of each picture, both in plan and in side view, is carried back through the viewpoint to meet the back wall, it defines in effect a rectangle on that wall. In all of the six cases . . . *this rectangle is the exact size of the corresponding painting*' (Steadman's emphasis). And he continues: 'This fact, I suggest, is very strong evidence that Vermeer used an optical arrangement in which a lens was placed at the viewpoint and an image was projected on to the back wall. Vermeer would then have traced this image.'

Because the artist would have needed to view the image in relative darkness, Vermeer – Steadman believes – screened off a small area at one side of the room, closing the shutter of the window in the outside wall that would have lit this area and making a sort of cubicle, into which the lens brought the image he wanted to paint. This image, seen on the darkened side wall, would have given him the wherewithal for an outline drawing and also provided him with data for the light and dark areas he needed for his basic underpainting. Steadman points out that Athanasius Kircher showed such a cubicle-type camera obscura in his *Ars Magna Lucis et Umbrae* of 1646. Steadman's room, furnished as for *The Music Lesson*, and with a darkened cubicle in which a 'simple biconvex lens' was installed, produced 'a clear sharp image at the actual size of the painting'.

It is typical of Vermeer to have left so few visible clues of all this. But, as we have seen, despite the *trompe-l'oeil* 'realism' of his paintings, when it seemed as if he was giving away too much information about his intentions, he hid them. He eliminated a dog in a doorway, a Cupid on the wall. In an age when every picture could have myriad meanings, he resisted obvious symbols. We may well be missing – as Walter Liedtke suggested in 1992 in his piece 'Vermeer teaching himself' – some of his meaning because we are unfamiliar with the formal iconographic conventions of his time, but – as Liedtke also notes – it may also be the case that Vermeer was as usual stepping away from the commonplace; moreover, 'his profound interest in optical effects compounds the sense of wonder, since his figures, no matter how conventionally arranged . . . are treated in terms of light, color, and definition (or "focus") as if they were still-life objects slowly transferred to canvas by some automatic means'.

Nevertheless, despite the concession of that 'automatic means', Liedtke disputes the growing body of opinion that believes Vermeer depended considerably on the camera obscura for the structure and effects of some of his paintings. Comparing some of Vermeer's 'luminous motifs' with passages in church interiors by Emanuel de Witte or still-lifes by Willem Kalf, Liedtke declares that 'Vermeer's individual manner of recording visual experience was not a science but a style – and a style of the period, however rare an example it might be'. But we should remember that the period was also one in which scientific experiment was happening nearby, explosively fresh and brilliant, in the hands of Christiaan Huygens in The Hague and Antony van Leeuwenhoek in Delft itself. Steadman convinces me that Vermeer's mature style had a scientific framework, and that Vermeer's art had at its heart an immense amount of craft, cleverly camouflaged. Indeed, Vermeer, I suspect, would have gone along with Jacob Cats, when he wrote in his book *Mirror of the Old and New Time* (1627): 'Proverbs are particularly attractive because of a certain mysterious quality, for while they appear to be one thing, in fact they are another. Experience teaches us that many things gain by not being completely seen, but veiled and concealed.'

The Art of Painting is a complex picture in which a great deal is going on: the tapestry curtain is swept back to let us see the little masque being performed; the light pours in; the candelabrum hangs motionless from the ceiling and the map is suspended in time and place on the wall. The girl holds her pose, the painter ponders, and the tiles and beams, table and chair edges, make their silent statements of direction. The net result is perfect equilibrium. He signed the painting on the bottom margin of the map, behind Clio's shoulder, 'I. Věr-meer'. This is the fullest signature of any that he placed on his pictures and serves notice that he gave it his all.

9. *The Geographer, the Astronomer, and the Lens-Maker*

Delft was a relatively small city. Living in the centre of town, as Vermeer did, it was impossible in the course of daily walks and errands not to run into people he recognised – a waiter at Mechelen; a peat merchant; van Buyten, the baker; several colleagues from the St Luke's Guild; Arnold Bon, the printer, coming out of his shop on the Market Place; a woman who sold fish – and then to exchange a nod of greeting or pause and trade some news or gossip of the day. A person he must have seen from time to time was Antony van Leeuwenhoek, a man with leonine features who lived not far from the western end of the Market Place, on the Hippolytusbuurt, close to the Fish Market, in a house called the Golden Head, and who worked part-time at the Town Hall. The entry for Leeuwenhoek's birth in October 1632 and the entry for Johannes Vermeer's that same month appear on the same page of the baptismal records book of the Nieuwe Kerk.

Leeuwenhoek was a cloth merchant by profession. His drapery shop was on the ground floor of the Golden Head. He also held various municipal posts – including that of chamberlain to the Delft sheriffs, and city wine-gauger, a role in which he or one of his staff was meant to test wines and spirits entering Delft and ensure that barrels were full – and he had several avocations, one of which was microscopy and another surveying; he measured, among other things, the height of the tower of the Nieuwe Kerk with his quadrant and worked it out to be 299 feet high. By his own account this homespun polymath couldn't read any language except Dutch and he couldn't draw. So, when he began to produce scientific papers in his early forties, offering his microscopic observations for publication by the recently founded Royal Society for the Improving of Natural Knowledge in London, he hired trained draughtsmen to make the necessary illustrations. For some years Leeuwenhoek had been busy not only at his haberdashery trade and civic duties but in teaching himself how to grind and polish glass to form magnifying lenses. And then, with what he called his 'microscopia', he began to examine natural material including chalk, mould, and water, and various small creatures and insects, so that he could describe precisely the eyes of a bee and the sting of a louse. In 1673, although Holland and England were at war again for their usual mercantile and maritime reasons, though without much rancour among their citizenry, Leeuwenhoek was introduced to the Royal Society by the Delft physician and anatomical researcher Reinier de Graaf (he died at the age of thirty-two later that year), who had sent to the Society some of Leeuwenhoek's insect observations. A few months later Constantijn Huygens wrote from The Hague to Robert Hooke – as noted, maker of a camera obscura and assistant to the Society's president – to tell him (in English) about the character of 'our honest citizen, Mr Leeuwenhoek . . . a person unlearned both in sciences and languages, but of his own nature exceedingly curious and industrious', and to express the hope that the Society would be pleased with the work of 'so diligent a searcher'. Leeuwenhoek himself, writing to Henry Oldenburg, the Society's secretary, in Dutch, acknowledged his lack of education and his need to overcome a desire to keep his discoveries to himself 'because I do not gladly suffer contradiction or censure from others'.

Over the next forty years or so, into long-lived old age, this inquisitive, perceptive, and somewhat cranky man made all sorts of discoveries with his microscopes and communicated them to the Royal Society from Delft in several hundred letters. He was eventually honoured by being made a Fellow of the society but he regarded fame as a bit of a nuisance, since it involved calls from visiting monarchs such as Peter the Great. He seems to have been the first observer of bacteria, protozoa, spirochaetes, spermatozoa. And in case anyone had any doubts about how he obtained the last, he wrote: 'What I investigate is only what, without sinfully defiling myself, remains as a residue after conjugal coitus.' When a collection of his microscopes, 247 strong, was sold in 1747, a vast range of material was found *in situ*: fixed to a moveable silver point or needle in front of a microscope's lens, or sometimes sandwiched between glass, were muscle fibres of a whale, scales of human skin, human blood corpuscles, papillae from the tongue of an ox, the hair of an elk, the spinning apparatus of a spider, the brains of a fly, the eyes of a dragonfly, red coral, oyster shell, embryo oysters, and the germ of a rye seed. He gazed at marble, diamonds, gold dust, and all sorts of wood. He used a hair from his wig to work out how many hair-breadths there were in an inch: 600 was his answer. He looked intently at water of various origins: well-water, river-water, canal-water, lake-water, and water from stagnant ditches and gutters. He inspected water caught in a new Delft porcelain dish, never used before and left outside in the rain. On one occasion, with a curiosity proper to a resident of Delft, he decided to examine the properties of saltpetre and set off a minute explosion of gunpowder as he peered through his lens; he saw what he wanted though he was lucky not to blind himself in the process.

To look through a microscope Leeuwenhoek had first to make one. He had to get the materials for the glass, blow it, grind and polish it, and then fix the lens in a silver or brass mounting. He learned glass-blowing from a professional glass-blower whom he met at a fair in Delft, and then practised at home. In effect his was a simple microscope, like a small modern magnifying glass, but superior to the compound microscopes then in use, and with a single biconvex lens and a screw device that brought the examined object into focus, by moving it closer to or further from the lens. His lenses were of short focus though some had a magnifying power of 270 diameters; he made in the course of his long career about 550 of them. He kept his lens-making skills to himself but it was a period when the craft had a number of devotees. Drebbel's microscope in London has been mentioned; Pepys was interested in such a device and bought one from his local instrument-maker, Mr Reeves, for £5 10*s* in 1664. Spinoza was making a living grinding lenses in The Hague from 1670 to 1677 so as to be able to eat while penning his philosophical works. Constantijn Huygens's son Christiaan – mathematician, scientist, and astronomer – ground and polished his own lenses and used them to make a telescope with which he studied the rings of Saturn.*

What turned the draper and civic functionary of limited education into one of the great scientific observers of the age? Leeuwenhoek's father was a basket manufacturer, his mother came from a brewing family, and they lived on the east side of Delft, *op de hoek van de Leeuwenpoort*, 'at the corner by the Lion Gate' – hence their name. Antony was the fifth child and went to a Catholic school; his father died and his mother remarried one J.J. Molijn, a painter for the province, a *staatsschilder*, and therefore a member of the St Luke's Guild along with Reynier Vermeer. Young Leeuwenhoek, taking up the cloth trade, perhaps developed an eye for the closeness of the weave of silk and worsted: thread-counting may have trained his vision, and an interest in magnifying glasses would have been natural. That he was good with figures one assumes from his job at sixteen as a cashier and book-keeper in Amsterdam, and his measuring talents may have had something to do with his later appointment as Delft wine-gauger. Shortly after his marriage to Barbara de Mey, the daughter of a Delft serge-dealer, in 1654, he began to study mathematics, navigation, and astronomy. The deaths of four of their five children in childhood may have further impelled him to take up these solitary pursuits. His surviving child Maria never married but looked after her widower father into his old age. He was in many ways a typical Dutchman of his time, hard-working, obsessed with dirt and cleanliness, with the state of his house (like those gutters of his that were scoured twice a year), and with his own bodily functions; he examined his own urine and excrement through a microscope. Although deeply religious, he was not superstitious, and he seems to

*Galileo had probably seen these first, but with a rudimentary telescope, and Christiaan Huygens would have had a much sharper view.

have been free of both sectarian and scholarly dogma. Above a portrait of himself by Jan Goeree he wrote, 'By diligent labour one discovers matters that before one has deemed inscrutable.' One learnt by seeing, by looking, and he learned about the human body by studying dissection with the Delft city anatomist Cornelis s'Gravesande. And once he had looked through his first lens at the new world it offered, there was no stopping him.

In Leeuwenhoek's letters one catches the poetry – and the competitive spirit – of his discoveries, as in his first observations of protozoa in rain-water:

> In the year 1675, about half-way through September (being busy with studying air, when I had much compressed it by means of water), I discovered living creatures in rain, which had stood but a few days in a new tub, that was painted blue within. This observation provoked me to investigate this water more narrowly; and especially because these little animals were, to my eye, more than ten thousand times smaller than the animacule which [Jan] Swammerdam [Dutch scientist, 1637–80] has portrayed, and called by the name of water-flea, or water-louse, which you can see alive and moving in water with the bare eye.
>
> Of the first sort that I discovered in the said water, I saw, after divers observations, that the bodies consisted of 5, 6, 7, or 8 very clear globules, but without being able to discern any membrane or skin that held these globules together, or in which they were inclosed. When these animacules bestirred themselves, they sometimes stuck out two little horns, which were continually moved, after the fashion of a horse's ears. The part between these little horns was flat, their body else being roundish, save only that it ran somewhat to a point at the hind end; at which pointed end it had a tail, near four times as long as the whole body, and looking as thick, when viewed through my microscope, as a spider's web [looks to the naked eye].

This investigator – 'the father of microbiology' – enjoyed good health. He noted that he was normally regular in his bowel movements but now and again had a looseness which he cured by drinking 'uncommon hot tea'. For minor problems, like fever or headaches, he dosed himself with great quantities of tea, which he thought thinned the blood. Maria looked after him and his faith supported him. In 1677, when he felt that the Royal Society in London might be dubious of his findings, he got Alexander Petrie, the pastor of the English church in Delft, to testify to being 'an eye-witnesse' to one of his experiments. After looking through the 'ingenious' Mr Leeuwenhoek's microscope at a tiny quantity of water, Petrie declared that he had seen 'a very great number of little animals moving in that water, so many that I could not possibly number them'. In 1688, in his sixty-fourth letter to the Royal Society, Leeuwenhoek wrote (as always in Dutch):

> God does not call any new creatures into being. He, the Lord, has from the beginning so ordered things that in all perfect or full-grown seeds He has already created so as to make them carry within themselves – albeit for ever hidden from our eyes – the matter which is the origin of the body that in the fulness of time will spring therefrom . . .

In the same year in London John Evelyn noted on one occasion in his diary: 'step'd in to the R. Society, where a paper of Mr Lewenhooks concerning insects etc was read'. In Delft Leeuwenhoek went on freely showing his discoveries to curious travellers, though the locals found him secretive about his lens-making. Sir Francis Child, an English banker, called on him in 1697 and saw 'the testicles and eggs of lice, the eggs of oysters and several other dissections of the most minute insects'. Leeuwenhoek seems to have inherited money from his mother's family, which, together with fees from his municipal functions, gave him ease from any financial worries; assistants did much of the day-to-day work of those posts. He eventually owned two houses in Delft and a garden and cottage outside town where he grew fruit and vegetables; his town, proud of him, paid him a pension for life. He received letters from near and far – one elderly lady in the East Indies sent him a piece of a palm tree – and visitors kept coming; in 1711, in four days, twenty-six people called on him. But to the end of his life he went on observing, taking note through a microscope of the soft matter he dug out of the roots of one of his own teeth (he pulled the tooth out himself). In his final illness, he had muscular spasms of the chest that affected his heart, and he described them. He dictated his last letter to the Royal Society on his death-bed. He died in August 1723, two months before his ninety-first birthday, and was buried in the Oude Kerk.

The basic connections between Leeuwenhoek and Vermeer are to be found in the baptismal records book, when they were at the beginning of their lives, and also after Vermeer's death, when Leeuwenhoek took a hand in sorting out the artist's estate. In between, hard facts, as so often in the case of Vermeer, are sparse. However, the circumstantial evidence is considerable that the two notable eye-witnesses – master painter and master scientist – had dealings with one another. We can spin a web of filaments that draws them close together in Delft.

For a start, there was Vermeer's father's early work as a weaver of the material called caffa and Leeuwenhoek's trade as a cloth merchant. There was Leeuwenhoek's education in the 1640s at a Catholic school – which would suggest that he was at least not raised as a diehard anti-Papist – and later his municipal functions: as the aldermen's steward after 1667 he would have been aware of the candidates for headmen of the St Luke's Guild, who in 1670 included Vermeer, and as the city wine-gauger he might have gone into inns on weights-and-measures inspections (though he assumed this job in 1679, after the Vermeer family gave up Mechelen). There was Leeuwenhoek's training as a surveyor, which would have given him knowledge useful to an artist looking for help with mathematics and perspective (the artist Pieter Saanredam in Haarlem consulted his fellow-townsman, the surveyor Pieter Wils, for similar advice). We have noted Leeuwenhoek's correspondence with Robert Hooke, who owned a portable camera obscura by 1668, and the links of both Delft men with Constantijn Huygens, another camera obscura owner, who probably visited Vermeer with Pieter Teding van Berckhout. Leeuwenhoek's expertise with lenses would have been of particular interest to an artist who employed a camera obscura. Both men were ambitious to attain what Leeuwenhoek in a letter once called 'a nicer Accuracy'. It seems likely that the amateur scientist used a simple system of 'dark-field lighting' which made very small objects more perceptible – for example, sand grains placed on a piece of black taffeta – when he was examining them under a microscope, and this would have fascinated a painter who may now and then have worked

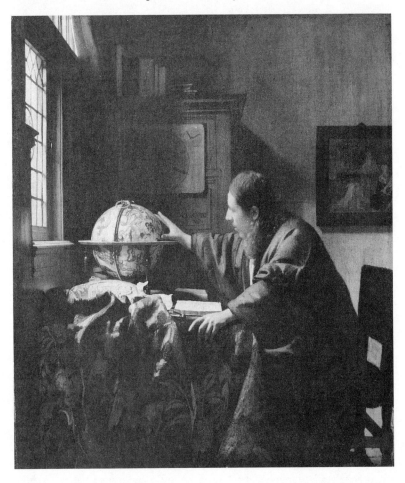

The Astronomer, 1668.

inside part of a room screened off and darkened while looking at an image produced by a lens.

There was also the tantalising association of scientist and artist after the latter's death. In September 1676 the town council asked their chamberlain to administer the assets of Catharina Bolnes, 'widow of the late Johannes Vermeer during his lifetime master painter'. This was one of several instances where Leeuwenhoek was made the executor of an estate, but it was not a job likely to produce many perquisites – worries, rather – and the fact that Leeuwenhoek accepted the curatorship of the more or less insolvent Vermeer estate suggests some acquaintance between the two men. In the event, Leeuwenhoek handled his duties in a way that showed no favouritism to Catharina in tussles that took place with the family's creditors, but perhaps he was simply being an honest executor, as impartial as he could be.

The most intriguing link is that which lies latent in two paintings by Vermeer. In 1667 and 1668, a man in his late thirties posed for the painter as he worked on two seemingly associated pictures with scientific themes. These were Vermeer's only two paintings – at least the only two to survive – with solitary male figures as their protagonists; today the pictures are called *The Astronomer* and *The Geographer*, though the titles have varied in the past. In 1713 they were auctioned as 'A work depicting a Mathematical Artist, by Vander Meer' and 'A ditto by the same'. When they came up for sale again a few years later they were described as 'An Astrologer' and 'A repeat' – i.e. another one of the same profession – and were referred to as 'extra choice'. Later still, the 'Geographer' as he is now called was re-identified as 'an Architect' or 'a Surveyor'. Obviously Vermeer intended the two men to be scholarly types. Although the 'Astronomer' has no telescope, he is shown touching a celestial globe, and the 'Geographer' holds a pair of compasses or dividers and has a terrestrial globe nearby; both men have books to hand. Indeed, a slightly idealised air permeates the pictures, which were probably commissioned work and thus balanced uneasily between the needs of client and painter. Some of the professional equipment may have been borrowed, including the cross-staff that hangs in deep shadow from the centre post of the window frame in *The Geographer*; such a staff could be used to measure heights (the height of the tower of the Nieuwe Kerk, for instance) or the angle of elevation of the sun. The date of 1669 now seen on *The Geographer* isn't original, though it is

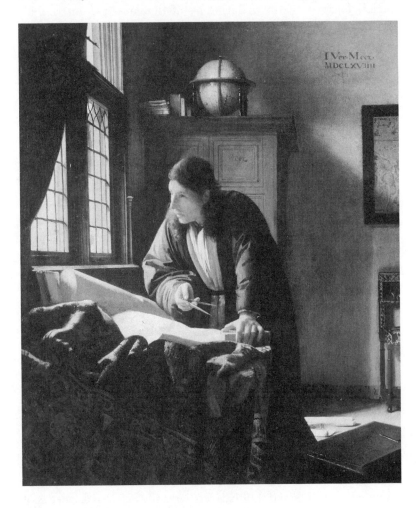

The Geographer, c. 1668–9.

thought to reflect the date the picture was painted. That year, 1669, happens to be when Antony van Leeuwenhoek qualified as a *landmeter* or surveyor.

The model in both pictures appears to be the same man. He has a large, long, straight nose and full lips. Moreover, although there are differences in detail between the rooms the two scientists inhabit – a section of stained-glass window in one and not in the other; the table carpets; a curtain moved from one side of the casement to the other – the actual room seems to be the same, with the same corner cupboard. The globes in the paintings, one celestial, one terrestrial, were a pair marketed by Jodocus Hondius in 1600. The book lying in front of the astronomer has been identified as the 1621 second edition of a work by Adriaen Metius, *On the Investigation or Observation of the Stars*, and it is open at the beginning of Book III, where not only knowledge of geometry and the aid of mechanical instruments are recommended for this research but also 'inspiration from God'. The painting that hangs on the wall behind the astronomer has for its subject the Finding of Moses, and perhaps acknowledges the same need for divine inspiration. Moses was described in the Acts of the Apostles as 'learned in all the wisdom of Egypt' – a body of wisdom that would have included astronomy – and was also considered to be 'the oldest geographer', because of his leadership of the Hebrews during their travels in exile. (As we have seen, for some contemporaries, the United Provinces were the new Israel, the promised land.) Did Vermeer paint this *Finding of Moses*? It would be one more picture by Vermeer to add to the list of his missing works, and has been suggested as possibly 'the large painting by Vermeer' that the baker Hendrick van Buyten had – along with 'two little pieces by Vermeer' – in his collection of pictures by mostly local painters.

Both of the men in the paintings, whether astronomers, geographers, or surveyors, seem to be thinkers as much as practical scientists. Of the two, the geographer is less conspicuously deep in thought but simply caught in an abstracted moment. The pictures may have had a message which is now obscure, for nature then had meanings that would not be so evident to us, with signs of God's will to be seen nightly in the movement of the stars – or, for that matter, in daylight, or for one Delft observer in the eel-like motion of protozoa. As Leeuwenhoek wrote, about some 'animacules' he observed in water from his gutter: 'Once more we see here the unconceivable Providence, perfection, and order bestowed by the Lord Creator of the Universe upon such little creatures which escape our bare eye, in order that their kind shouldn't die out.' Inspiration from God, indeed. Both Vermeer's astronomer and his geographer are dressed in a similar way, in scholarly dressing gowns. This was traditional wear for this sort of portrait, as painted by Gerrit Dou, Leonaert Bramer, Rembrandt, and many Rembrandt followers including Nicolaes Maes. Rembrandt's etching of Faustus has the scholar, in just such a loose robe, leaning over his table while looking at a strange light that has appeared before his window. Whether Vermeer knew of Rembrandt's etching can't be determined, but his geographer is seen in a similar pose, though without any alarming supernatural apparitions to catch his eye. Both of Vermeer's paintings demonstrate his usual sense of harmony and feeling for well-organised space, but we get a slight sense that, whatever his motive for undertaking these pictures, his heart wasn't completely in it. So, although it is possible that Vermeer himself served as his own model here, it seems more likely that the painter – perhaps asked to paint allegories of scientific endeavour – portrayed someone he knew with scientific concerns.

Whether that person was Antony van Leeuwenhoek is a question to which no conclusive answer can yet be given. If Vermeer had intended to represent the draper cum civil official turned scientist, he surely would have shown Leeuwenhoek with one of his microscopes; if Leeuwenhoek was merely the model, then possibly he was representing the Scientist (as the girl in *The Art of Painting* represented the Muse of History) and Vermeer didn't feel obliged to produce a close likeness. As mentioned, we know that Leeuwenhoek, having exercised himself for some time in 'the art of Geometry', qualified as a surveyor in February 1669, the year that Vermeer seems to have painted his man holding dividers, and that he gained a reputation for his skills in navigation, astronomy, and mathematics. At thirty-seven, Leeuwenhoek would have been the right age for the scholar-scientist in Vermeer's pictures. Moreover, when Leeuwenhoek was portrayed explicitly nearly twenty years later by the Delft portraitist Jan Verkolje, he was shown in a pose that in many respects derived from

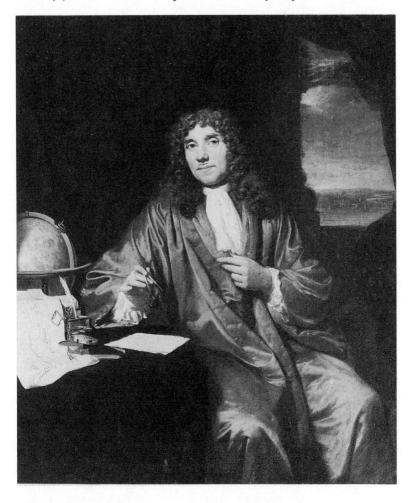

Portrait of Antony van Leeuwenhoek, 1686, Jan Verkolje.

Vermeer's *Geographer*, dividers in his right hand, a globe nearby, and wearing the same sort of robe and scarf. (It was acclaimed as an excellent likeness by none other than Constantijn Huygens, in some verses he wrote for the mezzotint Verkolje made from his painting.) In Verkolje's portrait, Leeuwenhoek has a nose very like that of Vermeer's model, but his face seems broad whereas that of the man in Vermeer's paintings looks long – though this discrepancy could be explained by the fact that Verkolje painted a fifty-four-year-old man and not one of thirty-seven.

Once again, we are left with questions as well as answers. It would obviously help if we knew who commissioned the two Vermeers or who first owned them; they first crop up in the art market in Rotterdam in 1713 at an auction where pictures belonging to Adriaen Paets, a Rotterdam city councillor and art patron, were being sold. The Dutch seaborne empire was then at its full extent, with cargoes of spices, silks, teak, coffee, and tea constantly arriving from distant colonies and trading posts to be landed in Rotterdam, Delfshaven, and Amsterdam. In any event, whoever modelled for the scientists in them, Vermeer's paintings demonstrate a willingness to be interested in the greater world, both terrestrial and celestial, and an awareness of the knowledge of both spheres needed for navigation – a world beyond Delft.

In his late thirties, the artist also had other things on his mind, closer to hand. In 1667 his brother-in-law Willem Bolnes was still a problem, though confined in Hermanus Taerling's house. In May of that year Maria Thins gave Vermeer authority to collect debts owed to her as guardian of her son and to reinvest the proceeds or pay out any obligations she owed. He and Catharina and the whole household mourned the death of a male infant child, buried on 10 July 1667 in the family grave in the Oude Kerk that Maria Thins had purchased six years before. Vermeer, signing himself 'Johannes Vermeer', witnessed a legal procuration to do with a property dispute for some wealthy sisters – relations of Maria Thins – named Rosendael, who lived in The Hague, and he also witnessed the will of a neighbour, an unmarried lady named Annetge Jans. The Dirck van Bleyswijck book on Delft was published and created a stir among the citizens who were hailed by the author for their sociability, restrained dignity, and elegance; and it was no doubt read by the town's painters, of whom Bleyswijck seemed especially proud. In 1668 Maria Thins empowered Vermeer to collect from the Gouda Orphan Chamber money owed to her children Willem and Catharina from funds left by their great-aunt. Later that year Vermeer was probably involved in discussions with his mother, Digna Balthens, now about seventy-four, on the subject of getting rid of Mechelen. She had been running the inn since 1641, and a sum of 2,500 guilders was still outstanding on the mortgage. In February 1669, after failing to sell it at auction with an asking price of 5,000 guilders, Digna leased Mechelen for three years to a shoemaker, Leendert van Ackerdijck, for 190 guilders a year. This was only 65 guilders more than Digna's annual payments for mortgage interest. (Van Ackerdijck got free use of the inn's beer and wine racks and promised to repair at his own expense any breakage or damage.) Digna, relieved of Mechelen, moved in with Gertruy in the Vlamingstraat. Gertruy's only child had been a daughter named Beyken, born in 1654, who died – it seems – in infancy, and Gertruy may have welcomed her mother's company.

Vermeer and Catharina had to deal with the death of another child in July 1669, the same month as that in which a child of theirs had died two years before; the later calamity was not long after Pieter Teding van Berckhout's visit.* And there were more family deaths, and intimations of mortality, in 1670. Gertruy and her husband Antony van der Wiel made a new will on 11 February that year, which in the light of what followed suggests that Gertruy wasn't well. One of the witnesses to the will, to which Antony set a star-shaped mark (he presumably was illiterate) and to which Gertruy put the name 'Geertruit Vormeer', signed 'in a trembling hand', was Vermeer's patron Pieter van Ruijven – who perhaps bought from van der Weil

---

*In the Dutch world outside Delft, 1669 was the year Rembrandt died in Amsterdam, in October, though not much of the world took notice.

10. *Delft Blue*

Among the domestic objects we encounter in Vermeer's paintings – the chairs, tables, carpets, curtains, maps, and foot-warmers – are tiles; not the large floor tiles that help establish his perspective but small, square white tiles with blue decorations that were made in Delft and generally used for covering the lower areas of inside walls. The tiles had a practical purpose, hiding damp spots on the ground-floor walls and providing a skirting or rubbing strip that protected the plaster from the daily assault of brooms and mops and scrubbing brushes. And – this was Delft – they were also simple works of art.

The tile industry was the other Delft success story in these years. Herman Pieterszoon of Haarlem is given the credit for bringing the making of tin-enamelled earthenware to Delft in about 1600. Over the century the numbers of glazed-earthenware makers or faienciers – *plateelbakkers*, in Dutch – increased, their status improved, and their incomes grew. In 1640 Delft had ten pottery businesses with a total of some 150 workers; in 1670 there were twenty-eight firms employing roughly 500 artisans. After 1648 two of the *plateelbakkers* joined two painters and two glassmakers as the headmen of the Guild of St Luke; and though the painters in the Guild in 1650 still greatly out-numbered the faience-makers (52 to 13), by 1680 there were almost twice as many faienciers as painters in the Guild (57 to 31). Among the leading manufacturers was Wouter van Eenhoorn, who owned five tile-bakeries, shipped his wares to London and Paris, and on his death in 1679 left the princely sum of 22,000 guilders to each of his three children. Most pottery- or tile-makers had their own claymaking sites near the Rotterdam Gate. The twenty-five or so potteries, often established in former breweries, employed clay-treaders, clay-mixers, kiln-stokers, glaziers, and painters. The *knechts* or apprentices learned how to mix clay, mould pots and tiles, mix glazes and apply colours, load ovens, and keep an eye on the products within; it was crucial to know when to take the baked ware out. The names of Delft potteries were soon well known: among others, De Twee Schepjes; De Paeuw; De Ham; De Metalen Pot; De Dissel; De Twee Wilde Mannen; Het Hart; De Witte Starre; De Porceleyne Lampetkan; De Porceleyne Schotel; De Grieksche A. Among the notable faience painters was Isaac Junius, born in Haarlem in 1616, who grew up in Delft and worked as an artist for the potteries there before going on to be sheriff in the coastal village of Katwijk. In 1657 Junius painted two Delftware plaques of that very Delft subject, the Tomb of William the Silent, a front view and a side view. Other well-known Delftware painters were Frederick van Frytom and Gysbrecht Verhaast, who, since they were a vital part of a business that employed many local people, were probably more celebrated in the town than any of its painters on canvas or panel.

How proud Delft was of its earthenware industry can be seen on the *Kaart Figuratief*, near the map's lower right-hand corner, where a man is shown wearing a broad-brimmed hat and displaying an assortment of Delftware plates, jars, and jugs – though no tiles. Indeed, despite the term 'Delft tiles', tile-making went on in other parts of the country, too – for instance, in Makkum, Friesland – though those that were made in Delft were less mass-produced and more artful. As had happened with other crafts, such as weaving, the flood of Flemish refugees had brought skilled workers, in this case potters and tile-makers, to the north and so to the burgeoning Delft tile-bakeries. The Flemings carried with them the technique of making polychrome majolica or faience (terms derived from the Balearic island of Majorca and the town of Faenza in Italy); this involved a double firing process and the clay being heated to a very high temperature. After the first firing, the buff-coloured sea clay or river clay was dipped in white tin enamel, which served as a base for a painted decoration. This was glazed with a transparent lead glaze, and then fired again. Along with the skills of the Flemish potters came a Spanish-Moorish style of decoration, but this was soon overtaken by the influence of Chinese porcelain. The Dutch had followed in the wake of Portuguese seafarers to the east, and when two shiploads of late Ming 'china' had arrived in Amsterdam in the early years of the seventeenth century, their designs and finish made a tremendous impact. Seldom has long-distance plagiarism produced such an original result – the creation of a type of folk art. In mid-century the blue monochrome faience of Delft was given a great fillip by civil war in China; exports in Dutch East India Company ships of the coveted Chinese porcelain to the United Provinces were halted and the Delftware-makers rushed to fill the demand.

By 1670, one in four of the male inhabitants of Delft got his living from the potteries; many manufacturers other than Wouter van Eenhoorn were highly prosperous; and at the monthly meetings with their fellow headmen of the Guild of St Luke, Vermeer and Cornelis de Man may have had to hide their envy at the easy circumstances of the faienciers' leaders, who in 1671 were Jacob Corton and Claes Janszoon Metschert. The work of some fine-art painters was taken up by the industry. Plates and plaques – so-called 'porcelain paintings' – made use of landscapes or biblical scenes; prints by Nicolaes Berchem were adapted, as were drawings by Leonaert Bramer; and engravings after the paintings of Gerard van Honthorst were copied, such as his portrait of the youthful William III – at this point House of Orange commemorative ware was once again a popular item, though possibly not in the Thins-Vermeer house on the Oude Langendijck. What seems to have taken Vermeer's fancy were the white Delftware wine jugs, like the jug to which he draws attention – too close to the edge of the table – in his *Girl being offered Wine*. These jugs echo female shapes, like those of Cycladic figurines. More intricate, more highly decorated jugs were also made in Delft, sometimes with such sculptural embellishments as a horizontal tunnel through the middle of the jug, and the figure of a horse placed within this hole.

Tiles were the humblest form of the earthenware business. Twenty-five guilders would buy a thousand tiles. Sometimes they were used as inexpensive ballast in ships sailing abroad to bring back costly cargoes, and in that way the Delft tile travelled afar as a sample of Dutch artistry. The designs on them make a splendid subcategory of genre painting and a record of many aspects of daily life. Children's games are depicted: flying kites, walking on stilts, trundling hoops, spinning tops, hitting *kolf* balls, playing knucklebones and leap-frog. Tiles show adults and children angling, skating, or sledding, and people out in the countryside hunting, walking, or riding. Soldiers, archers, and marksmen were popular subjects, but other crafts and trades were also featured, including sea-fishing, farming, knife-grinding, thatching, and basket-weaving. Pedlars made their mark in the drawings on tiles as they did in Rembrandt's etchings; preachers were shown in mid-sermon on tiles as in de Witte's paintings. Naval battles were commemorated, and so too, more fancifully, were sea-monsters. Natural life was portrayed: birds on a branch; rabbits coupling; and of course flowers, especially tulips, the Near-Eastern bulb the Dutch had made their own. (Vermeer was never an all-inclusive artist, but it is worth mentioning that none of his paintings incorporates a single flower; the only evident natural growing things are the thorn and trees in the *Diana and her Companions*, the vine in *The Little Street*, and the few trees among the houses in the *View of Delft*.)

Vermeer's fellow painters Hoogstraten and Metsu took note of tiles in their interiors, but there is a sense in which Vermeer didn't just show them as humdrum items of decor but seems prompted to add to the occupations that might figure on tiles: reading letters, making lace, pouring milk. Behind his milkmaid, to the right of her red skirt and blue apron, tiles cover the plaster at the foot of the wall. A small foot-warming stove obscures two of them but three that are visible seem to depict Cupids, which may indicate what Vermeer imagined a kitchen-maid's daydreams to be about. Tiles are also to be seen in *The Geographer* (though not *The Astronomer*) and in the three late paintings of the *Young Woman standing at a Virginal* (see p. 198), the *Lady writing a Letter with her Maid* (see p. 126), and the *Young Woman seated at a Virginal* (see p. 199).

The blue of the drawings on the tiles clearly intrigued him. He picked it up in the blue of the elegant silk dress the young woman wears as she sits at the virginal and looks out at us – the stuff of her dress heaped up on her chair – and he parlays it again in the ruffled blue blouse of her sister virginal-player, who stands. Delft blue was China blue. The colour acknowledges the Oriental influence, but also reminds us that Vermeer was subject to it not just as a colourist but as a pattern-maker. Blue materials were set against a white or off-white background; areas of dark, bluish shadow contrasted with areas of light behind. It was an aspect of things where he also masterfully emulated Carel Fabritius. Both men would have had the opportunity to study Delftware and talk to pottery- and tile-painters. The pared-down simplicity of *The Goldfinch* and the wide-angle, wrap-around, almost willow-pattern distortions of the *View in Delft* both suggest in different ways that Chinese art, via Delft pottery, had made an impression on Fabritius. As for Vermeer, Lawrence Gowing felt the need for Oriental analogies when looking at the way the artist rendered the white floor tiles in *The Love-letter* and the *Lady writing a Letter with her Maid*, and he felt the same urge when observing the liberation of 'certain unexpected qualities of his talent' in some of the otherwise rather too elegant and elaborate late paintings: 'The marbling of the virginals of the *Lady* [i.e. *Young Woman*] *Seated* . . . has the kind of life which a Sung painter might discover in the leaves of bamboo.'

Unfortunately, in the 1670s, when Vermeer may have had a greater financial need to produce pictures for sale, his inner need to paint seems to have waned – the old drive stuttered and his sense of direction faltered. The characters are too posed, the style too polished, in the few pictures he finished. This may have had something to do with the art market, because 'fine-painting' was now the fashion, as was to be seen in the popularity of the works of Gerrit Dou, which today seem so over-detailed, and in the swanky upper-class households being portrayed by Pieter de Hooch. Vermeer re-used his own themes and situations (and continued to borrow other artists', including Dou's), while generally looking into the corner of a room, with a curtain partly hiding our view of the 'action', such as it was, of women writing letters or playing musical instruments. But for the first

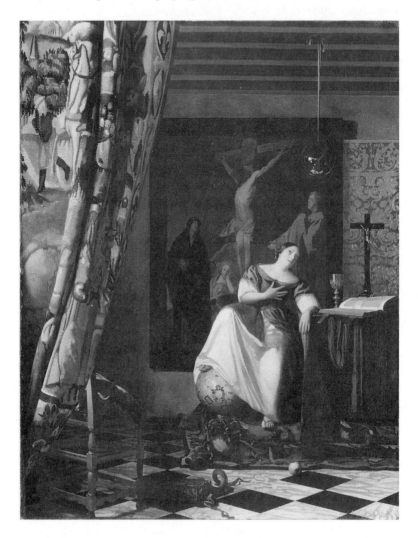

Allegory of Faith, c. 1671–4.

time we can find major things to object to. The dream-like self-containment is now occasionally shattered by self-consciously splashy passages. One wonders if his decision to concentrate on refined ladies and elegant interiors was not only a way of satisfying wealthy patrons like van Ruijven but a way of shutting out the rougher, less literate world he had climbed up from: the Flying Fox, Grandma Neeltge, Grandpa Balthasar . . . His 'Catholicism', not particularly obtrusive in his paintings since *Christ in the House of Martha and Mary*, now showed up in a painting called *Allegory of Faith*, and did so in a sickly, melodramatic way, all the more curious in that it was painted by a man who had hitherto not flaunted his attachment to the Roman Church.

Here, with a vengeance, was what the historian Pieter Geyl called the 'fervent, though externalized religious life of the Counter-Reformation'. One can see why Dutch Protestants wanted to get rid of stained-glass and statues in the churches they took over. A plump pale-skinned lady in a gold-trimmed, blue-and-white satin dress sits on a carpet-covered dais staring aloft in goggle-eyed ecstasy, right hand operatically clutching her full bosom, left arm lying on a table that seems to be an altar set up for communion, with gold chalice, open Bible, crucifix. Her right leg is raised and the right foot – toes just visible under the hem of her dress – rests on a globe, a model of the earth, while on the marble-tiled floor a snake lies coiled and bleeding under a piece of masonry. For good measure, amid this iconological surfeit of detail and gesture, an apple – the forbidden fruit – sits discarded, with a perilous bite taken out of it. And on the back wall, next to a gilt leather panel of secular splendour, hangs a *Crucifixion* (collection: Johannes Vermeer) painted by the Flemish artist Jacob Jordaens, colleague of Rubens. Was the local Jesuit priest lurking behind the tapestry on the left, prompting the performance?

It would have been easier – particularly for a Catholic – to look at this picture three hundred years ago. Perhaps, as one scholar has suggested, it was painted for the Catholic chaplain in The Hague, Père Léon. However, the *Allegory* was in the hands of a Protestant collector before the end of the seventeenth century and at a subsequent sale, where it was commended in the catalogue as 'powerfully and glowingly painted', it sold for the high price of 400 guilders. Viewers at the time would have responded more enthusiastically to Vermeer's Italian references and scholarly debts. He once again plundered Cesare Ripa's *Iconologia*, in which the female figure of Theology was similarly posed, with her hand on her breast (i.e. faith in her heart) and the world under (or behind) her feet. He borrowed the glass globe that hangs above his lady from a Catholic book of sacred emblems, published in Antwerp, in which a sphere reflected a cross and the sun. Here the glass orb, intensely scrutinised, appears to reflect the room, with its three windows and a darkened area that might be the cubicle of a camera obscura. The room is in fact little different, though differently lit, from the studio in that other allegory *The Art of Painting*. That picture, too, could be considered 'unreal' – no paint on the floor, no palettes or brushes scattered around. But how much more of a piece it is, how much more eloquent in its non-declamatory way.

In the *Allegory of Faith* Vermeer turned to propaganda of the faith; his picture is as much rhetorical as allegorical and, at least to our eyes, suffers for it. As *St Praxedis* may demonstrate, Vermeer might always have had that inclination, but the early painting (assuming it is by him) was very much a copy. This was his own work. But he failed to sign the *Allegory of Faith*, so maybe he also had his doubts. For an artist of Vermeer's high standards, some bits of the actual painting in it were uncharacteristically unsuccessful, like the woman's bizarrely shadowed right thigh, which seems to be joined to her torso not at the hip but at the ribs, and the lower part of her left leg which, although disguised by her satin dress, isn't quite in the right place anatomically. The ceiling beams seem unduly tentative. Normally he would have regarded such symbols as the crushed snake (heresy being squashed out of existence) as horribly didactic, and on second thought painted them out. Or should we simply deduce that Vermeer found it easier to paint the Muse Clio being portrayed in his studio than a figure of Faith set in a well-to-do Delft living-room?

With his interest in young women, Vermeer as a Catholic convert or someone close to Catholics might have been expected to take an interest in the mother of Christ. His apparent 'annunciations' and his predilection for blue, which was 'Mary's colour', lead to that thought. But then, for all of his well-demonstrated ability to get Catharina pregnant, Vermeer showed no great desire to paint children or infants, even the baby Jesus. We don't know whether he believed in the Virgin birth. (Early in the next century a Delft potter produced a simple figurine of a Madonna with child that has much more life, and innate religious feeling, than Vermeer's *Allegory of Faith*.) For Vermeer, the reality of active, wriggling small children may have been enough; he didn't want them in his pictures, too. He needed subjects which enabled him to withdraw from the loudly insistent world of the banal and ordinary into an altogether quieter and more mysterious sphere of existence. Something special happened on the way to this picture, enough to make him set aside his basic instincts about the ingredients of a painting. Perhaps he felt he owed the Catholic Church something; perhaps he was tempted by a hefty payment at an otherwise thin time. Whatever the motive, the result was a display of overt religious fervour being mimicked rather than felt. The patron who gave the possibly too explicit commission for this work delivered it to a painter who for once failed to produce his usual sleight-of-hand.

Two 'tronies' he apparently worked on in the late 1660s show that magic. The Dutch word comes from a French term, *trogne*, meaning a character head or face rather than a full portrait. These were two small head-and-shoulders and both of young women wearing exotic headgear, their open eyes in shadow, their red lips just parted, and each sitting on or near one of his chairs with lion's-head finials. The girl in the bright red feathered hat wears a vivid blue robe. The young girl with a flute has a wide conical Chinese hat and a jacket or dress of grey-blue material. A broadly painted late sixteenth-century tapestry from the southern Netherlands forms the entire background of each picture. Both are painted on wood panels. Both girls wear large pearl drop-earrings. Both are seen at very close range. Both have something white around their necks – one a cravat, the other a wide collar – that throws light up on to the side of their faces, on to chin and cheek.

Although some scholars dispute the idea that Vermeer painted these heads, they appear to have his (and no one else's) trademarks. How close these girls are to us, how attentive, and yet how much they hold back within themselves! In a more technical sense, one expert has seen the 'fluid execution' of the *Girl with a Red Hat* as 'related to Vermeer's use of a camera obscura' – although the adjustments the painter made to the chair finials, placing them out of alignment to make room for the girl's arm on the back of the chair, show that he

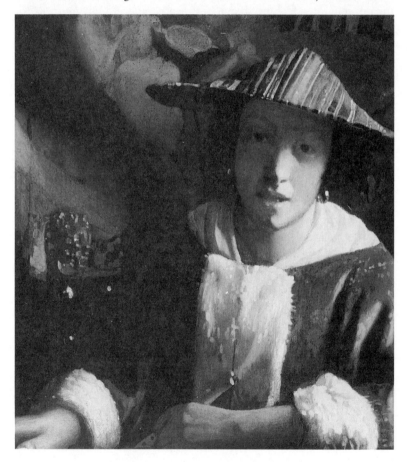

Young Girl with a Flute, c. 1665–70.

wasn't subservient to the device, even as he attempted to capture the shimmer and intensity of the image he saw through it. Modern science also puts us in its debt as we attempt to make a conclusive attribution of this picture: X-radiographs and infra-red reflectograms of the *Girl with a Red Hat* disclose an underlying portrait. Our painter re-used a panel on which a man's head had been previously painted. He turned it upside-down before painting on it his own tronie. Arthur Wheelock writes: 'Although one cannot attribute a painting solely on the basis of an x-radiograph, the brushstrokes and impasto of the underlying head are similar in style to those found in figure studies by Carel Fabritius . . . from the late 1640s.' We know that Vermeer owned two *tronien* by Fabritius and also the two 'tronie paintings' by Hoogstraten, and it wouldn't be surprising if the Vermeer & Son art-dealership had several unfinished works in stock by Vermeer's Delft precursor. And it would be natural enough for Vermeer to turn to one of these one day, inspired by the feel and size of the small panel. The fact that both heads are on wood is an exception to Vermeer's usual practice but 'six panels' were listed in the 1676 inventory, ready to hand in his upstairs front painting-room.

The *Young Girl with a Flute* is more roughly painted and may well have been left unfinished by Vermeer and reworked by another artist. But both pictures share characteristic Vermeer ways of doing things; for example, his 'blocky' brush-strokes. The face of the girl with a flute is painted in a very similar manner to the face of the woman in *The Guitar Player*. The blue-grey-green fur-lined jacket the flute girl wears is also worn by Vermeer's model in the *Woman holding a Balance* (*c*.1664) and the girl singer in *The Concert* (*c*.1665–6); and it is listed in the 1676 inventory as 'an old green mantle with white fur trimmings'. The Chinese hat which the girl with the flute wears is noted by Wheelock as owing much 'to the contemporary vogue for oriental fashion'. Rembrandt etched a portrait of himself in oriental guise and a follower of Frans van Mieris did a painting showing a woman artist wearing a similar conical Chinese hat. In Delft, the hat might also be taken as a salute to the distant Chinese potters whose works made such an impact on the local *plateelbakkers* during these years.

11. *The Years of the French*

In the mid-1630s, the United Provinces, dominated by Holland, had been seized by a get-rich-quick mania, as merchants, peasants, servant-women, peat-carriers, and artists, the landscape painter Jan van Goyen among them, turned valuable possessions into cash and borrowed large sums in order to invest in tulip bulbs. Stolid Dutch citizens, widely known for their prudence, became reckless speculators. Possibly they wanted some relief from their long hours of hard work, something wild and exciting. And perhaps the strange beauty of the flower, which had come from Turkey, brought on the passion to which they became addicted. The tulip was subject to mutations and variations, some virus-created, which produced spectacular new forms that were thought valuable; as bulb prices rose, many people were infected with a gambler's fever to shoot for the moon. Those who had the bug were called 'hooded ones', as if they were madmen. Tales of sudden riches inspired emulation and more and more plunged into the tulip market. A bunch of yellow crown tulip bulbs, one pound in weight, bought for 24 guilders, was sold for 1,200 guilders. One single bulb was traded for a coach and horses, another for a herd of cows. Some bulbs were traded several times a day. Buying on margin and buying tulip 'futures' were common practice.

The tulip bubble had finally burst in February 1637, when Vermeer was still a small boy, leaving many ruined; Jan van Goyen was one of them. The art market also had its highs and lows, along with other areas of buying and selling, as people felt more or less rich, more or less immune to times of shortage or ill-health. There were recurrent outbreaks of plague, particularly in the bigger cities and towns: nearly 18,000 died in Amsterdam in 1656, and even more in 1663 and 1664. But these devastations were shaken off, immigrants poured in to take the place of the dead, and the wealthy merchant class continued to set the pattern for the nation: onward and upward. The Dutch Republic seemed generally insulated from war. When conflict occurred, with Habsburg forces south of the Maas before 1648 or with English fleets in the North Sea, it happened largely out of sight and hearing of the Dutch people. Prosperity continued, though taxes might rise to pay for campaigns and ships, and English blockades caused temporary shortages.

With the 1670s, however, the Republic's long and energetic run of fairly consistent good fortune came to an end. Problems were bred as increasing numbers of people retired from active business and began to live on their investments. A pamphleteer in 1662 complained that small shopkeepers, even publicans and shoemakers and their wives, dressed in such a way that they couldn't be distinguished from their social superiors. The old drab black habits were out; velvet and silk finery was the rage; prosperous middle-class men wore powdered wigs, as Antony van Leeuwenhoek did for Verkolje's portrait; the regentesses of the Amsterdam city orphanage gave up their starched white caps and severe black gowns and appeared for their portraits in nearly off-the-shoulder gowns, their hair in ringlets. Pious patriots noted the growth of effeminate behaviour in Dutch youth and blamed French diplomats for corrupting their young men and turning them into sodomites. French fashions were making inroads – it was a plot, some said, inspired by Madame de Maintenon, Louis XIV's mistress, to soften up the Dutch before French arms cut them to pieces. It was also simply the case that Dutch economic success gave people more money to spend, and many spent it on ornate mirrors, leather wall-hangings, opulent silverware, and fancy furniture, some of which was imported from France.

In 1672 Louis XIV set in motion his plans to bring the people of the northern Low Countries low indeed by taking away their independence. He had organised an anti-Dutch coalition and his English allies struck first, attacking a Dutch merchant convoy in the Channel in late March. On 22 May, seeking glory and France's 'natural' frontiers, Louis led his armies across the Maas north of Maastricht. Among his distinguished generals were Condé and Turenne; his forces were four times greater in number than those of the United Provinces; and he also had the help, further north, of the armies of the Bishop of Munster and the Elector of Cologne. Atrocities – recorded in engravings by Romeyn de Hooghe – were committed by French troops at Woerden and Bodegraven, sending waves of horror through the country, and many terrified Dutch towns and cities succumbed to the enemy. There was a brave defence at Nijmegen, but Naarden fell, Arnhem capitulated in the face of the French without a shot being fired, and at Utrecht, with the citizens rioting and impeding the defences, the town council voted for appeasement; the keys of the city were offered to Louis when he was still a day's march away. Utrecht's people were thereafter given the collaborationist nickname 'keycarriers'. On 3 July Louis entered Utrecht and six days later the first Catholic Mass was celebrated in the city's cathedral since the Alteration one hundred years before. (Louis's policy was generally one of toleration and free public worship for all, including Reformed and Catholic.) But by the time Utrecht gave in, the Dutch employed their traditional defensive measure of last resort: they opened the sluices, broke gaps in the dikes, and began to flood the country.

The French king was greeted by inundations between his troops and the shattered Dutch army. But the water level was not as high as the Dutch commanders would have liked – it had been a dry summer so far, and many peasants didn't want to submerge the land from which they got their living. Moreover, numerous citizens in the towns of Holland weren't keen to man defences they thought untenable. However, the inundations, the edges of which began just east of Gouda, slowly rose in level and spread, covering great areas of the western part of the country. Refugees fled the combat zones and the regions where the French were expected next. Wealthy families shipped their possessions by barge to Amsterdam; though there, too, burgher morale was low – in midsummer there was a run on the Amsterdam Bank as depositors took fright, but the bank authorities cleverly invited in their customers to look at all the hard cash in the vaults, and the institution's coin and bullion reserves just coped. There was also rioting in many towns, including Delft, with rioters urging the instatement as Stadtholder of the young William III, Prince of Orange, and restrictions on the power of the regents – their high mightinesses or lordships, as they insisted on being called – who had been managing the Republic under the leadership of Johan de Witt (one-time target of Downing's pickpocket). In June hordes of angry men and women, including labourers from outlying farms and city workshops and the crews of laid-up Delfshaven fishing boats, besieged the Town Hall. The city fathers were compelled to vote for the installation of the present Prince of Orange as Stadtholder. Yet some good news came in from the waterline: Muiden and its castle, the outpost of Amsterdam, though expected to fall, was reinforced at the last minute and held firm. And on the second front, at sea, where the third Anglo-Dutch naval war of the century was in progress, de Ruyter surprised the Anglo-French fleet at anchor off Sole Bay, on the East Anglian coast; although the Dutch lost two ships, the allies suffered a greater loss with the burning of the English flagship, the 100-gun *Royal James*, the death of the corpulent Earl of Sandwich, Pepys's patron, and far greater casualties. Preventing the enemy from winning a victory at sea was regarded as a major step in saving the United Provinces. Another good omen was the safe return of a convoy of Dutch East Indiamen that entered the Ems estuary in mid-August with valuable cargoes.

For many years Johan de Witt, the Grand Pensionary from Dordrecht whom the British ambassador Sir William Temple called 'the perfect Hollander', had steered his country through troubled seas, reorganised its finances, rebuilt its navy, balanced foreign alliances and entanglements, and demonstrated to all that the United Provinces were a European power. His idea was to promote stability through 'Harmony', which among other things meant keeping the

Prince of Orange happy but separate from the real power he might have enjoyed as Stadtholder. De Witt led a thoroughly modest life but his haughty manner – a father-knows-best attitude which was characteristic of the Dutch regents – was no help in these times. Now the Orangist forces he had in the past so greatly antagonised were excited by the French invasion which to them signalled the collapse of de Witt's foreign policy. Popular pressure (as seen in the Delft riots) compelled the States-General to make William, the twenty-one-year-old Prince of Orange, commander of the army and navy; he had the job of opposing the best army in Europe with four thousand ill-trained men, and he took the immediate step of withdrawing his forces behind the waterline. He refused an Anglo-French offer to give him the sovereignty of the country in return for peace on the allies' terms. Soon, with mounting popular support, the posts of Stadtholder in Holland and Zeeland were revived and William III of Orange was appointed to hold them.

De Witt resigned in July and a month later was the victim of mob revenge. So was his brother Cornelius, who had been joint commander with de Ruyter of the Dutch fleet in the brilliant attack on Chatham five years before, when they had humiliated the English by towing away their first-rate ship of the line, the *Royal Charles*. In August 1672 Cornelius had been arrested and imprisoned by the Orangists on a trumped-up charge, and when Johan de Witt went to visit him on 20 August, an enraged crowd turned up at the prison and seized the two men. The Hague militia proved useless in protecting them; in fact its pro-Orange members participated in the lynching which ensued. The de Witt brothers were attacked with guns, knives, and cudgels, and savagely slaughtered. The incident has been explained as a perverse manifestation of patriotism and as somehow emphasising the order which prevailed all around (these were the only murders in The Hague at the time). Possibly it resulted from hysteria and panic rather than from a deep-seated tendency to murder in the Dutch people, though a blood-thirsty class-hatred also seems to have fuelled the mayhem. Both Cats and de Witt as leaders had held 'the people' in some disdain, and now the people got their own back.

Possibly the de Witts were also made to pay for the massacres, atrocities, and gang-rapes the French were committing and which – very like those committed by the Spanish a hundred years before – were being multiplied and retailed to a ready Dutch public in pamphlets and prints: the shocking scenes at Swammerdam, Bodegraven, Woerden; mutilated women, decapitated babies, bonfires of bodies . . . The Dutch could be uncivilised, too (as their colonial behaviour in distant places, in the East Indies and southern Africa, occasionally showed). But this was a breakdown at home of the celebrated civic sense that had hitherto seemed to bind Dutchman with Dutchman, as unexpected in its way as the Thunderclap in Delft. Accounts of these exceptional events in The Hague were still being used to frighten travellers a decade later. The Englishman Ellis Veryard visited The Hague in 1682 and recorded what he was told of the end of the de Witts:

> Both their bodies being stripped naked, were dragged out of town and hung up by the legs at the common gallows, where their bowels were pulled out and their limbs minced into a thousand pieces, everyone present endeavouring to get his share; some got a finger some a toe and others a piece of their flesh, which they preserved in oil and spirits of wine as trophies of their matchless vengeance. Nay, divers of them were sold at incredible rates to others, who took a more than ordinary pride in showing some part of these great men, whom they called traitors; but how justly I shall not determine.

According to other witnesses, some parts of the de Witts were roasted and eaten. But trophy-keeping was more common. In 1705 another Englishman, Sir Justinian Isham, a student at Utrecht University, was shown one of Johan de Witt's fingers; it was in the collection of an Arminian minister at Utrecht named Altenus.

In Delft, seven miles from The Hague, the *Rampjaar*, the year of catastrophe, had less terrifying but still significant effects. The town's fortifications were quickly strengthened. The shanties of the poor families who lived along the walls were cleared away and destitute people who had been allowed to camp in the gatehouses were moved out, so that the city's defences could be put in order. Much military material was delivered to the Rotterdam Gate on 19 August. The civic militia had been greatly expanded with new recruits and brought to full alert, but when three of the four militia companies met at the Doelen on 5 September, they called on the regents of the town, the *vroedschap*, to resign; the regents did so, and Delft had no proper government for a week. The town council's forty members were then replaced on the instructions of Prince William III, though several of the purged *herren* managed to convince the young Prince's representatives that they were 'honourable patriots' and make the new list. The upheaval was documented in Renier Boitet's *Beschevering*, which prints two lists of burgomasters for that year, rather than the usual one. Among the survivors of the purge were Dr Theodore Vallensis, one of the four burgomasters in 1672 and 1673, though he died in mid-August of 1673. Dirck van Bleyswijck also got through the troubles as one of the *schepenen* or aldermen. Delft Catholics may have felt more exposed than usual, with diehard Calvinists suspecting them of plotting treason because they shared the religion of the King of France; but there were few cases of disloyalty. Even so, it was fortunate that the French armies didn't reach the city and test its walls and the mettle of its citizenry.

For many in Delft times were hard enough; in 1654 other parts of the country had rallied round after the gunpowder explosion and sent aid and goods, but in the *Rampjaar* difficulties were general. The flooding of the countryside ruined the harvest; grain had to be imported and there were severe food shortages. Everyone felt the pinch. For artists, in Delft as elsewhere, the problems were those of all entrepreneurs and traders dealing in items that suddenly weren't necessities any longer: the buying of pictures was now a luxury to be dispensed with. The situation was perhaps made worse by the fact that some artists had in the course of the century ceased to be humble craftsmen and had been raised to a position where they provided expensive commodities; and now their patrons no longer felt rich enough to go on buying their products. Well-known names were among the casualties. The celebrated marine artists, the Willem van de Veldes, father and son, decided to move to enemy England, where they continued to paint pictures of ships. The fashionable Amsterdam portrait painter Bartholomeus van der Helst went broke and so did Vermeer's near namesake the Utrecht painter Johannes van der Meer. Jan Steen put his earlier experience as a brewery-owner to practical effect and took up innkeeping.

In Vermeer's household, belts were tightened. In normal times Maria Thins got part of her income from farmland. Some of this near Schoonhoven was within the waterline and had been flooded to deter the French advance; since no crops could be grown on what was now part of an immense sky-reflecting lake, the farmers who leased the land were paying no rent. In March 1675 Vermeer went to Gouda on his mother-in-law's behalf and had discussions with a farmer named Jan Schouten, the result being that Schouten was allowed to forgo the rents he owed for 1673 and 1674, 'due to the war times', and had the cost of building a temporary dike (perhaps to preserve farm buildings from the waters) taken into consideration against his future debts. By January 1676 Maria Thins was owed more than 1,600 guilders in unpaid rent for other lands she owned in Oud Beyerland. In May 1674 Vermeer had been to Gouda to lease out the house of the irascible Reynier Bolnes, Catharina's father and Maria's former husband, who had died the month before – no great loss to those in the Oude Langendijk, one imagines. In July 1675 Vermeer again made himself useful by travelling to Amsterdam to borrow – apparently on his mother-in-law's behalf – 1,000 guilders from a merchant named Jacob Rombouts. Maria Thins, once relatively rich, now found herself obliged to cut the assistance she usually gave her daughter and son-in-law to help with living expenses and support their occasionally patrician aspirations.

On his own account Vermeer had worries. The cash he had eventually got in 1671 from his sister's estate was apparently reduced by debts his mother had left, and amounted to only 148 guilders, less than he might have expected. Mechelen was now his, as his share of his mother's estate; in the deed of July 1670 by which he became the legal owner, his name was originally written as 'van der Meer', but this was crossed out, presumably at his request, and 'Vermeer' written in instead. Even if he hadn't been fussy about such matters, the misnaming could have been a source of confusion, for in 1673 he rented the inn to his local near-namesake, Johannes van der Meer, the apothecary. The six-year lease obliged van der Meer to pay 180 guilders a year, ten guilders less than his predecessor as tenant, the shoemaker van Ackerdijk, had been paying. It was evidently all the soft property market would bear. Vermeer's debts had mounted as his income from his own work – whether painting or dealing in pictures – had dropped away.

He was one of the headmen of his guild in 1671–2 and 1672–3, and this – together with his local celebrity as a painter and experience as a dealer – may have helped him acquire a consultancy job in May 1672, even as the French armies were massing on the border. He was asked to be one of a two-man team whose task was to determine the authenticity of some paintings that had been offered for sale by Gerrit Uylenburgh to Friedrich Wilhelm, the Grand Elector of Brandenburg – who was shortly to acquire, by Louis XIV's actions, a number of Dutch-garrisoned towns in Cleves on the lower Rhine; the paintings had been declared by the Elector's agent to be fraudulent imitations. The Elector had paid a deposit against the purchase of the pictures, which he had on approval, but he now refused to pay the rest of the agreed price; Uylenburgh refused to take the paintings back and wanted the balance due. Most of the paintings were purportedly Italian, and another reason for Vermeer's participation may have been his expertise in that field. Perhaps his Catholic connections also helped. In any event, the only other notable Delft artists at the time, Cornelis de Man and Hendrick van Vliet, weren't invited and Johannes Jordaens, a local painter who had worked in Italy, served as Vermeer's fellow-judge of the pictures. But then just about everyone in the case was well connected. Gerrit Uylenburgh was the son of the dealer Hendrick Uylenburgh, in whose art 'factory' Rembrandt had worked as a young painter when first in Amsterdam. Uylenburgh had taken over his father's business in 1661. As Michael Montias wryly points out, Friedrich Wilhelm was the grandson of the Elector of Brandenburg whose Dutch representative, Hendrick Sticke, had been one of the plotters in the coin-counterfeiting operation of 1619–20 in which Vermeer's grandfather Balthasar and uncle Reynier Balthens had been junior partners, working as die-makers and 'forgers'.

The Dutch art world was riven by the dispute over the attributions. Pamphlets and verse were written, defending Uylenburgh or mocking him. Some reputable painters thought the Uylenburgh pictures were worth buying, others – equally reputable – did not. The collection was put on show at the painters' guild-hall in The Hague. Philips Momper, Abraham van Beyeren, and Pieter Codde were among those who believed the pictures were copies or imitations of Michelangelo, Titian, Raphael, Holbein, and company. Constantijn Huygens, whose critical eye had earlier distinguished the budding talents of Rembrandt and Lievens, supported Uylenburgh, thinking that he was being unfairly picked on: Huygens said the paintings were genuine even though of varying quality. This view was supported by Gerbrandt van den Eeckhout, who had come to Delft to sketch the effects of the 1654 explosion, and by the landscape painter Philips Koninck; both Rembrandt pupils (and so possibly part of an Amsterdam-based, pro-Uylenburgh camp), they declared that the paintings merited a place in a collection of Italian art. At the request of the Elector's agent, the artist Hendrick de Fromantiou, Vermeer and Jordaens, 'outstanding art-painters in Delft', were asked to inspect the pictures and consider their value. They gave their views before a notary in The Hague on 23 May 1672, the day after Louis XIV's armies invaded the United Provinces, when many in The Hague and elsewhere in the country had other things on their minds. The paintings, they said, were 'not only not outstanding paintings, but to the contrary, great pieces of rubbish and bad paintings, not worth by far the tenth part of the aforementioned proposed prices'. (The 'Michelangelo' *Venus and Cupid* had been valued at 875 guilders and a *Shepherd and Shepherdess* supposedly by Titian at 400 guilders.)

In the end, the nay-sayers won the day. The Elector kept a few items
to cover his deposit and sent the rest back. Gerrit Uylenburgh was
judged insolvent in 1675 and decided like the van de Veldes to try his
luck in pastures new, in England.

Vermeer was forty in late October 1672. Several children more were
born to him and Catharina in these years: in 1672 a son they called
Ignatius; an infant – perhaps stillborn – who died in June 1673 and
was buried in the family grave in the Oude Kerk; and a child whose
name we do not know who came into the world in 1674 and lived only
four years. Once again Vermeer and Catharina would have found it
hard to accept the Divine Will. Perhaps they were shattered, as was
the poet Vondel, who lost two children a year apart, and poured forth
his grief. Their dead children might now be angels, but would that
they were still mischievous, noisy, and alive. In February 1674
Vermeer's colleague, friend, and mentor Leonaert Bramer died and
was interred in the Nieuwe Kerk; he was seventy-seven, had been
living in the Cornmarket, which ran parallel to the Oude Delft, and
was described in the church records as an elderly bachelor. A more
joyful family occasion took place in June 1674. Maria, eldest daughter
of Vermeer and Catharina, now about twenty years old, married the
son of a prosperous Delft silk merchant, a young man named Johannes
Gilliszoon Cramer who followed his father's profession. The wedding
ceremony was held in Schipluy, as Maria's parents' wedding had
been, and presumably with Catholic sacraments.

Maria was the only one of their children they had yet managed to
get off their hands. In August 1674, it was once again bad news:
Vermeer and his wife learned of the death of van Ruijven, on the
Voorstraat. He was forty-nine. As a patron he had been indispensable,
buying about half of Vermeer's small output. Vermeer must have
wondered at this point how he was going to be able to support the
large family he and Catharina had brought into being. He may have
recalled stories of earlier hard times, in which his grandparents had
struggled – not always honestly – to make do. The traders to whom he
owed money weighed on his mind. Debts like deaths closed in on him.

But he seems to have been still considered a sound citizen. His name appears in a register of the city militia for 1674; he was inscribed (third on the list) as a *schutter* or marksman of the first *rotten* or squadron of the third company or *vendel* (literally, the 'banner').* This was the Orange company whose members were recruited from the quarter of the city that contained the Oude Langendijk. Each company – Green, White, Orange, and Blue – had six squadrons, formerly of twenty members, by now increased to thirty-two. A company was commanded by a captain, in Vermeer's case by Abraham Coeckebacker, whose subordinates included a lieutenant, an ensign, and several sergeants – at least until 1674, when the rank of sergeant was abolished. Leonaert Bramer had been a sergeant in the same company; in uniform he wore a sash worth twelve guilders and during his time in service was a member of a select group of militiamen known as the Brotherhood of Knights. Bramer's small triptych model for the wall paintings he had done for the new Doelen on the Verwersdijk had as its central feature a panel showing the civic guards parading along a Delft street, banners flying. If after retiring from service at the age of sixty Bramer kept an eye on militia events, he would have seen Vermeer when training at target practice or guard feasts in the Doelen or during outdoor exercises in the New Cattlemarket, where Vermeer's father had been born. Reynier Vermeer had known Johan van Santen, once captain of the Orange company, who stood surety for a loan Reynier had received in 1648. The five officers of the White company who were painted in a group picture around that time by the portraitist Jacob II Willemszoon Delff all had flourishing moustaches, which might lead us to wonder if Vermeer was similarly equipped.

Among Johannes Vermeer's other full-time or part-time military acquaintances were Johan van den Bosch, a captain in the service of the States-General, and his own uncle Reynier Balthens, army engineer; Vermeer witnessed legal declarations for these two in 1653. In 1654 he witnessed a debt acknowledgement for a widow when a

---

*This *Schuttersboek* of 1674 is the only militia register of that period to have been found.

fellow-witness was an army captain named Lambertus Morleth. Captain (and flag-bearer) Bartolomeus Melling had of course with Bramer at that time witnessed Maria Thins's agreement to Vermeer's and Catharina's wedding banns being published. In 1674 a fellow member of Vermeer's squadron was Adriaen or Ary van Buyten, a close relative of Hendrick van Buyten, baker and art collector.

We don't know what qualities Vermeer had as a part-time soldier. Was he in fact a good marksman? 'An iron armour with a helmet' and 'a pike' are recorded in the 29 February 1676 inventory of his goods. But being even a humble pikeman signified social acceptance. In 1674 one Delft *schutter* was dismissed from the militia because he was too poor, but Vermeer, though heavily in debt, was evidently acceptable. Dirck van Bleyswijck wrote in elevated terms of those admitted to the civic guard: 'The judicious magistrate has until now not found it advisable to have any other than the most learned burghers from the most admirable families and those who are men of property.' Yet these entry requirements, which would have confined militia membership to those of well-to-do middle-class or regent backgrounds, could be stretched to include others, like the shoemaker and tailor mentioned in one document of 1631, so that roughly one-in-twenty of able-bodied men of the right ages qualified, and the total numbers were kept at around 850. Being a Catholic or a Catholic sympathiser created no problems. The right political attitude was possibly more important than religious affiliation. The civic guards had to be prepared not only to try to repel foreign incursions but also to put down revolts against the regents' rule, such as the 1616 riots in Delft against a new tax on grain; then the militia, 480 strong and armed with pikes and guns called 'firelocks', were pelted with paving stones, disarmed by the mob, and forced to retreat. (The poet Westerbaen had said the Delft guards were as well-suited to their firelocks as donkeys to a lute.) Perhaps their hearts weren't in it. As mentioned, in September 1672 three of the four militia companies demanded that Delft's town council resign; their stance by then seemed, like that of much of the country, to be pro-Orange rather than pro-regent.

We also don't know for sure about Vermeer's participation in the activities of the Delft guard during the *Rampjaar* and after. He may have been one of the 300 Delft militiamen who were called into service when the French invaded and were sent to Geertruidenberg, Heusden, Den Briel, and Gorkum; on 30 June, when faced with a heavy French attack, the Delft *schutters* were forced to make a rapid withdrawal. After the Orangist shake-up of the *vroedeschap*, the new leaders of the city replaced many of the officers of the militia with men sympathetic to Prince William. Vermeer may have been with the four companies from Delft who went to Gouda in May 1673, led by Captain van Hurk, to 'protect the land' from the French, but there is no certainty of this or of whether he saw action. Again, there is no sign of war in his pictures, other than the earlier use of military uniform in the *Officer and Laughing Girl*.

As it was, William III's armies made gradual progress in winning back lands taken by the French. Utrecht was abandoned by Louis XIV's troops towards the end of 1673 – the devastating tornado that hit Utrecht the following year was regarded by some as payment for its citizens' lack of pluck in the face of the French. Peace with England was signed in February 1674, when New York became an English colony again though the Dutch remained powerful in the East Indies. That year had a dry hot summer, and the late autumn seemed to presage more bad times. Delft was more full of refugees than ever, especially after a final burst of French fury in Tiel, in Gelderland. Across the North Sea in East Anglia, Sir Thomas Browne (whose son Edward had visited Delft in 1668) noted on 27 November a great fog that was shrouding much of England and Holland; it seemed to him like 'the white mist that rises from within a body opened presently after death, and which during our lifetime clouds our brain when asleep and dreaming'.

According to Catharina, in her testimonies to the High Court of Holland and Zeeland in April 1676 and July 1677, Vermeer earned hardly anything from his art-dealing business during the wartime years, and had to sell 'the works of art he traded in . . . at great loss'.

It seems that he was also painting little or nothing at the time. There were many distractions; his service in the civic guard may have meant serious interruptions; his health may not have been good; and his old impetus to paint – never constant – apparently fizzled out. What appear to be his last two paintings, the similarly-sized *Young Woman*

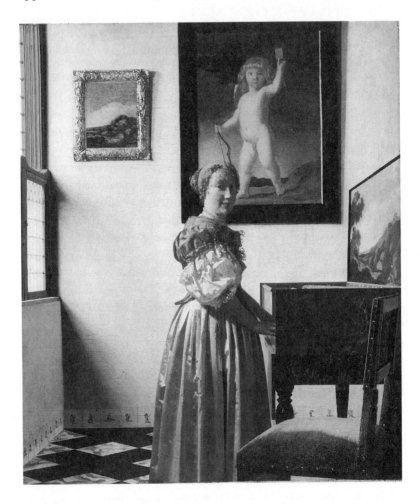

Young Woman standing at a Virginal, c. 1672–3.

standing at a Virginal and *Young Woman seated at a Virginal*, reworked his familiar subject-matter of *juffertjes* but did so in a somewhat bloodless way. Compare them with the tiny *Lacemaker* of a few years before. The two women at their keyboards are refined young ladies demonstrating their musical talents and meeting the artist's (and therefore the viewer's) gaze – no downcast eyes here – though coolly,

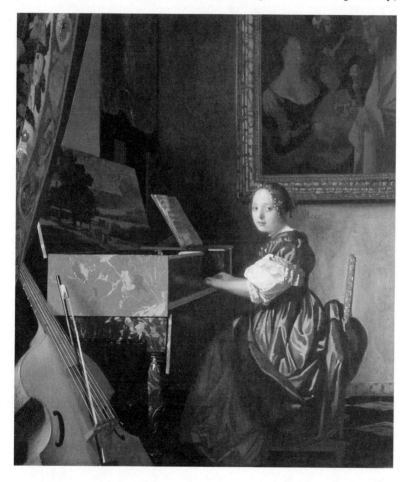

Young Woman seated at a Virginal, c. 1675.

without personal involvement. Whereas the lowered eyes of the woman making lace are intent on her private and painstaking work. Here is concentration, dedication, from which any thought of a viewer or audience has been shut out. The references or symbolic aspects all add to the suggestions of intense commitment and sacrifice: the thick yellow vellum-bound book by her right hand that must be a Bible; and the threads that spill forth from her padded sewing box. John Nash writes:

> These threads do seem to spill . . . The red thread is a *tour de force* of painting. It might have been poured on to the horizontally laid canvas from a fine nozzle rather than applied by any brush. If optical images did suggest the mode by which these threads are depicted, it can only have been because Vermeer recognised in them some metaphoric or figurative force that appealed to him.

And Nash, impelled by such a force, concludes that as the term for a *naaikussen* or needlecushion could be broken down into *naaien*, 'to copulate', and *kussen*, which is not only the noun for 'cushion' but also the verb meaning 'to kiss', so 'the threads that gush from the gape in this swollen *naaikussen* evoke the blood red and milk white spilling from the womb that precede the birth of a child'. Even if we think the painter chose red and white for purely painterly reasons, this picture can be seen as Vermeer's final tribute to Catharina as the mother of his children.

The *Young Woman seated at a Virginal* also draws attention to a change of tactics that perhaps signals a change that has occurred in Vermeer. The room – unlike that with the standing player – is darkened in the corner close to which she sits. Shutter and curtain have both been closed across the window behind the virginal. The other curtain, the tapestry that separates her from the lit foreground, does so in rather the same way as the tapestry which is pulled aside to reveal the diva performing in the *Allegory of Faith*. Dirck van Baburen's *Procuress* on the wall behind the seated virginal player and a too noticeable viola da gamba – awaiting its musician – add to our impression of symbolic overload, though a discreet row of Delft tiles at the foot of the wall forms a modest contrast to the general poshness of things. (As for the lighting, Vermeer may have been trying to make his painting different from a very similar though somewhat more cluttered Gerrit Dou picture painted around 1665, in which the music-playing woman sits before an unshuttered and uncurtained window.) This Vermeer or its sister picture probably belonged at an early stage to Diego Duarte, the Antwerp banker and jeweller, friend of the Huygens family. Constantijn Huygens was a composer as well as a statesman and poet, and as noted had a Ruckers virginal acquired with Duarte's help; his son Constantijn junior often visited the Duartes in Antwerp and may well have attended some of the private concerts the banker, collector, and music lover held in his house there. It seems likely that one of the Huygens, father or son, got Duarte to buy, perhaps even to commission, at least one of Vermeer's virginal pictures. They should have prompted him sooner. On the inside of the lid of the virginal in *The Music Lesson*, painted ten years earlier, is the inscription MUSICA LETITIAE CO[ME]S MEDICINA DOLOR[UM], 'Music is the companion of joy, the balm of sorrow' – as well as being the proverbial food of love. But it looks in these late pictures more like the companion of ennui. The moneyed young ladies whiling away their time in the two late virginal paintings also had a stylised colleague, playing a guitar (and wearing the well-known, fur-trimmed yellow jacket), and smiling tentatively, as if she was aware that her poise was all put on (see next page). Vermeer had responded with greater intensity to the absorption in her craft that was shown by the lacemaker.

In 1675 the town council of Delft must have felt that the worst of the war was over and things were looking up. The *vroedschap* commissioned a celebratory map, the *Kaart Figuratif*, which expressed their pride in the city. Dirck van Bleyswijck was put in charge of the project, and various well-known and competent Delft illustrators were employed, including Jan Verkolje, Willem van Oderkercken, and Pieter van Asch as draughtsmen, and Conraet Decker, Johannes de Ram, and Romeyne de Hooghe as engravers. Coats of arms,

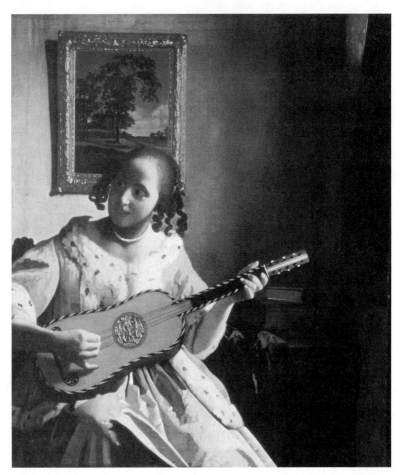

The Guitar Player, c. 1672.

Cupids, fishes, lions, storks, human figures (such as those of clay-mixers and cloth-cutters), symbolic figures, and a poem by Constantijn Huygens under his pen-name Constanter decorated the borders. The map was published in 1678. But in fact by then the town was past its economic peak; its population was beginning to decline, now that the wartime refugees had gone home; deaths exceeded births; and the bigger cities like Amsterdam, Rotterdam, and even The Hague exercised their pull. But the Dutch Republic seemed to be losing its drive: exhausted by the French war, its people wanted a quiet life; energy turned to contemplation and some craftsmen moved abroad to more vigorous economies. Delft hugged its own comforts to itself, like the hospitals, *hofjes*, and Old People's Homes that were marked on the map. The authorities required foreigners and outsiders to have official permission before they could settle in the town and the council allowed the very poor to beg on the streets only if they could prove they had lived in Delft for four years. But the *Kaart*'s fine detail of churches and gateways, rooftops and chimneys, gardens and public spaces, canals and bridges, and trees and windmills, must have given great pleasure to the citizens who bought it, and hung it (like one of Vermeer's maps) in their houses.

In Maria Thins's house on the Oude Langendijk no one in the second part of 1675 was feeling very buoyant. Vermeer had slowed down. In July, as mentioned above, he went to Amsterdam to raise a thousand guilders from Jacob Rombouts, but this complicated deal, it seems on behalf of his mother-in-law, resulted in the loss of valuable interest and she had to pay back the loan Vermeer negotiated. It was a year of much sickness. Once again, John Evelyn tells us, there was in Europe 'an exceeding dry Summer & Autumn'. Severe illnesses swept Holland and England. Evelyn wrote in mid-October: 'I got an extreame cold, such as was afterwards so epidemical, as not only afflicted us in this Iland, but was rife all over Europe, & raged like a Plague.'

Walking gloomily around the house, looking through doorways from room to room, Vermeer would have encountered some of his many children, and been aware of the strenuous efforts Catharina was making to keep them properly fed and clothed. He would have seen on the walls the pictures that his mother-in-law owned and that he had used as part of the scenery in his own paintings. He might have stopped to look at *The Art of Painting* . . .

We don't know why he collapsed, but collapse he did, a week after St Nicholas's Day. Did he have an infection, for which the apothecary's remedies proved useless? An 'extreame cold', like Evelyn's, which turned into pneumonia? An epileptic fit? Acute melancholia which brought on a depression in which he simply submerged? Or something else?

Some of the putting-on of paint in his later pictures seems uncharacteristically coarse, and drink was as close as the nearest tavern, or indeed as the nearest apothecary's, to quell any sense of failure as a head of family or as an imperfect painter and thereby injure control of the brush. Catharina had her own ideas, though we may have to read between the lines of her statement to the High Court a year and a half later to guess what they were. She said that the effect of being unable to trade, being so burdened with children and being without resources had caused her husband to lapse into 'decay and decadence'. The last word is striking: decadence might suggest an act of volition by the victim, such as an intensive bout of drinking that could have brought on alcohol poisoning and liver failure. On the other hand, it might mean simply a sudden physical decline: did he have a stroke? In any event, Catharina went on, Vermeer had taken his problems so to heart that, 'as if he had fallen into a frenzy, in a day and a half he had gone from being healthy to being dead'.

It was as simple and as short as that. Was there time to consult him to see if they should call a priest for the last sacraments? The register for the Oude Kerk records the burial on 15 December 1675 of 'Jan Vermeer, art-painter on the Oude Langendijck, in the church, 8 children under age'. This 'Jan' was a rare written use of what well may have been the name by which Catharina and Maria Thins called him. There were in fact ten minor children at this point. Vermeer was forty-three.

His burial involved a rearrangement of the family grave. The infant who had been buried two and a half years earlier was taken out momentarily while Vermeer was lowered into the grave, and then the tiny remains of the child were put on top of its father's coffin. When the Chamber of Charity next day filled in its report of what had been donated in lieu of Vermeer's best outer garment, there were three succinct words: '*Niet te halen*' – 'Nothing to be got'.

12. *Diaspora*

Eventually there would be a great deal to be got, though not by the Chamber of Charity. The process of releasing the value of Vermeer's work would take a long time and the painter's heirs wouldn't benefit. Now, creditors were at the door and Catharina made an effort to pay off the family's debts while holding on to the work Vermeer had left – two objectives that weren't always compatible. A month after her husband's death Catharina handed over to the baker Hendrick van Buyten two of Vermeer's paintings, probably *The Guitar Player* and the *Lady writing a Letter with her Maid*. Van Buyten paid her 617 guilders and 6 stuivers, or would have done if the Vermeers hadn't owed him this sum for bread, a large amount of the staff of life. (Montias reckons that this sum covered about 8,000 pounds of white bread at the prices of the time, roughly three years' worth of supplies for a household of that size.) As it was, van Buyten promised to give the paintings back to Catharina if she paid off the debt and another sum she owed him of 109 guilders, either by instalments of 50 guilders a year or, following Maria Thins's death (when Catharina would presumably inherit), at 200 guilders a year plus 4 per cent interest. Van Buyten may have coveted these pictures but he put a high value on them, which showed his generosity to the artist's widow. In 1734 the *Lady writing a Letter with her Maid* was appraised as being worth 100 guilders, about a third of van Buyten's estimated price for it.

Another debt, another bunch of pictures: twenty-six paintings, probably the greater part of Vermeer's stock as an art-dealer, were seemingly sold on 10 February 1676 to another artist-cum-dealer, Jan

Coelenbier of Haarlem. But most of the 500 guilders he paid for them was claimed from Catharina by a woman named Jannetje Stevens, a cloth merchant in Delft to whom the Vermeers also owed money. This transaction was further complicated by Coelenbier alleging that Jannetje owed him money, too, so some of the 500 guilders should come back to him on that account. If the unfinished *Young Girl with a Flute* was in this batch of pictures, 'large and small', Coelenbier may have seen it as meriting some of his time and may have worked it up to saleable condition.

Catharina delivered the pictures to Coelenbier in Amsterdam at an apothecary's shop called the Three Lemons. She was perhaps grateful for errands that helped take her mind off her loss. Two weeks later, and two days before an inventory of Vermeer's 'moveable goods' was to be made at the house in the Oude Langendijk, she went to The Hague to make a formal declaration to a lawyer. She said that in partial repayment for money she owed her mother, she was giving up to Maria Thins income from some property, some annuities, and 'a painting done by her late husband wherein is depicted "The Art of Painting"'. *The Art of Painting* had so far remained in the family; this move was apparently an attempt to preserve the masterpiece from Vermeer's creditors.

The inventory of household goods listed them in two sections: items belonging to Catharina and lately to Johannes Vermeer; and items belonging to Catharina jointly with her mother. The list seems to have tried to present some 'best things' in the second category rather than the first. But oh, the melancholy of such lists, the memories provoked: a 'Turkish mantle of the aforesaid Signeur Vermeer . . . Twelve bedsheets, good and bad . . . a white satin bodice . . . two night-shirts . . . an old beer jug . . . two copper bedpans . . . a cradle . . . a drawn coat of arms of the aforenamed Sr. Vermeer with a black frame'.

The family grave in the Oude Kerk was reopened again in late March. This time it was for the interment of Catharina's brother Willem, who had reached his late forties or early fifties in Hermanus Taerling's care in the Vlamingstraat and had now finally ceased to cause trouble. The funeral took place from the Oude Langendijck house, as if Willem in death had been allowed home by his mother.

In late April Catharina faced up to the fact that she was unable to pay all their creditors and therefore requested, and received, 'Letters of Cession' from the High Court; she was now legally insolvent. When Maria Thins made a new will in September that year she left Catharina the legal minimum, one-sixth of her estate, to ensure that a larger part of her property didn't go to Catharina's creditors; this reserved more for the grandchildren. In this will a lawyer, Hendrick van Eem, was named as guardian of Vermeer's children, although Catharina was also mentioned as 'most responsible for looking after the children'. Maria Thins recommended that Catharina 'take due care of the education of her [i.e. Maria Thins's] heirs, [and] that she teach them some commerce or handicraft so that they may earn their living, since the number of children is too great for them to go about in idleness and to undertake nothing'. However, she also declared that the four youngest children should be 'fed, clothed, and supported in such trade, occupation, and handicraft as their guardians shall deem appropriate' from the revenues of her properties until the youngest of the children was fourteen.

The Vermeers' sixth surviving child and first son, also called Johannes, was having his education paid for out of income from farmland in Schoonhoven that had been Willem Bolnes's. The boy may have been sent to a Catholic college in Mechelen in the southern Netherlands; in which case, it may have been Johannes who was the child of Vermeer's who in 1678 was mentioned as being 'piteously wounded' in an explosion on a vessel carrying gunpowder from Mechelen. But young Johannes, if he was the wounded person, survived that minor *ontploffing*. He seems to have become a lawyer in Bruges, preserving his links with the Catholic south, and had a son, another Johannes, who preserved the artist's name but was brought up in Delft by his aunt Maria and her husband Johannes Cramer – despite which the boy doesn't appear to have learned to write (he put a cross rather than a signature on a power of attorney in 1713). He married a Delft girl but moved to Leiden where their five children – Vermeer's great-grandchildren – were baptised as Catholics. Another son of Vermeer, Franciscus, became a master surgeon in Charlois, a village near Rotterdam, and later moved to The Hague. Apart from Maria, Beatrix was the only one of Vermeer's daughters to marry. Aleydis, the fourth girl, lived until 1749, when she died in The Hague. Continuing remittances from their grandmother Thins's estates and from the Gouda Orphan Chamber apparently helped the unmarried daughters (including Aleydis, Gertruyd, and Catharina, named after her mother) to subsist. Of the girls, Maria seems to have been the most fortunate through her marriage to Cramer; the couple had a number of children who were well provided for, and one of whom became a Catholic priest.

Five months after Catharina's request for Letters of Cession, on 30 September 1676 the Delft city fathers appointed Antony van Leeuwenhoek 'curator of the estate and assets' of the insolvent widow of 'the late Johannes Vermeer during his lifetime master painter'.

Leeuwenhoek was named curator for several other Delft estates; this apparently was one of his duties as steward to the Chamber of Aldermen. In this case, he set about his task without seeming to favour Vermeer's widow and orphans. The tangled web of their finances and those of the Thins family took some sorting out. Catharina told the court when explaining her circumstances in her petition of July 1677 that she had never had to think about anything other than 'housekeeping and her children'; but now, how things had changed! There was 2,900 guilders on deposit in the Orphan Chamber of Gouda. There was the property in and near Gouda and Oud Beyerland. There were inheritances and obligations transferred to Catharina from her brother or given her by her mother. And then there were the many debts.

Leeuwenhoek seems to have suspected that Maria Thins and Catharina had been trying to keep in the dark Catharina's real assets. Maria denied this. Leeuwenhoek also had to work out a settlement of the dispute with Jannetje Stevens, who said she still hadn't been paid

the 442 guilders which Catharina owed her and which she was meant
to have got from the money Catharina had received from Jan
Coelenbier for Vermeer's stock of paintings. Leeuwenhoek
apparently determined that Coelenbier had loaned Catharina the 500
guilders while the twenty-six pictures were being held as security.
Coelenbier now handed back the pictures to Leeuwenhoek who
intended to auction them, the agreement being that Jannetje would
get 342 guilders (100 less than the sum she had claimed) from the
estate, and that the estate would get the first 500 guilders of the
auction sale (and presumably pay back Coelenbier from this).
Leeuwenhoek also intended to sell at this auction *The Art of Painting*,
which it seems Jannetje had had seized to cover her demands, but
which the curator had got back. However, a few days before the
auction was due to take place, on 15 March 1676 at the hall of the
Guild of St Luke, Maria Thins said he shouldn't sell *The Art of
Painting* because it was hers, given her by Catharina to cover loans she
had made her daughter 'both for herself and as guardian of her
children procreated by the late Johannes Vermeer'. If he did sell it,
then the money he received should go to her. Maria Thins's lawyer
and Leeuwenhoek argued about this, with the curator of the Vermeer
estate pointing out that it had cost the estate 342 guilders plus costs to
settle with Jannetje and get the painting back. And then that area of
the stage goes dark. We don't know what happened at the auction and
whether *The Art of Painting* – which would have been the star offering
– was included in the sale. The painting drops out of history for more
than a century.

Maria Thins went through other legal manoeuvrings at this time. She
arranged to collect deposits left with, and rents received by, the
Gouda Orphan Chamber, for the benefit of Vermeer's children. She
wanted to further her claim on Vermeer's estate so that other creditors
were pushed back down the queue and the Vermeer children were
further protected. And she proceeded in 1678 to get permission to
hand over to Catharina interest on an annuity because Catharina was
'no longer able to feed her children and to pay apothecaries and

surgeons', none of her children yet being able to 'earn any but small amounts'. The old lady made a final will on 24 January 1680. She wanted to ensure that her property remained undivided until Ignatius Vermeer was sixteen, but asked her executor to use his discretion since if Catharina didn't have enough to live on, then assets might need to be mortgaged or even sold for her benefit. The executor was instructed to produce annual accounts to Catharina and 'two honest people', but not to give them to Maria Vermeer's husband Johannes Cramer, 'for weighty reasons and motives'. What had young Cramer done to displease Maria Thins? Unlike Vermeer, he apparently hadn't the diplomatic skills needed to propitiate and please her.

Maria Thins was at home on the Oude Langendijck when she received the last sacrament of Extreme Unction on 23 December 1680. Her neighbour the Jesuit priest Philippus de Pauw anointed her with holy oil and prayed at her bedside. Four days later she was buried in the Oude Kerk. Fourteen pallbearers made a prosperous show of mourning, and a generous donation of twenty-five guilders and four stuivers was given to the Chamber of Charity. The family grave she had bought years before was now designated as 'full'. It was perhaps just as well Vermeer had gone first because his greatest day-by-day benefactor was no more.

Catharina outlived her husband by twelve years. Considering the number of children she had given birth to and raised, this was good going. Unfortunately the records that have been found concern themselves only with the debts and obligations in which her many children involved her. She seems to have stayed on in Delft for a few years. In 1681 she borrowed 800 guilders. In 1684 she was living in Breda, a largely Catholic city near the border with the southern Netherlands, while still trying to support eight children, one of whom – Gertruyd – was sick at the time. Catharina applied to the burgomasters of Gouda for assistance from the funds her ancestors had left the town for helping the worthy poor; she was awarded 96 guilders a year for five years. In October 1687 she acknowledged before a notary in Breda debts to a respectable widow named Pitronella de Lange that included a loan of 300 guilders and boarding costs of 175 guilders. Catharina was now in her late fifties and apparently unwell, and the debt acknowledgement may have been a formal way of regularising a situation that Juffrouw de Lange feared might lose her money if her tenant died. At the end of that year Catharina returned to Delft; she – the writer, if we can take her husband's paintings as evidence, of many personal letters in the past – was unable to sign in her usual educated hand when she made her last testament on 27 December 1687 and named a lawyer in The Hague as guardian to her five minor children. (The local notary C. Ouwendijck endorsed her feeble pen marks as her signature.) In this will Hendrick van Eem lost his guardianship for unexplained reasons; his last recorded task had been to empower Leeuwenhoek in November 1682 to sell two sureties in Gouda worth about 1,400 guilders, arising from property passed by Willem Bolnes to Maria Thins, on behalf of the Vermeer estate. Catharina was now staying at the Blue Hand, the house on the Verwersdijck that was the home of her daughter Maria and son-in-law Johannes Cramer. A few days later, another end-of-the-year departure, she was dead – Father Philippus de Pauw having given her the last sacraments. She was buried in the Nieuwe Kerk on 2 January 1688; the grave in the Oude Kerk was full, but it seems strange that no one thought it right to bury her near Vermeer. There were twelve pallbearers in attendance, no doubt paid for by the Cramers. No donation found its way to the Chamber of Charity.

A gradual dispersal took place of Vermeer's and Catharina's large family. So, too, with the paintings. Pieter van Ruijven's collection of twenty, the biggest batch, passed to his daughter Magdalena, who married Jacob Dissius in April 1680 but who died two years later. Jacob, a bookbinder and bookseller, took over his father's printing press at the Golden ABC in the Market Place and died in October 1695. Six months afterwards, the collection was advertised for sale in the Amsterdam auction already mentioned in relation to individual pictures.

During Vermeer's lifetime his paintings seem to have stayed almost entirely in his home town, but as time passed the Dutch art market certainly became aware of them. The announcement in the *Amsterdamsche Courant* declared that on 16 May 1696 there would be sold at the Old Men's Lodging House in that city 'several outstandingly artful paintings, including 21 works most powerfully and splendidly painted by the late J. Vermeer of Delft; showing various compositions, being the best he has ever made'. That there were now twenty-one rather than twenty Vermeers in this group may be explained by the suggestion that Jacob Dissius at least once followed his father-in-law's instincts as a collector or by the possibility that the twenty-first picture had been in the van Ruijven collection all along but not credited to Vermeer.*

The Amsterdam sale brought good prices. The twenty-one Vermeers sold for 1,503 guilders, an average of roughly 72 guilders each – though there were considerable variations, with the *View of Delft* fetching 200 guilders, the *Milkmaid* 175, and the *Lacemaker* only 28. Three Emanuel de Wittes went for a total of 160 guilders – that is, about 53 each. The top seventeenth-century price accorded a Vermeer was the 400 guilders paid in 1699 for the *Allegory of Faith* ('A seated woman with several meanings representing the New Testament') when the picture collection of the Amsterdam banker and postmaster Herman van Swoll was sold.

In the course of the next hundred years Vermeer's pictures moved away from Delft. Most stayed in the Low Countries until the early nineteenth century. The master painter would probably have been better served if his reputation had been further flung, outside his home town, at an earlier date, though as the Amsterdam sale made clear, that city was considered an appropriate setting to get the best price for his work in 1696. And his paintings went on being prized even if sometimes *his* name was no longer attached to them. Metsu, de Hooch, van Mieris, Flinck, and Rembrandt were occasionally given the honour. Both King George III of Great Britain and the Duke of

---

*Montias speculates that the picture was *The Little Street*, camouflaged in the 1683 Dissius inventory as an anonymous landscape 'with houses'.

Saxony bought Vermeers as the work of other artists. Even so, in 1719 the *Milkmaid* was called 'the famous Milkmaid by Vermeer'.

Yet the art chroniclers and local historians weren't much help in getting Vermeer through to the notice of posterity: in 1678 Samuel van Hoogstraten failed to mention him in the *Inleyding* and in 1718–21 Arnold Houbraken made only the briefest of allusions to him in his *Groote Schouburgh*, at the end of a bald list of Delft painters, putting his name in small italics rather than the capitals he used for major painters and saying nothing about him.* Renier Boitet, who in 1729 followed van Bleyswijck with another city history of Delft, in which he devoted six pages to Antony van Leeuwenhoek, also ignored the last stanza of Bon's panegyric to Fabritius and printed Vermeer's name only once, unadorned by any description, at the end of a short list of Delft painters. As for Gerard de Lairesse, he left Vermeer out of his *Groot Schilderboek* of 1707, but whoever revised it for its 1740 edition was in the know, including among celebrated painters of recent times 'the old Mieris, Metzu, [and] Van der Meer'.

Even if Vermeer by name sometimes failed to get mentioned in the right books, his works went on speaking up for him. Connoisseurs recognised their quality and made a point of drawing attention to them. Sir Joshua Reynolds, travelling through the Low Countries in 1781, remarked on the 'Woman pouring milk from one vessel to another: by D. Van dermeere' (the 'D.' perhaps standing for Delft) as an impressive work. In 1792 the Parisian art-dealer Jean-Baptiste Lebrun commented in a book of prints he published of Flemish, Dutch, and German paintings (one of which was of Vermeer's *Geographer*, a painting he owned): 'This van de Meer, never once mentioned by historians, merits special attention. He is a very great painter, in the manner of Metsu. His pictures are very rare, and are better known and more appreciated in Holland than anywhere else.

---

*It has been suggested that Houbraken must have had a grudge against Vermeer, but it seems more likely to have been an accidental slight. If Houbraken had been reading van Bleyswijck's *Description*, he might have neglected to turn the page that deals with Fabritius and to note the last stanza, on the next page, of the Arnold Bon poem that acclaimed Vermeer.

He was especially fond of rendering the effects of sunlight, and sometimes succeeded to the point of complete illusion.'

As time went on, Vermeer's preferred way of spelling his name was often set aside; the experts tended to call him 'the Delft van der Meer'. At an auction in 1765 a Pieter de Hooch painting was referred to as 'being as good as the Delft van der Meer'. Indeed, not only were Vermeer's works occasionally attributed to de Hooch, as *The Art of Painting* was in 1813 when bought by Count Czernin, but some de Hoochs were sold as by Vermeer; the Delft master's *oeuvre* was further swelled by paintings in fact by such minor painters as Jacob Vrel and Esaias Boursse.* And Vermeers were even being copied in the late eighteenth century, with Derk Jean van der Laan mimicking him in paintings called *The Little Street* and *A Rustic Cottage*. Two chroniclers of Dutch art history, E. van der Eynden and A. van der Willigen, wrote in 1816, 'It is hardly necessary to point out that the works of the so-called Delft van der Meer deserve a place in the most distinguished collections.' He was, these authors thought, one of the greatest Netherlands masters – the Titian of the Dutch school, whose *View of Delft* was 'an artistic wonder'. At the behest of King William I of the Netherlands, that picture was acquired in 1822 – with funds put up by the state – for the King's Gallery in the Mauritshuis, the price being 2,900 guilders, a great sum at the time. One of many visiting art lovers who saw it in the King's Gallery was the British connoisseur and dealer John Smith. He wrote, in his eight volumes cataloguing Dutch, Flemish, and French paintings (1829–42), that Vermeer 'is so little known, by reason of the scarcity of his works, that it is quite inexplicable how he attained the excellence many of them exhibit'. For Smith, however, it seemed that Vermeer was partly explicable as a 'pupil and imitator' of de Hooch and Metsu, though he knew that Vermeer also painted views of towns. 'One of his best performances in this branch', wrote Smith, was the *View of Delft* in the Mauritshuis, 'a superb and most unusual landscape' – though he took it to be a view 'at sunset'. Even so, Vermeer's curious status at

*Vermeer certainly influenced Vrel.

this point, known yet not known, is indicated in a small *Beschryving* of Delft by G.F.J. Guffroy and C. Bottelier published in Delft in 1840, which, in a section on Delft artists, describes the painter with a tortuous double negative as *mede niet onvermaard*, 'also not unrenowned'.

One of the factors that kept Vermeer in the realm of the lesser known was, as Smith had noted, the small number of his paintings. Another perhaps was his name, as it came to be used, and which to all intents was the same as that of a number of contemporaries who painted. Confusion occurred and obscured the Delft painter's identity. Together with the other non-painting Vermeers and van der Meers in Delft (a doctor, an apothecary, a schoolteacher, a tapestry-weaver, and a beer-mixer), at least seven or eight Vermeers/van der Meers worked as painters in the United Provinces in the seventeenth century. There were several landscape painters in Haarlem called Jan van der Meer, two of whom were father and son, the elder at least being a highly talented artist. And last but most ubiquitous, there was Johannes van der Meer, also known as Jan or Jacques or Johan or Jacob, a genre, portrait, and history painter active in Utrecht. According to Houbraken, who gave him real attention, this van der Meer was born in Schoonhoven (where Maria Thins had owned land); but Houbraken seems to have been mistaken – recent research has shown that van der Meer was born in a place even more closely connected with Johannes Vermeer: the village of Schipluy. Houbraken also wrote, unwittingly founding a further chain of confusion: 'One should reckon as a Utrecht painter Johan van der Meer . . . Where did he learn his art? I cannot say, but he went to Rome in the company of Lievens Verschuur. He stayed there more than a year and perfected himself in his art. At Rome he met Drost, Carel Lot . . . etc.' This painter then returned to Utrecht where he worked as an art-dealer and art-supplies merchant as well as an artist, and was there in 1672 when the French soldiery burned down his house and his wife's factory, which made lead-white; he also, as we've seen, suffered bankruptcy in the depression of that time. At some point or other a number of Vermeer's paintings, particularly his early history or religious paintings, have been attributed to his Utrecht namesake. P.T.A. Swillens regarded the *Christ in the House of Martha and Mary* as the work of 'the Utrecht Vermeer'. Abraham Bredius shared that view, and also at one time thought the Utrecht artist had painted the *Diana and her Companions*. More recently the *St Praxedis* painting after Ficherelli has been considered as possibly by the Utrecht van der Meer.

It perhaps isn't surprising that some writers have read Houbraken and then wondered if the two similarly named painters weren't one and the same. Could Houbraken have been referring to Vermeer of Delft when he said 'One should reckon as a Utrecht painter Johan van der Meer . . .'? Student-work in a Utrecht studio, and the Italian training, would take care of much of the vacuum of our man's apprenticeship years. Christiaan Josi, a Dutch engraver and print-publisher born in 1768, was highly aware of Vermeer's paintings – 'so remarkable for the simplicity of their subjects and their truth of expression' – but like most people was much less knowledgeable about his life: he thought the Delft Vermeer was the father of the Utrecht painter. (The Schipluy/Utrecht van der Meer was not only about two years older than Vermeer of Delft but lived some twenty years longer.) Nevertheless, Josi warned against confusing their works. One difficulty here has been that the Utrecht painter's works have been hard to find under his name. They were thought to be entirely unknown when Jean Decoen wrote about him in the *Burlington Magazine* in 1935, though some have recently been identified, among them a group portrait, *The Regents of the Utrecht City Orphanage*, painted around 1680 – van der Meer was one of the regents and portrayed himself with his fourteen colleagues. He seems to have been a competent portraitist but an uninspired artist. After the French war he apparently recovered some of his prosperity. He became a city councillor of Utrecht and in 1682 acquired the profitable post of 'collector of convoys and licences' for the Amsterdam Admiralty in the village of Vreeswijk near Utrecht. Perhaps, if our Vermeer had escaped his fatal illness, the Delft master would have made a similar financial come-back.

★

We have seen early indications of the growth of French taste and culture in the United Provinces. William the Silent's *cri de coeur* as he was shot was in French, and French persisted as the language of the Dutch court. Constantijn Huygens's many musical compositions were strongly influenced by French music. The Sun King hardly needed to invade the country. After the Golden Age of the Dutch Republic came the *Pruikentijd*, the Periwig Age – fine polish was the mode, and was already evident in those last virginal pictures of Vermeer's; Dutch theatre copied that of Paris; the children of the Dutch regent class learned to write in French before they wrote in their native language; and soon the ideas of Voltaire, Rousseau, and Montesquieu permeated the Low Countries. At the end of the eighteenth century French armies occupied the southern provinces, which became part of the French republic and next of the Napoleonic empire, while the former Dutch Republic – renamed the Batavian Republic – became a client state of France. It is perhaps then less astonishing that the mid-nineteenth-century 'rediscovery' of Johannes Vermeer was prompted in large part by French writers, who in their own expansive way now took an interest in the Netherlands and the artists who had lived there.

However, an interest in and fondness for Vermeer wasn't obligatory among these writers. For example, the French artist and writer Eugène Fromentin travelled in Flanders and Holland in 1875, two hundred years after Vermeer's death. Fromentin was fifty-five, a painter whose works had not made much of a mark, but a keen student of the Dutch masters – or most of them. He found it hard to handle Rembrandt's genius but wrote in his book *Les Maîtres d'autrefois* perceptively and expressively about Jacob Ruisdael, Jan van Goyen, Pieter de Hooch, Paulus Potter, Jan Steen, Gerard Terborch, Gabriel Metsu, and Frans Hals. Yet there was a Delft deficit: Fromentin doesn't mention Carel Fabritius and in the course of his Low Countries travels sees not a single Vermeer (though he perhaps had seen some in Paris). His only allusions to Vermeer have to do, first, with his influence on some contemporary French painters, among them (it seems) Camille Pissarro, with a reference to a similar 'disdain for drawing, for difficult and delicate construction' (a remark that now seems pretty bizarre); and second, where Fromentin suggests condescendingly that since Vermeer 'has points of view which are rather strange even in his own country, a journey would not be without its use to one who cared to inform himself upon this peculiarity of Dutch art'. (Vincent van Gogh used the same epithet when describing Vermeer's palette, calling him 'this strange artist' – but 'peculiarity' is a peculiar word to choose.)

Even greater ignorance was shown by the celebrated Swiss art historian Jakob Burckhardt. In 1874 he had lectured on Netherlands genre painting, pointing out that Houbraken had not referred to Hobbema and de Hooch, but failing to note Houbraken's neglect of Vermeer. (Burckhardt was also wrong about de Hooch, to whom Houbraken devoted twelve lines of text.) But outside the Renaissance Burckhardt had a blind eye. He called Rembrandt 'that idol of the talented and untalented daubers and sketchers', and he referred dismissively to 'the over-rated single figures of the Delft painter Meer: women reading and writing letters and such things'.

Fromentin at any rate appears successfully to have insulated himself from the writings of his compatriots, Maxime Ducamp, Théophile Gautier, and Théophile Thoré. Ducamp wrote in the *Revue de Paris* in 1857 about the *View of Delft*'s vigour, solidity, and firmness of impasto, and concluded: 'this Jan van der Meer, of whom I know nothing but the name, is a rugged painter.' Gautier the following year exclaimed in the *Moniteur*, after seeing the same picture: 'Van Meer paints spontaneously with a force, a precision and closeness of tone that are unbelievable.' As for Thoré, in 1866 he brought Vermeer to the attention of the readers of the *Gazette des Beaux Arts* in three articles which thereafter appeared in book-form. In May that year in Paris an exhibition had opened made up of pictures loaned from private collections, including Fabritius's *Goldfinch* and eleven paintings attributed to Vermeer, of whom only a few scholars seemed then to be aware – one being the Berlin museum director Gustav Waagen, who in 1860 realised that *The Art of Painting* was not by de Hooch but by Vermeer, whom he called a 'Proteus among painters'.

But Thoré was among the most knowledgeable of these rare enthusiasts. He was an unusual art expert. A radical who had been involved in an attempted coup in Paris after the 1848 revolution, he was exiled by Louis Napoleon. As he journeyed through Europe, he studied painting, particularly that of the Dutch; this seemed to him the art of a people which had freed itself from the old clerical and aristocratic bonds; it was a 'domestic and civic painting'. While staying in Belgium, fearing Napoleon III's secret agents, Thoré adopted the *nom de plume* of William Bürger, and wrote essays about European art collections under that name – *bürger* meaning citizen.

Yet Thoré–Bürger didn't immediately succumb to Vermeer. When he had first seen the *View of Delft* in 1842 he thought its impasto excessive, and this remained his verdict in 1858 in his first published reaction to the painting. Then he wrote of Vermeer's picture: 'One could say that he wanted to build his city with a trowel and that his walls are of real mortar. Enough is enough. Rembrandt never committed such excesses.' But by 1860, Thoré – at that point a collaborator with Gustav Waagen on a book about Dutch and Flemish painters – was resisting such construction-material metaphors and had begun to admit that he had failed to give the *View of Delft* and its painter their due. Now he was caught by the Vermeer fire and wanted to know all he could about the mysterious Delft master. His exile had given him the chance to dig – not very deeply – in the Delft archives. He visited the galleries in most European cities, looking for signatures on likely pictures. He spent large sums on photographs of paintings. In libraries he was able to 'read, in all languages, books on art, and attempt to untangle somewhat the still confused history of the Northern Schools, especially the Dutch School, of Rembrandt and his circle – and my "sphinx" van der Meer'. Thoré learned about some of the artists who had had similar names and he also learned of Vermeer's celebrity in his own time and place, despite which obscurity had set in, making him indeed a sphinx, the lack of biographical details and rarity of his works being factors in that process.

It was obviously important to find out more about Vermeer's life and to construct a proper body of work – an *oeuvre* – for the painter. In the latter task Thoré's enthusiasm and keen eye helped him uncover a number of Vermeers which were hidden under other names. These were tremendous discoveries. In the Six family mansion in Amsterdam he found *The Milkmaid* and *The Little Street*, 'by Jan van der Meer of Delft! The astounding painter!' And he asked himself a question which perhaps now sounds naive but was feasible then: 'After Rembrandt and Frans Hals, is this van der Meer . . . one of the foremost masters of the entire Dutch School?' For Thoré the answer was obviously yes, and he went on gathering the evidence to support it. In Brunswick he found the *Girl being offered Wine*, and in Dresden performed a similar rescue errand with *The Procuress*. He was able to give Vermeer credit for these paintings. Thoré actually bought, for himself or friends, the *Woman with a Pearl Necklace* (he called it 'delicious'), *The Concert*, the *Young Woman seated at a Virginal*, and the *Young Woman standing at a Virginal*. His fervour occasionally got the better of him; he inaccurately transcribed the text of an 1822 sale catalogue concerning the *Girl with a Red Hat* to make it a portrait of a young man, and he ultimately gave Vermeer an *oeuvre* of seventy or so paintings, some of which were by one of the Haarlem van der Meers, some by Jacob Vrel, and some even by Pieter de Hooch. Like others later, he naturally hoped that Vermeer might have done more pictures in a category where few were to be found – in townscapes, say – and his hopes occasionally sabotaged his connoisseurship.

Yet Thoré has to be given credit for pulling Vermeer out of the pack of Dutch seventeenth-century painters and establishing him as 'astounding' and 'one of the foremost masters'. He loved Vermeer, even without knowing much about Vermeer's life; and although he thought there might be 'something of Rembrandt' here, he realised that there was a great deal too that was absolutely original. And Thoré's eye – and eye for connections – was proved sound when he came across Carel Fabritius's *Goldfinch* in Brussels, in the collection of Chevalier J.-G.-J. Camberlyn. Thoré wrote with excitement to his friend Félix Delhasse: '*Deux siècles sur un perchoir, un vrai Siméon*

Stylite, quoi! Mais, Félix, admirez donc son plumage: les couleurs en sont aussi vives qu'au premier jour!' Camberlyn had been so taken with Thoré's admiration for the little picture that he had given it to Thoré. Thoré continued his letter to Delhasse: '*Béni soit le chevalier Camberlyn! C'est un superbe chardonneret qu'il m'a donné.*' Thoré went on to open up the career of Fabritius for scholarly examination and to link Rembrandt's pupil with Vermeer; having read Bon's elegy, he perhaps made the link too strong by suggesting Fabritius had been Vermeer's master. But Thoré correctly noted that Fabritius's works were even rarer than Vermeer's. And when his exile came to an end and he returned to France, the *Goldfinch* went with him and remained with him until his death.

What made Thoré, a radical activist, take to Vermeer, whose work is seemingly so quiet, so passive, so serene? Part of the answer may be that Thoré recognised in Vermeer beyond those characteristics a revolutionary upturning of things, with normality so heightened, all points of fact quivering with such intensity, and reality pierced with insights that arose out of conscious and unconscious powers. Another part of the answer may be that the age had come for Vermeer to be appreciated again, this time first on a European and then a world scale. The era of the photograph was upon us, and photography – as Lawrence Gowing noted later, in the twentieth century – helped create the moment for Vermeer's recovered and enlarged reputation. Artists came to see in a new way, and Impressionism would soon adopt Vermeer, and absorb Vermeer, as its ancestor. From being half-forgotten, Vermeer would eventually be in an equally invidious situation, with fame so great it seemed almost to suffocate its subject.

13. *'Every Inch a Vermeer'*

Seeing peculiarity in Vermeer, as Fromentin did, might have been less weird a response if – along the way – the French artist had acknowledged that he was talking about a great master. The peculiarity he saw may have been part of Vermeer's originality and stature. Yet we would probably be wrong to assume that all we see in the work was seen in the same way by Vermeer himself, and that what we conclude from his pictures was always intended by him. Moreover, there were undoubtedly occasions when he was leading us on or camouflaging his purpose: the skills of deception were in his genes. Even so, what we regard as strange or even duplicitous in Vermeer's works may have seemed normal to him. Vermeer went out of his way not to be caught drawing moral lessons. It seems to me that he removed the speech from his characters' lips and froze their actions in perpetual ambiguity. Question marks replace other forms of punctuation. Vermeer's 'statements' are steeped in hesitation and doubt.

But there were other conventions in Dutch art in the seventeenth century within which Vermeer can also be seen to flourish, and which suited his tendency to indulge in a very high grade of artistic subterfuge. One motive of seventeenth-century Dutch artists was to celebrate day-to-day reality, the common glories of creation; but another was for the artist to get pleasure from an ability to make the viewer feel for an instant that what he or she saw on the canvas was not paint but 'the real thing'. Samuel van Hoogstraten discussed the subject of 'fooling the eyes'. He wrote, in his *Inleyding*: 'The Art of

Painting is a science for representing all the ideas or notions which the whole of visible nature is able to produce – [a science] for deceiving the eye with drawing and colour.' And a little later he declared: 'I say that a painter, whose work it is to fool the sense of sight, also must have so much understanding of the nature of things that he thoroughly understands by what means the eyes are fooled.' When Shakespeare's Hamlet showed his locket of his father to his mother, and then made her look at her locket of Claudius, he remarked on 'the counterfeit resemblance of two brothers'. The seventeenth-century Dutch word for portrait was *conterfeijtsel*, as used in the description of an item of art work in the estate of Aeltge Velthusius, Carel Fabritius's first wife, '*een conterfeijtsel van Gerrit*'. This term suggests a straightforward level on which artistic 'counterfeiting' could be done, that is, by creating a realistic image of a person. But tricking the viewer by fooling the sight was – as Hoogstraten acknowledged – part of the artist's role; one picture-form that did this and was fairly common was a *bedriegertje*, a 'little deceit' or 'cheater' – like Fabritius's *Goldfinch*, Cornelis Gijsbrecht's picture of the back of a painter's canvas, or the brilliant *trompe-l'oeil* painting by Hoogstraten himself, which appears to be a collection of household objects hanging on the back of a cupboard door. This ambition to make an illusion of reality – and perhaps at the same time to remind us, and gain the credit for the fact, that a sleight of hand had occurred – is evident in Vermeer's *The Love-letter*.

It is an unsettling picture. We almost feel that we are looking into a perspective box of the kind Hoogstraten made, which gives us a sense of gazing through a keyhole into a Dutch house 240 years ago, with a broom standing waiting for the person who still has chores to finish. A similar broom waits in the doorway of *The Love-letter* – or perhaps we should say in what seems to a doorway, because at least one scholarly viewer has taken this boldly narrow rectangular space to be (as mentioned before) a mirror, in which we see – as through a doorway – a well-dressed woman holding a cittern on her lap and a letter a maidservant has handed her. There are no hinges visible, indeed no door. The frame in which a door might hang seems rather to be the frame of a picture, or of a piece of mirrored glass. The curtain that hangs across the space, suspended from the upper right, looks more appropriate for covering a mirror (or a painting) than it does for closing off a frequently used entrance into another room. But then why does the mirror – if such it is – reflect a well-lit space when the foreground area from which we see it is dark?

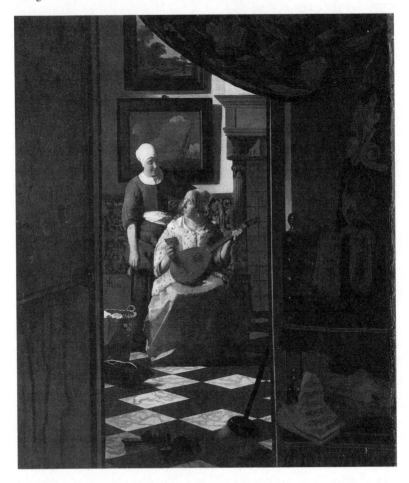

The Love-letter, c. 1669–70.

Some experts have scorned this mirror-idea (first mooted, I believe, by R.H. Wilenski in 1929). After all, the woman is, like any right-handed person seen directly by the human eye, accepting the letter with her right hand and holding with her left the neck of the cittern she has been playing. But Vermeer could have achieved this correction by using two mirrors. Although there are no other signs in Vermeer's work of a tall standing mirror of this kind, such mirrors had begun to arrive in the Low Countries from France at this time, and Rembrandt is known to have used a large mirror in his studio. The artist of the still unattributed painting of this period that has been called *Refusing the Glass* shows himself in that picture, with his back to us, sitting behind the man and woman with a glass of wine in the foreground, as he paints the scene in front of a mirror. A mirror, like a camera obscura, would have been a useful device for framing a concept, for focusing and selecting the elements of a composition. And it is worth recalling again that the Dutch have always been used to seeing things in their reflected forms, on the surfaces of their lakes and canals and more recently in the small mirrors called *spiegeltjes* placed outside windows, so that the occupants inside can keep an eye on who is passing in the street or arriving at the front door. At any rate, Wilenski thought that Vermeer when painting *The Love-letter* turned the leg of his easel, when he saw it in the reflected view in his mirror, into the broom – a symbol of domestic virtue or, in this otherwise idle scene, an ironic allusion: we know which of these two women isn't going to be sweeping the floor.

But even if it isn't a mirror view, Vermeer doesn't make us feel wholeheartedly that it is 'real life'. Is it then rather a picture within a picture, a different kind of step back, a way of removing things to another level of reality? De Hooch painted a similar doorway scene, looking into a well-lit room from a dark room, with a broom in the doorway, in his picture *Couple with a Parrot* that was painted probably a year or so before Vermeer did *The Love-letter*. One wonders if Vermeer's picture is in a way a tribute to de Hooch. But there was no open admission of debt; indeed, the fact that he borrowed pictorial motifs and approaches in this way perhaps also spurred him to take the evasive measures he did. Lebrun in 1792 had noted Vermeer's 'deceptive realism', and Gowing more recently has remarked on the same score: 'An element of concealment, of deception, of which the painter was as much the victim as any of his students, is never entirely absent from Vermeer's thought.'

Théophile Thoré had helped Vermeer's cause in one other respect: by buying, and persuading his friends to buy, Vermeers, he had raised the price for which these paintings sold. By the end of the nineteenth century Vermeers were beginning to fetch very big money. American millionaires including Henry Marquand, J. Pierpont Morgan, Henry Frick, and Isabella Stewart Gardner had joined the Vermeer owners' club, and the great American museums were discreetly lobbying for the pictures to be given to them or at least lent to them and later given as bequests. The Dutch museum director and art historian Abraham Bredius did well in this process. He had bought the *Allegory of Faith* in 1899 for roughly 700 guilders, loaned it to the Mauritshuis and the Boymans Museum for many years, and then sold it for $300,000 to the American collector Michael Friedsam – Friedsam later left it to the Metropolitan Museum in New York. Vermeer's prices were also affected by shortage: there just weren't that many of the paintings around. With hindsight, we can see that the conditions were becoming ripe for new 'Vermeers' to turn up, whether as a result of generous attribution or from counterfeiting in the twentieth-century meaning of that term, as entrepreneurs thought there should be more of them to fulfil the demand.

Coincidentally, some in the art world were ready to believe that more Vermeers might be found. In 1928 the art historian, museum director, and optimist W.R. Valentiner wrote: 'It is still quite possible that for a number of years to come new Vermeers may now and then appear', though he didn't expect these paintings to be experiments, far from Vermeer's usual path. Valentiner went on: 'Vermeer used a very small number of models and repeated certain details like costumes, curtains, pillows, windows, mantelpieces, and even the paintings hanging on the walls so often that newly discovered works by him frequently seem like puzzle pictures composed of pieces taken from different groupings in known pictures by him.' Almost a prescription for how to forge a Vermeer. In 1935 a big exhibition in Rotterdam displayed fifteen 'Vermeers', six of which were later judged to be not genuine. In 1937 Andrew Mellon, who had been US Secretary to the Treasury under Presidents Harding and Coolidge, bought two paintings of young women as Vermeers, with attributions to that effect signed by Willem Martin of the Mauritshuis and Wilhelm von Bode of the Berlin Museum. Mellon later gave them to the National Gallery in Washington where they are now in storage, both credited to an 'anonymous twentieth-century artist'. The end of that dishonest decade saw connoisseurs and collectors of Vermeer, more than ever spellbound by his great magic, taken for an astonishing ride. And a few years later, as the Second World War ended, it had become clear that Vermeer appealed not just to the presumably law-abiding patrons of art; all sorts of crooks, forgers, thieves, and even murderers liked him, too.

In 1937, the art world was brought to its feet by a short piece by Abraham Bredius in the *Burlington Magazine*. Bredius had the nickname of 'the Pope' – he was thought to be infallible – and the *Burlington* was the art historians' monthly Bible. Bredius had devoted much of his life to the study of Vermeer, and was now eighty-three, with imperfect sight, and living in retirement on the Côte d'Azur near Roquebrune. He had recently been approached by a lawyer who said he was a trustee of a Dutch family estate. Bredius was asked to look at a painting of Christ with his disciples at Emmaus; the painting was said to have been in the family's possession for forty or fifty years. The short piece Bredius wrote about the picture for the *Burlington* was entitled 'A New Vermeer', was accompanied by a full-page black-and-white reproduction, and was a rhapsody. Bredius wrote:

> It is a wonderful moment in the life of a lover of art when he finds himself suddenly confronted with a hitherto unknown painting by a great master, untouched, on the original canvas, and without any

restoration, just as it left the painter's studio! And what a picture! Neither the beautiful signature 'I.V.Meer' (I.V.M. in monogram) nor the *pointillé* on the bread which Christ is blessing, is necessary to convince us that we have a – I am inclined to say – *the* masterpiece of Johannes Vermeer of Delft, and, moreover, one of his largest works (1.29 m by 1.17 m), quite different from all his other paintings and yet every inch a Vermeer.

The colours are magnificent – and characteristic. Outstanding is the head of Christ . . . In no other picture by the great master of Delft do we find such sentiment.

Bredius dated the picture to Vermeer's 'earlier phase', about the same time as the *Christ in the House of Martha and Mary*. And he apologised for the accompanying reproduction, which 'can only give a very inadequate idea of the splendid luminous effect of . . . this magnificent painting by one of the greatest artists of the Dutch school'. Bredius had signed a certificate on the back of a photograph of the painting, guaranteeing it to be a genuine Vermeer. In December 1937 it was sold to an art-buying body, the Rembrandt Society of the Netherlands, for 520,000 guilders, roughly $170,000 or £52,000 at values then, with the help of a large donation from W. van der Vorm of Rotterdam, and presented to the Boymans Museum in that city. The Boymans had never owned a Vermeer.

In the next few years, seven other 'Old Master' paintings surfaced in Holland – two were de Hoochs, five more were Vermeers – and sold for large sums. That a world war was going on during most of this period and that Rotterdam had been an early victim of the German Luftwaffe did not seem to disturb the galloping interest in new works by Vermeer. Dutch magnates, art experts appointed by the Dutch state, and a German warlord vied with each other for the privilege of buying them. Indeed, it was only at the war's end, when various cases of collaboration with the German invaders were being investigated and because one of the 'Vermeers', *The Woman taken in Adultery*, had ended up in the possession of Reichsmarschall Hermann Goering, that an artist named Han van Meegeren was found to have been involved in the transaction by which Goering had acquired the picture.

Van Meegeren was accused of trading with the enemy. At his trial in 1947, an original defence was put forward. He could not be accused of selling a Vermeer to Goering because Vermeer had not painted the picture; he, van Meegeren, had painted it. He had hoodwinked the Nazi, who had 'paid for' the false Vermeer by returning some 200 paintings, worth more than 1.5 million guilders, that the Germans had looted from Dutch collections. To prove his case, van Meegeren painted for the court another Vermeer (it was to be at least his ninth). Possibly, it was suggested in his defence, he was neither a collaborator nor a criminal but a hero; in a Dutch opinion poll ranking popular public figures at the time, van Meegeren came second after the Prime Minister. The collaboration charges were dropped and he was given a one-year sentence for fraud. But even that was too long for the forger who had deceived both the art historian Bredius and the art lover Goering; he died in prison of a heart attack, aged fifty-eight.

Henricus Anthonius van Meegeren had been born in Deventer in 1889. The forename Han was either a diminutive for Henricus or a portmanteau shortening of his first names. His father wanted him to become an architect and sent him to the Technology Institute in Delft. So van Meegeren lived in Vermeer's town for five years but studied painting rather than building-design. He was a promising pupil and at the end of his studies was made a teaching assistant in the institute's course on Drawing and History of Art. He won a gold medal for a water-colour in seventeenth-century style of a church interior, proving his facility for mimicking the work of that period. He married, moved to The Hague in 1914, had two children, exhibited his own original paintings, at first with some success, began to drink heavily, sold fewer pictures, and got divorced. In 1932 he moved to the French Riviera with his second wife, an actress. By then he resented the Dutch art world – the critics and dealers who he thought were conspiring to keep him from fame and fortune. He settled first in Roquebrune, where coincidentally Bredius was to follow him, and where he lived reclusively, working on the paintings that would achieve his revenge.

Van Meegeren had the necessary technical knowledge. He believed he could reproduce Vermeer's smooth surfaces and the 'local colours' – yellow, white, and blue – that Vermeer had manipulated so brilliantly. He also had the vital obsession with and the indispensable admiration for Johannes Vermeer, whose name sounded rather like his own. He first (c.1935–6) produced two pseudo-Vermeers of women, one reading music, one playing music, and then a Terborch and a Frans Hals. But these were apprentice pieces, too close in subject-matter to the work of the masters he was forging and too similar to works that could be seen in museums. Then he had the brilliant idea that the world needed another religious painting by Vermeer to accompany *Christ in the House of Martha and Mary*. It would confirm the experts' ideas that Vermeer might have studied in Italy. It would support the notion that the Jesuits or wealthy Catholic patrons had quietly bought up Vermeer's work.

For this purpose he borrowed a subject from Caravaggio. He used an old canvas, partially cleaned, that had been used for a painting, by an unknown artist, of *The Raising of Lazarus*, and shortened its stretcher on one side. The old craquelure was allowed to remain and show through. (For later paintings van Meegeren produced the network of cracks by placing the canvas in an oven at 100–120 degrees for several hours; he also rolled up the canvas to induce cracking.) After chemical experiments, he produced an artificial medium, a phenoformaldehyde resin mixed with white lead; this gave him the ability to age a painting in a few days rather than the long time it would have taken with a conventional drying oil medium mixed with linseed oil, of the sort Vermeer had used. When the painting of *The Supper at Emmaus* was finished, he rubbed black ink in the surface cracks to give the effect of old dirt. He then cleaned the surface of surplus ink and laid on a coat or two of varnish. He had supplied himself with a useful armoury of appropriate objects to paint or copy, including a white Delft wine jug and a glass *roemer*, which he used in the *Emmaus*, and a map of the world by Nicolaes Visscher, which he used in a fake Pieter de Hooch. Van Meegeren then worked out a story to explain the provenance of his fake pictures and talked a gullible or greedy agent into helping him bring them into the light.

After his masterstroke *The Supper at Emmaus* had been blessed by Bredius and had gone to the Boymans Museum, van Meegeren returned to Holland and went on making forgeries, though with less care and attention. Why bother too much when the experts were so completely hoodwinked and desperate to grab every new Vermeer or de Hooch that came before them? Following the success of his *Emmaus*, van Meegeren's de Hooch-like *Interior with Drinkers* was bought by the wealthy art collector Daniel George van Beuningen of Rotterdam for 220,000 guilders. In early 1941 the same gentleman

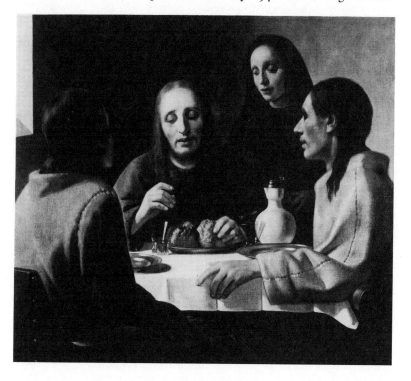

The Supper at Emmaus, c. 1937, Han van Meegeren.

paid about half a million guilders for a small *Head of Christ* signed with the initials IVM forming the famous monogram; the sale was through the agency of a leading Amsterdam dealer named D.A. Hoogendijk. Hoogendijk also arranged the sales of a 'Vermeer' *Last Supper*, a 'de Hooch' *Cardplayers*, and a 'Vermeer' *Isaac blessing Jacob*. In late 1942 a Dutch banker served as the go-between in the sale to Goering of the *Woman taken in Adultery*; van Meegeren, changing his mode a little, used another set of dealers on that occasion; he was presumably paid off in cash. In mid-1943 the Dutch government got into the act, buying a supposed Vermeer, *The Washing of Christ's Feet*, for 1.3 million guilders.

The government did this despite the advice of several art experts who distrusted the work; other experts voted to buy the picture so that the Nazis wouldn't have the chance. Throughout this sorry sequence of events, the dealers concerned avoided any intent examination of the pictures: no X-ray photos were taken; no analyses were made of the paint and therefore no one was aware that the *Woman taken in Adultery*, for instance, had cobalt blue in it, a colour that didn't exist in Vermeer's time; and none of those involved was bothered by some of the strange features of the characters in the pictures – the weirdly exaggerated lowered eyelids, like sea-shells, the heavily shadowed eye-sockets, and the hollowed, cadaverous cheeks, which were not at all Vermeer-like but rather like those in the figures by a painter in The Hague named Han van Meegeren, exhibited between 1914 and 1930 and illustrated in a book published in The Hague in 1942.* Of course we can understand what van Meegeren was after. Think of Clio's demurely lowered eyelids in the *Art of Painting* or the eyelids of the maid in the *Mistress and Maid*. But these details don't grab the viewer's attention the way van Meegeren's faces do. Moreover, why did none of the experts fail to shout in alarm at the awkward, wooden hands, the stiff bodies, the heads that are obvious copies of heads in

*The great nineteenth-century scholar of connoisseurship, the Italian surgeon Giovanni Morelli, who studied the characteristic ways in which Renaissance artists handled anatomical details, would have been interested in the hollow cheeks of van Meegeren's figures, which were like van Meegeren's own hollow cheeks.

Vermeer paintings (*The Astronomer*, for example), and the completely un-Vermeer-like details such as the right eye of Jacob, in *Isaac blessing Jacob*, which appears to have a severe case of conjunctivitis? Why, why, why?

D.A. Hoogendijk said at the time of van Meegeren's trial, trying to explain how they were all taken in and went on buying the van Meegerens even though the quality of the forgeries got worse:

> It's difficult . . . we all slid downwards – from the *Emmaus* to the *Last Supper* to the *Blessing of Jacob*. When I look at them now, I do not understand how it could possibly have happened; a psychologist could explain it better than I can. But the atmosphere of the war contributed to our blindness.

The experts could also plead that all the real Vermeers in Holland were hidden away and not available for comparison – though this hadn't been the case when the *Emmaus* turned up in 1937. The war was a factor, no doubt; the pervasive atmosphere of making out, of petty criminality, played its part. And afterwards the air was full of self-justification and even arrant disbelief. A commission of inquiry was set up by the Dutch government and scientific tests were made. The commission reported that the paintings were contemporary and probably from the hand of van Meegeren. Despite this, and despite the fact that van Meegeren while in custody painted a last 'Vermeer', *Christ among the Doctors*, to prove his ability as a forger, several scholars including Jean Decoen went on maintaining that the *Emmaus* and *The Last Supper* at least were genuine Vermeers. D.G. van Beuningen allowed himself to be reconvinced that he had bought an original Vermeer when he purchased *The Last Supper* in 1941, but he died just before the hearing of a court case in which he brought an action against the Belgian scientist P.B. Coremans, who had worked for the inquiry and declared the painting was by van Meegeren; van Beuningen's heirs pursued the case and lost. A conclusive discovery about this picture was made after the inquiry. In May 1940 an Amsterdam dealer had sold a seventeenth-century canvas of a hunting scene by Hondius to van Meegeren for a modest price; this was the year before van Meegeren painted his *Last Supper*. The dimensions of the two canvases were similar. Radiographs revealed several areas of the hunting scene underlying *The Last Supper*. And Coremans's question to the 'believers', asking them to explain the presence of a modern resinous medium in the paint structure of these so-called Vermeers, remained unanswered.

Van Meegeren made nearly 7.25 million guilders from his forgeries; that was roughly $2 million or £600,000 then, and would be probably twenty times that sum today. He spent it on houses and travel and the good life. The *Emmaus* was certainly a clever forgery, which – as Albert Blankert put it – 'evoked' the atmosphere of Vermeer, and was a smart gift to those who hungered for more Vermeers with religious subjects. But from this distance only the paucity of Vermeer's *oeuvre*, and the authority of Bredius, account for van Meegeren's success with the *Emmaus* and his consequent successes in unloading the increasingly implausible 'van Vermeegerens' that followed it. He said he had hoped to have the truth told after his death, by making a confession in his will, and thus not only to put the record straight but to perpetuate the sweet revenge he had taken against those who had thought him a third-rate painter. But his arrest on collaboration charges forced the premature admission that he was a forger.

Some art commentators, as if to make up for the credulity of the experts, hailed van Meegeren as the greatest forger of all time; but the greatest forger must be one who hasn't been caught. Those who believe crooks should get their just deserts even in small things will be pleased to know that some seventeenth-century Berkemeyer goblets which van Meegeren had paid good money for, so that he could use them as models for drinking-glasses in several of his de Hoochs and Vermeers, were later found to be nineteenth-century imitations.

The master criminal of our time was not to be deprived of a part in this cavalcade of wrong-doing. Adolf Hitler, as a young man, had twice tried to become a student at the Academy of Fine Arts in Vienna, without success. *The Art of Painting* was 'liberated' from Vienna on the Führer's orders and brought to Berchtesgaden, where Hitler personally admired it between 1942 and 1945; it is thought he intended it eventually to go to the gigantic Adolf Hitler Museum he wanted to set up in his native town of Linz, with himself as director, a Valhalla in which he intended to put on show European masterworks of all periods. *The Art of Painting*, labelled 'A.H., Linz', was eventually stored along with 6,750 other works of art hidden in a salt mine in the mountains near Salzburg. (One of the other works was Goering's van Meegeren/Vermeer, *The Woman Taken in Adultery*.) During the last weeks of the war, Hitler gave the command from his Berlin bunker to blow up the repository of paintings, but fortunately the local gauleiter disobeyed the order. After the salt mine's treasure trove was found at the end of the war the Allies returned *The Art of Painting* to Vienna. Another Vermeer taken by the Nazis was *The Astronomer*, owned by the Rothschilds since 1886, which the German art-looting organisation Einsatzstab Reichsleiter Rosenberg stole in Paris in 1940. Alfred Rosenberg, the ERR director, wrote to Hitler's aide, Martin Bormann: 'I am pleased to inform the Führer the painting by Jan Ver Meer of Delft, to which he made mention, has been found among the works confiscated from the Rothschilds.' *The Astronomer* was stamped on the back with a swastika, put in a crate marked H (for Hitler) 13, and sent on a special train to Germany. Why Hitler particularly wanted it is not known, though he is said to have been interested in astrology. It, too, was recovered in Austria, was returned to the Rothschild family, and is now in the Louvre.

In 1943 the owner of Vermeer's *A Lady writing* was murdered. For three years the picture had belonged to the sixty-nine-year-old goldmining magnate Sir Harry Oakes, who was found dead in mysterious circumstances at his mansion in Nassau, in the Bahamas; some believed that a deal with the Mafia to set up a casino on the island had gone sour and the mob had rubbed him out. (His widow, Eunice, Lady Oakes, thereafter sold the painting to another millionaire, Horace Havemeyer, whose sons gave it to the Washington DC National Gallery.)

Villainous and sometimes injurious interest in Vermeer of a more direct kind increased in the 1970s. The Rijksmuseum's *Love-letter* was damaged when stolen in 1971 from an exhibition in Brussels to which it had been loaned; the thief, a hotel waiter, had hidden in the exhibition hall when it closed for the night. The painting was found two weeks later under the waiter's bed; the waiter himself was found hiding in a farmyard in eastern Belgium. He wanted to raise cash to help refugees in Pakistan, and his deed, according to the art historian Albert Blankert, writing in 1978, was 'alarmingly well-received' by the Dutch public. We had by now entered an era in which works of art were considered as potential make-weights – as hostages or compensation – for all sorts of political, social, or personal injustice. The painting had been removed from its frame, rolled up, and sat on, considerably damaging some parts of it, but these were evenly coloured areas, and were well restored after it had been recovered.

One Saturday night in February 1974, *The Guitar Player* (see p. 202), one of the two paintings Catharina had given to Hendrick van Buyten to cover the family bread bill, disappeared from Kenwood House on Hampstead Heath in London where it was exhibited. Shutters and a window to the formal dining-room had been forced open. Despite two night-watchmen on the premises, an alarm which had sounded at Hampstead police station, and a 10-foot wall that had to be scaled, the thieves got away with their prize. A political motive for the theft was soon suspected. Among the many messages received by the police was one demanding that two young women named Dolours and Marion Price, who had been part of an IRA bombing unit, and who were serving life sentences in Britain, be moved to an Irish prison. The painting's frame was found, damaged, on Hampstead Heath after a clairvoyant charwoman told the police where it was. (Police tracker dogs had missed it.) *The Times* received through the post an envelope containing a strip of canvas cut from the edge of the picture and a typewritten threat: because the Price sisters didn't care and 'a capitalist society values its treasures more than humanity . . . we will carry our lunacy to its utmost extent [–] the painting will be burnt on St Patrick's night'. However, a few months

later, a phone-call to the police led them to the churchyard of St
Bartholomew's, in Smithfield, London, and there was *The Guitar
Player*, wrapped in an evening paper, leaning against a gate. No IRA
prisoners were moved and apparently no ransom was paid.

The second Vermeer which Catharina pledged to van Buyten, the
Lady writing a Letter with her Maid, is – at this date – the only one of
Vermeer's paintings to have been stolen twice. The first occasion was
in April 1974. A woman and four gunmen broke into a country house
near Dublin, called Russborough, which belonged to Sir Alfred Beit,
the second baronet, and heir to a South African gold- and diamond-
mining fortune. The not very competent gang was led by a young
woman named Bridget Rose Dugdale, ex-debutante daughter of a
well-to-do London Lloyds insurance underwriter and friend of the
Beit family; she had already taken part the year before in the looting
of her parents' Devon farm, for the benefit of the IRA. (She had
received a suspended sentence for her part in the crime; her boy-
friend, who had a prison record, got six years.) Sir Alfred and Lady
Beit were tied up. Nineteen paintings were levered out of their frames
and taken away from Russborough, but all were recovered a week later
in a Cork cottage; the fact that they were not insured made high
ransom payments or rewards improbable. The Vermeer, one of the
last in private hands, acquired only a few scratches by way of damage.
Rose Dugdale was arrested and this time got nine years, though the
IRA denied any involvement with its sympathiser. Later it was
revealed that a ransom note sent in the Russborough case was in the
same handwriting as one received at Kenwood House after the theft
of *The Guitar Player*. Rose Dugdale was probably the common link.
She has since changed her name and works as a teacher.

Twelve years after the first Russborough robbery it all happened
again. The Russborough alarm system sounded at two a.m. on 21 May
1986. The male housekeeper, Michael O'Shea, searched but discovered nothing suspicious. He and a policeman who turned up
thought it was a false alarm. Next morning eighteen paintings were
found to be missing, including the Vermeer, a Goya, two Rubens, a
Gainsborough, and two Metsus; the thieves had apparently triggered

the alarm on purpose and then hidden until the hullaballoo had died down; there was a broken window at the back of the house through which they had escaped with their loot.

This time the paintings were missing for a lot longer. The leader of the crooks was known to be a Dublin robber named Martin Cahill, nicknamed 'the General', who clearly liked Old Masters. An attempt by the Gardai to retrieve the pictures in 1987 went wrong when a planned handover in the woods of Killakee, County Wicklow, was thwarted by poor communications and muddy ground. The following year Sir Alfred Beit gave most of his collection to the National Gallery of Ireland, which thus became the legal owner, if not the possessor, of the still missing paintings. By now, the General evidently wanted to unload the pictures but didn't know how to do so, though he went on 'collecting' art, including sixty pictures, jewellery, and antique furniture stolen from the elderly widow of a Dublin judge in 1988. Some of his henchmen were arrested and convicted. One man who was suspected of putting robbery proceeds into his own pocket was nailed to a floor during interrogation by the General's men. The General himself broke into the offices of the Irish Director of Public Prosecutions to see what the authorities had on him – he learned that sixty gardai were meant to have him under twenty-four-hour surveillance. A Metsu turned up in Istanbul in 1990; it was being offered for sale not by the IRA but by some minor figures from a Protestant paramilitary group, the Ulster Volunteer Force; an undercover negotiation followed and the picture was brought back to Ireland. In 1992 the Beit Gainsborough was found in a delivery van at Euston station in London. In 1993 the Rubens portrait and an Anthony Palamedes, *A Group making Music*, from the Beit collection were recovered, also in London. And later that year, at Deurne airport near Antwerp, Belgium, three Irish 'businessmen' with paintings to sell were met by two 'collectors' who revealed themselves to be Belgian policemen. The Irishmen were arrested. Paintings recovered included the other Metsu, the Goya, and the *Lady writing a Letter with her Maid*. Like the others, the Vermeer was unframed and a bit damp; it also had a dent in the canvas but was otherwise unharmed. The *Irish*

Times suggested that the General had bitten off more than he could chew. Sir Alfred Beit lived until 1994 and thus saw the recovery of most of his pictures. Martin Cahill, whose gardai surveillance had by then been lifted, died in the same year; he was suspected of helping Loyalist gunmen arrange a bomb attack and was shot dead by – it is thought – the IRA.

At this writing, one Vermeer is known to be missing. Since 1990, illustrations of *The Concert* in catalogues and books have been accompanied by the note: 'Present whereabouts unknown'. Its former whereabouts were Fenway Court, the tall Venetian palazzo-style house in Boston that Isabella Stewart Gardner called home but also intended to be a personal museum designed to 'enrich American cultural life'. Fenway Court has ground-floor cloisters around a central courtyard, several floors of galleries, and a fourth-floor apartment built for Mrs Gardner. The building housed her collection of art works and *objets d'art*, chosen with the help of such connoisseurs as Bernard Berenson. Among roughly 2,500 items, many unlabelled or ill-lit, one of the most celebrated was *The Concert*, which she had bought in Paris in 1892 for 29,000 francs at the auction of Théophile Thoré's collection, bidding via an agent to whom she signalled with her handkerchief. Fenway Court was opened to the public after Mrs Gardner died in 1924 and has long been a favourite haunt – like Sir John Soane's house in London or Henry Frick's collection in New York – for people wanting to brood or browse among fine works of art that have been collected by one person. Nowadays viewers looking for the place where *The Concert* used to hang find an empty frame and alongside it a poignant notice informing them that Vermeer's painting was one of eleven works of art stolen from the Isabella Stewart Gardner Museum in the small hours of the morning of 18 March 1990.

This was a Sunday and the day after St Patrick's Day. Two 'unknown white males' – as the FBI report later described them – knocked on a side door of the museum. They were dressed in Boston police uniforms and told the two security guards who opened the door on to the dark street that they were police officers responding to a call about a disturbance. The guards – reportedly 'undertrained, underpaid, and inexperienced', according to a local journalist – let in the purported policemen, despite the rules of the museum, and had no time to hit the emergency button. They were made captive, handcuffed, gagged with sticky tape, and put in the basement. With a clear run, the intruders in the next two hours cut or pulled from their frames *The Concert*, two early oil paintings and one etching by Rembrandt, a painting by Rembrandt's pupil Govaert Flinck, five drawings by Degas, and a small Manet; they also grabbed a Shang dynasty bronze beaker from about 1150 BC. It seemed to be a connoisseur's choice. However, the thieves ignored, or at least neglected to take, a celebrated self-portrait in exotic costume done by Rembrandt when he was twenty-three, which was one of the cornerstones of the Gardner collection; they also left behind many other great works by such masters as Fra Angelico, Botticelli, and Titian. The rough value of the works they took was said by the press to be $300 million, though the haul was in fact priceless. A $5 million reward was offered. The objects were not insured, we were told, because the annual premium would have been higher than the museum's endowment income every year.

The FBI described the thieves as wearing dark, shiny moustaches, 'appearing to be false'. But these Keystone-cops-who-were-real-robbers destroyed the film in the security video camera before they left. After the heist, more than a thousand tips were received by the FBI from various parts of the world, and some from prison inmates. Boston police proposed an IRA connection; it was reported that one of the thieves, leaving, had said to one of the gagged guards: 'Can you breathe, mate?' – not exactly a North American expression.

At various moments in the last few years there have been rumours that negotiations for the return of the pictures were under way and even 'at a delicate stage'. In the summer of 1997 a Massachusetts antiques dealer named William P. Youngworth III – a name with a fancy, fraudulent air but apparently a real one – was arrested and charged with possession of a stolen van. Youngworth offered to help arrange the return of the Gardner art if the van charges were dropped, if he and those he called 'caretakers' of the pictures were given immunity from prosecution for the Gardner robbery, and if an imprisoned former associate of his was released, a rock band leader and art thief named Myles Connor Jr. Youngworth also wanted the $5 million reward to be given to him and Connor. But Connor had an alibi – he had been in a Chicago prison during the Fenway Court snatch on a ten-to-twenty-year sentence for fraud and drug offences.

Nothing has so far come of the 'negotiations'. Youngworth was sent to prison for three years for stealing the van. He hasn't given any proof that he has access to the stolen pictures. The State of Massachusetts has been holding in reserve a charge against Youngworth of being judged a habitual criminal, a charge which merits a mandatory jail sentence of fifteen years, but he has said he won't co-operate at all if so charged. And where, meanwhile, is *The Concert*? Is it in a New England country barn or suburban garage or under a city apartment floor, wrapped in a sack or plastic sheeting? Do its caretakers ever take it out and look at it and listen to that silent music?

The two young women and the man with his back to us, like the artist in *The Art of Painting*, are in the middle distance, in a group removed from the viewer and looking like figures in a dream; they are set further apart from us by the bright de Witte orange of the back of the chair on which the man sits. (It is the orange Vermeer also used less emphatically in the skirt of the virginal-playing woman in *The Music Lesson*.) Maria Thins's van Baburen *Procuress* and the Ruysdael-like landscape, both in black ebony frames, hang on the wall over the clavecin – the landscape is echoed in the painting on the upraised lid of the instrument. The foreground is dominated by the black-and-white floor tiles and the carpeted table with what may be a guitar on it and then another instrument, a double bass or viola da gamba on the floor, lying in the shadows. As for the musicians, one young woman sings and beats time; one girl plays the clavecin; and the young man holds what seems to be a cittern though we can't see much of it. He wears a sash, and a sword at his left hip, and strikes a slightly military note – civic guard, at any rate. Despite the earthiness of the

14. *Swann's Essay*

Great art raises the question: is this the real point of things, to make constructs of this kind? Vermeer's art especially puts the question almost as an ultimatum: What in life is more important than these abstractions of life, these dreams modelled in paint that are slightly offset from 'reality'? A number of writers – that is, people often engaged in trying to make art with different materials – have in the last hundred years or so reflected this assumption by placing Dutch art at the centre of the universe. This pre-eminence of art over life was such that when Henry James went to Holland in 1874 he complained in an exaggerated fashion that the country and its inhabitants had been too accurately depicted by the Dutch painters – 'You have seen it all before; it is vexatiously familiar; it was hardly worthwhile to have come!' His comment failed to take into account the fact that some Dutch artists, including Vermeer, were doing more than simply mirror and portray what they saw; that beyond exact depiction was something else, possibly a vision. And perhaps seeking such a glimpse, Marcel Proust's last trip out of his Paris apartment into the 'outside world' was to an exhibition at the Jeu de Paume, in 1921, at which three Vermeers were being displayed. Man is mortal; art can be immortal – or at least comes closer to immortality than man does.

In the last few decades this sense of Vermeer filling our world, waking and sleeping, has been enhanced by a number of works of fiction that have used him and his paintings as a launch-pad. Recently a novel called *Girl with a Pearl Earring*, by Tracy Chevalier, has presented us with a young woman named Griet who rises from being a maidservant in Vermeer's household to being his model and studio assistant, manipulating his props (the rumpled table carpets and precariously placed wine jugs) and cleaning the windows to let in the necessary light. Another novel, *The Music Lesson*, by Katharine Weber, published in 1998, created a fictional painting by the master (not, the author stresses, the one of that name in Buckingham Palace), housed it in the Frick Collection, and made it the subject of a pensive thriller in which the painting is stolen on its way home from an exhibition in The Hague and held for ransom by an IRA 'splinter group' in the Irish countryside. The woman who narrates this tale, a curator who succumbs to Irish ancestral sympathies and sexual attraction for the leading boyo, at one point looks in a mirror at the reflection of her own face and thinks 'it seems far away, indistinct, less real' than the face of the woman in the Vermeer painting she is meant to be guarding. (I hope the Isabella Stewart Gardner *Concert* isn't sacrificed as Mrs Weber chillingly sacrifices her Vermeer.) Among other recent works of fiction or reflection making use of Vermeer have been Susan Vreeland's *Girl in Hyacinth Blue*, John Bayley's *The Red Hat* (with Palestinian terrorists, Mossad, and a good deal of strangely detached sex), and Susannah Kaysen's *Girl Interrupted*, in which the author's so-called 'character-disorder' and consequent stays in mental hospitals are related to the Vermeers in the Frick.

More inventively, the Polish poet Zbigniew Herbert brought forth in 1991 a collection of writings sparked by seventeenth-century Dutch art. *Still Life with a Bridle* included a learned essay on the cost of the Dutch pictures of those days, an empathetic piece about Gerard Terborch, and a story about the discovery of a letter from Vermeer to Leeuwenhoek. In this epistle – not to be found in the Dutch archives – Vermeer remarked on an occasion when Leeuwenhoek showed him a drop of water under a microscope: 'I always thought it was pure like glass, while in reality strange creatures swirl in it like in Bosch's transparent hell.' Leeuwenhoek had been pleased at Vermeer's consternation. However, Vermeer went on in his letter to argue that each scientific discovery, in the search for truth and knowledge to replace superstition and chance, opens a new abyss. The task of Art is not to solve enigmas but 'to prepare the eyes for never-ending delight and wonder . . . [and] to reconcile man with surrounding reality'.

Before Herbert, the reality of the Dutch seventeenth century was infiltrated with great skill by the French writer Marguerite Yourcenar, notably in her *Two Lives and a Dream* (though painting wasn't her prime concern), and – a few years ago – by the British author Michael Pye in his novel *The Drowning Room*, set in Amsterdam and New Amsterdam. A bestseller by Deborah Moggach, *Tulip Fever*, as a novel touch is illustrated with plates of seventeenth-century Dutch paintings but suffers from a novelletish plot (a phoney pregnancy making use of a pillow) and some striking anachronisms (bed-*springs* creaking). A character in Thomas Harris's 1999 blood-fest thriller *Hannibal* is offered as a bribe enough money to enable him 'to see every Vermeer in the world'. He sees them all, apart from 'the Vermeer in Buenos Aires'. (Does Mr Harris know there is a Vermeer in Buenos Aires?) Harrison Birtwistle composed the music for an opera, first put on at Glyndebourne in 1994, *The Second Mrs Kong*, with libretto by Russell Hoban, in which King Kong is a tenor, Vermeer's model for the Pearl Earring girl is a soprano, and Vermeer himself is a baritone, irritated by Pearl's lack of interest in him. A more recent opera by Peter Greenaway, *Writing to Vermeer*, with music by the modern Dutch composer Louis Andriessen, puts on stage Vermeer's wife, his mother-in-law, and one of his models as they send letters to him in The Hague in 1672 when he is judging the Elector of Brandenburg's pictures, telling him how much they miss him, while – a bit early – a 'special effects' waterline rises to thwart the French, and above the stage five movie screens display Vermeer's paintings. It is as if a parallel Dutch seventeenth-century universe has been made by contemporary creative artists as an alternative *mise-en-scène* for their works. (And books on that period by present-day historians such as Simon Schama, Jonathan Israel, and A.T. van Deursen provide stockpiles of material.) The reader's familiarity with Dutch painting of that time makes this possible. We prefer then to now.

★

The writer who above all opened up this opportunity for his successors was Marcel Proust. *À la Recherche du Temps Perdu*, his multi-volume masterpiece, has none of Vermeer's economy. It is a book about consciousness – about hyperconsciousness, even – in which a good deal that now seems like unwanted flotsam rises up to and floats just beneath the surface of the author's mind. But we bear with all that – we may skip much of it – and immerse ourselves in the whole because Proust creates a universe in which thought and memory play as great a part as event and action – an oblique role, but then, for Proust, obliqueness is all. He slides up to his concerns. And then he worries out of them every possible facet, present and past, as he examines them like the strange creatures swirling under the microscope in Herbert's or Vermeer's or Leeuwenhoek's drop of water. Early on in the Combray section of the volume called *Swann's Way*, Proust in fact mentions 'protozoa', not in any Delft context but as if some reading of Leeuwenhoek's discoveries had planted the word in his memory, ready for this moment. In the last volume, *Time Regained*, Proust talks not just of microscopes but of telescopes that could have been used in making his own work, 'to perceive things which were indeed very small because they were far away but every one of them a world'.

We aren't surprised to find that Proust's characters Swann and Bergotte have a passion for Vermeer. Charles Swann is intelligent, wealthy, an amateur of the arts, Jewish, a member of the Jockey Club, and part of the fashionable world while being offhand with it. He is humbled by his infatuation with the courtesan Odette de Crécy. From time to time throughout *À la Recherche* he is understood to be writing an essay on Vermeer, as if proving he is his own man. He has started it, we are told; he has abandoned it; he has taken it up again. In Swann's imagination, Vermeer provides a calming counterbalance for Odette's flightiness. When Swann on one occasion wants to punish his mistress (or himself) by not going to her house for tea, the need to work on his essay is his excuse. Odette says that she has never heard of Vermeer – 'Is he alive still?' For a moment she seems jealous of the long-dead painter. 'She asked whether he had been made to suffer by a woman, if it was a woman who had inspired him, and once Swann had told her that no one knew, she had lost all interest in that painter.' When he went back to work on his essay, Swann needed to return to The Hague, Dresden, and Brunswick to look at Vermeers. 'He was convinced that a picture of 'Diana and her Companions' which had been acquired by the Mauritshuis at the Goldschmidt sale as a Nicholas Maes was in reality a Vermeer. And he would have liked to be able to examine the picture on the spot, in order to buttress his conviction . . .' But Swann couldn't leave Paris while Odette was there, or, indeed, even when she wasn't. As for Odette, it transpires that she hadn't lost all interest in 'that painter'. Even though she doesn't fully understand Swann's urges, she recognises Vermeer's importance for him: 'she was acquainted with the titles and with all the details of his studies, so much so that the name of Vermeer was as familiar to her as that of her own dressmaker.' Later, after she is married to Swann, she tells the young narrator of the novel (who is surprised to find out that Odette knows about Vermeer), 'I ought to explain that Monsieur Swann was very much taken up with that painter at the time he was courting me – isn't that so, Charles dear?'

We never learn whether Swann completes his essay. I see him head on hand, looking melancholy, like 'the other man' in the *Girl being offered Wine*, having to put up with Odette as she flirts with a rival admirer. As for Odette's questions about Vermeer, perhaps they aren't entirely frivolous. Was Vermeer made to suffer by a woman in the way that Swann is made to suffer by her? Was he inspired by one – or by many? As we have seen, Vermeer enjoyed painting women's clothes. He liked depicting silks and satins, soft and shimmering, smooth and ruffled. He was a master at painting the look in women's eyes and the expression in their faces. Through Swann's interest, Odette detected – without seeing the paintings – the importance of women for Vermeer.

Towards the end of his fifty-one years of life, Proust told the writer Jean Louis Vaudoyer that Vermeer had been 'my favourite painter since the age of twenty'. In September 1902, when he was thirty-one, Proust read Fromentin's *Les Maîtres d'autrefois* and travelled to

Bruges, Antwerp, and Amsterdam, and then went to Dordrecht and to Delft. There he saw 'an ingenuous little canal, bewildered by the din of seventeenth-century carillons and dazzled by the pale sunlight; it ran between a double row of trees stripped to their leaves by summer's end, and stroking with their branches the mirroring windows of the gabled houses on either bank'. He moved on to The Hague where he saw the *View of Delft* and 'recognised it for the most beautiful picture in the world'. Its painter – 'this artist who keeps his back to us' – kept popping up in *À la Recherche*, whose eight parts were published between 1913 and 1927. In *Cities of the Plain* the narrator takes a rise out of his girlfriend Albertine, who says she has been to The Hague, by having Madame de Cambrener ask her whether she saw the Vermeers there. 'Albertine replied in the negative, thinking they were living people.' But in *The Captive*, the narrator says to Albertine:

> You told me you had seen some of Vermeer's pictures: you must have realised that they're fragments of an identical world, that it's always, however great the genius with which they have been recreated, the same table, the same carpet, the same novel and unique beauty, an enigma at that period in which nothing resembles or explains it, if one doesn't try to relate it all through subject matter but to isolate the distinctive impression produced by colour.

And at least one of Vermeer's colleagues also gets a look-in, as on the occasion where Swann's love for Odette is evoked by Proust recalling 'these interiors by Pieter de Hooch which are deepened by the narrow frame of a half-opened door, in the far distance, of a different colour, velvety with the radiance of some intervening light'.

Through Vermeer Proust premeditated his own end. In May 1921 the exhibition of Dutch painting at the Jeu de Paume was attracting crowds, drawn to see, among other things, Vermeer's *View of Delft* and *Girl with a Pearl Earring*. According to George Painter's biography of him, Proust had read in the Paris press articles on the Vermeers by Léon Daudet and Jean-Louis Vaudoyer. At last he decided he had to go and see them. At nine one morning, a time when he was usually just going to sleep, Proust sent a message to Vaudoyer asking him to accompany him to the Jeu de Paume. Leaving his apartment, he had a terrible attack of giddiness, but recovered from it and went on downstairs. At the exhibition, Vaudoyer steadied the writer's shaky progress towards the *View of Delft*. Proust was apparently revived by Vermeer, for he managed to go on to an Ingres exhibition and then to lunch at the Ritz before returning home, though according to Painter he was still 'shaken and alarmed' by the attack. He never went out again.

Proust soon transmuted this experience into *The Captive*, the sixth part of *À la Recherche*, to which he was still making changes. His character Bergotte, a writer, had been ill. Bergotte slept badly, had nightmares, and couldn't write any more. But he read in a newspaper that the *View of Delft* was to be seen in Paris, a painting he adored and imagined he knew by heart, though the article had referred to 'a little patch of yellow wall' in the picture as being like a 'priceless specimen of Chinese art, or a beauty that was sufficient in itself', and worryingly he couldn't recall that particular little patch. Bergotte therefore

ate a few potatoes, left the house, and went to the exhibition. At the first few steps he had to climb, he was overcome by an attack of dizziness. He walked past several pictures and was struck by the aridity and pointlessness of such an artificial kind of art, which was greatly inferior to the sunshine of a windswept Venetian palazzo, or of an ordinary house by the sea. At last he came to the Vermeer which he remembered as more striking, more different from anything else he knew, but in which, thanks to the critic's article, he noticed for the first time some small figures in blue, that the sand was pink, and, finally, the precious substance of the tiny patch of yellow wall. His dizziness increased; he fixed his gaze, like a child upon a yellow butterfly that it wants to catch, on the precious little patch of wall.

Bergotte thinks he should have written in the same way, less dryly, with more layers of colour in his latter books, with language that he had made more precious in itself, as in that little patch of yellow wall. But he remains conscious of the gravity of his condition:

> In a celestial pair of scales there appeared to him, weighing down one of the pans, his own life, while the other contained the little patch of wall so beautifully painted in yellow. He felt that he had rashly sacrificed the former for the latter. 'All the same,' he said to himself, 'I shouldn't like to be the headline news of this exhibition for the evening papers.'
>
> He repeated to himself: 'Little patch of yellow wall, with a sloping roof, little patch of yellow wall.' Meanwhile he sank down on to a circular settee; whereupon he suddenly ceased to think that his life was in jeopardy and, reverting to his natural optimism, told himself: 'It's nothing, merely a touch of indigestion from those potatoes, which were under-cooked.' A fresh attack struck him down; he rolled from the settee to the floor, as visitors and attendants came hurrying to his assistance. He was dead.

And Proust, who has stunningly involved us in the last minutes of life of a character he has in the course of his work only alluded to on and off, continues with a coda to Bergotte and art. Was Bergotte – as it were, enshrouded in Sir Thomas Browne's white mist – dead for ever? Proust thought that neither experiments in spiritualism nor religious dogma offered proof that the soul survived death.

> All that we can say is that everything is arranged in this life as though we entered it carrying a burden of obligations contracted in a former life; there is no reason inherent in the conditions of life on this earth that can make us consider ourselves obliged to do good, to be kind and thoughtful, even to be polite, nor for an atheist artist to consider himself obliged to begin over again a score of times a piece of work the admiration aroused by which will matter little to his worm-eaten body, like the patch of yellow wall painted with so much skill and refinement by an artist destined to be forever unknown and barely identified under the name Vermeer.

Proust concludes that the idea that Bergotte was not permanently dead was by no means improbable. Bergotte is buried,

> but all through that night of mourning, in the lighted shop-windows, his books, arranged three by three, kept vigil like angels with outspread wings and seemed, for him who was no more, the symbol of his resurrection.

Thus Proust conjured up with Vermeer's help a sort of heaven for Bergotte to reside in. And of course Vermeer is there, too, perhaps now somewhat less irrevocably 'unknown and barely identified' than in Proust's time, indeed maybe even sanctified with the help of the French writer. Proust is said to have gone on working on this episode – this fatal epiphany – into the last month of his life and to have dictated some revisions to it a few hours before he died on 18 November 1922. Towards the end of *À la Recherche*, in the volume called *Time Regained*, he wrote that a work of art 'is the only means of regaining lost time', and he summed up the effect of art:

> Thanks to art, instead of seeing one world, our own, we see it multiplied, and we have at our disposal as many worlds as there are original artists, worlds that differ more widely from each other than those which revolve in infinite space, worlds which – whether their name be Rembrandt or Vermeer – send us their special radiance centuries after the fire from which it emanated was extinguished.

15. *A View of Delft*

There are no Vermeers in Delft today, as far as I know, though possibly someone, some day, clearing out a cluttered attic may find a dusty canvas which a seventeenth-century ancestor – a provisions merchant or cloth-dealer, perhaps – took in lieu of payment.

Vermeer's *oeuvre* is not large for a master. Nor does it cover a wide range of subjects. He is in some ways a restrained and restricted painter, with so much of the world lying beyond his narrow field. He seems such a clean, neat painter, with none of the rumpled sheets or sagging flesh of Rembrandt. And yet how magnificent – how magnified in effect – that small body of work is! It is made up for the most part of small paintings, a fact it is possible to forget in their presence as we feel their immense impact. Houbraken, surely, would now kick himself for having ignored Arnold Bon's last stanza. Vermeer continues to multiply, expand, and intensify as time passes. His thirty-five paintings are now thirty-five squared, or thirty-five to the Nth power.

After my parents died a few years ago, and their possessions were sorted out, I came across a coloured reproduction of a painting, in a cheap black frame, that had belonged to my mother and had hung in the houses where we lived as I grew up, at the foot of the stairs in one, over the oak cupboard in the dining-room of another: the *Girl with a Pearl Earring*. I looked unwittingly at this picture during much of my childhood and youth. I never asked my mother why she had it. Had Roy Bower, her employer as United States consul in Southampton, and later my godfather, given it to her? The girl somewhat resembled my mother. I took the print for granted (as I took my mother) and only later realised that the painting it reproduced was beautiful. (Appreciation of my mother took as long.)

In a box of books and stamp-albums stored in the loft of my parents' last house I found a volume, published in New York by the now-extinct firm of Liveright, which I had received in my early teens in a sequence of books sent me by the Golden Hours Book Club at the behest of Roy Bower. This book was *Tolerance* by Hendrik Willem van Loon. It was illustrated by the author's spiky ink drawings of Netherlandish martyrs on racks and in blazing fires, and of Protestant heroes; for example, Luther nailing his theses to the door of Wittenberg Cathedral. Van Loon's simple, strident text told of how the Inquisition and the Church of Rome were among the bad guys of history and the Dutch – all this for freedom's sake – were among the best. (When I later read John Motley's stirring *Rise of the Dutch Republic* I got a similar if more detailed story.) Another book acquired at a charity jumble sale during my teens remained in use in college and adult life: a Dutch atlas, indeed a *Schoolatlas der Geheele Aarde*, that is, of the whole world, published in Groningen in 1897. It shows not only the continents, oceans, countries as then, but the distribution of races, growth of cities, extent of empires, and climatic zones. Of course, being Dutch it has many Dutch features: Indonesian colonies in the Far East, and at home the coastal dunes, polders, reclamation schemes (the thirteenth-century draining of the Haarlemermeer, for instance), and provincial boundaries. Opening today the double-page spread which shows '*Noord en Zuid Holland en Utrecht*', I find Delft at one end of the Vlaardingen Vaart, a main canal, and Schipluiden not far away. The first name written inside on the flyleaf (above my own name with the date 1946) is that of H.J.N. Douwes Dekker, relative of the celebrated Dutch novelist who wrote around the turn of the nineteenth and twentieth centuries under the name of Mulatuli. To these touchstones I have added a more recent one, not a stone but a small grey-brown brick. It is rough and pitted, probably baked in the seventeenth century, and I picked it up from the footpath, where it was lying loose, one night in Amsterdam while walking past that city's Oude Kerk. Theft, or the city equivalent of beach-combing? Whatever, I'm glad to have it on my desk as I write, together with a Delft tile which I bought not long ago, marked down because it had a single crack across one corner, neatly mended. The tile shows a man energetically pushing a child on a sled over snow.

The two great churches in Delft are still visible from just about everywhere in the town. If I don't recognise the street I am in, I consult the skyline and take rough bearings on the church towers to determine where I am. Today I set off for a farewell visit to the Paardemarkt, the horse-market built where the former Clarissen convent and States gunpowder store once stood. A nineteenth-century artillery depot on the east side of the Paardemarkt now houses military relics, and the brick-paved open space where horses were sold is a public car-park. The nearby Doelenstraat remains a narrow roadway lined with small cottages, many of which look as if they date back to the post-*Donderslag* reconstruction; no plaques to Fabritius or van der Poel are to be seen. On the other hand, there is a new development in the Schutterstraat, on the old Doelen grounds, with twenty modern houses and a little park and playground. From here I walk eastwards to the Rijn-Schie canal and then north, keeping by the waterside footpath, to the top end of the old city. A huge barge rumbles past, squeezing through the abutments of a bridge which opens just in time, and the barge's bow wave splashes against the canal banks. It has been a day of sunshine and showers, but now it is bright. I'm not sure the Delft light *is* unlike that elsewhere in Holland, as Paul Claudel thought, but at this moment I could be nowhere else. The late afternoon sun bounces off the underside of puffy low clouds and is reflected down on Delft, as in Vermeer's *View*.

In the restaurant of the Hotel des Compagnons in the Voldersgracht I talk with two middle-aged men at the next table. Frans Hals faces. Large moustaches. They are painters – house-painters – and come from Heerenveen, in Friesland. They work for a company that made the windows for a new housing development in Delft and sent them down here all painted the wrong colour. They are now painting the windows again, installed, on the spot. At least, they tell me, they are doing so when it isn't raining and they aren't forced to sit in their van. Not a very profitable job: hotel bills, food bills, charges for time and materials; hard not to be impatient.

I have been thinking about Vermeer's final 'frenzy', his lapse into 'decay and decadence', and wondering again whether the term decadence referred not to a moral collapse but to a physical or even mental breakdown. Was it the last frenzy of the perfectionist in art, who had sought the immortal, and then came up against an ultimately imperfect thing, a fatal natural flaw, which doomed him, and doing so sent him wild? I ask the house-painters about stress. I consult my dictionary for what I hope is the right word, *spanning*. Oh yes, they say, a lot of it about. Holland is too crowded. One of the painters goes abroad whenever he gets the chance to travel to emptier places – Ireland, Finland. The other does a lot of exercise: skating in the winter, fast-walking the rest of the year. He is a *snell loper*. He sometimes walks twenty hours at a stretch, at a great clip. Walking it off, as it were. Three centuries ago Holland was not so densely peopled, but its population had expanded rapidly and its horseshoe of towns, including Delft, was congested by seventeenth-century standards.

'Strangers among them are apt to complain of the spleen', wrote the British ambassador Sir William Temple, though he didn't record the effect on the natives of the overcrowding and the fiercely competitive life. Constipation was a common problem. When one considers Vermeer's works, on the one hand, what restraint, what control they possess! On the other hand, one wonders what Vermeer kept bottled up inside him and whether it contributed to the frenzy which reduced this costive artist 'in a day and a half . . . from being healthy to being dead'. He remains in some respects the missing man in some of his own paintings: the person who has just left the room, or who is expected at any moment. He is impatient to be found, to be seen, but while he waits he paints stillness.

Bibliography

Books

Ainsworth, Maryan W. and others. *Art & Autoradiography: Insights into the Genesis of Paintings by Rembrandt, van Dyck, and Vermeer.* New York, 1982

Aitzema, Lieuwe. *Notable Revolutions.* London, 1653

Alpers, Svetlana. *The Art of Describing: Dutch Art in the Seventeenth Century.* Chicago, 1983

Arasse, Daniel. *Vermeer: Faith in Painting.* Princeton, NJ, 1994

Bailey, Anthony. *Rembrandt's House.* Boston, MA and London, 1978

Bailey, Anthony. *A Concise History of the Low Countries.* New York, 1972

Baker, L.M., editor. *Letters of Elizabeth, Queen of Bohemia.* London, 1964

Blankert, Albert. *Vermeer of Delft.* Oxford, 1978

Bleyswijck, Dirck van. *Beschryvinge der Stadt Delft.* Delft, 1667

Boitet, Renier. *Beschryving der Stadt Delft.* Delft, 1729

Brandenberg, T., editor. *The Scholarly World of Vermeer.* Zwolle, 1996

Bredero, Gerbrandt A. *The Spanish Brabanter*, ed. H.D. Brumble. Binghamton, NY, 1982

Brown, Christopher. *Carel Fabritius.* Oxford, 1981

Brown, Christopher. *Scenes of Everyday Life: Dutch Genre Painting in the Seventeenth Century.* London, 1984

Coremans, P.B. *Van Meegeren's Faked Vermeers and de Hoochs.* London and Amsterdam, 1949

Dam, Jan Daniel van. *Dated Dutch Delftware*. Zwolle, 1991

Deursen, A.T. van. *Plain Lives in a Golden Age*. Cambridge, 1991

Dobell, Clifford. *Antony van Leeuwenhoek and his 'Little Animals'*, London, 1932; reprinted New York, 1960

Eisler, Max. *Alt-Delft: Kultur und Kunst*. Vienna, 1923

Evelyn, John. *Diary*, ed., E. S. de Beer. Oxford, 1959

Feliciano, Hector. *The Lost Museum*. New York, 1997

Fest, Joachim C. *Hitler*. New York and London, 1974

Fromentin, Eugène. *The Masters of Past Time*. Paris, 1876; new edn, ed. H. Gerson. London and New York, 1948

Gaskell, Ivan, and others. *Vermeer Studies*. Studies in the History of Art, Vol. XXXIII. Washington, DC and New Haven, CT, 1998

Geyl, Pieter. *The Revolt of the Netherlands*. London, 1932; reprinted 1966

Geyl, Pieter. *The Netherlands in the Seventeenth Century*, Part One, *1609–1648*, Part Two, *1648–1715*. London and New York, 1964

Goldscheider, Ludwig. *Vermeer*. London, 1958

Gowing, Lawrence. *Vermeer*. London, 1952; reprinted 1997

Gregory, Richard, editor, and others. *The Artful Eye*. Oxford, 1995

Haks, D., and others. *De Hollandse Samenleving in de tijd van Vermeer*. Zwolle, 1996

Hale, Philip L. *Vermeer*. London and Boston, MA, 1937

Havard, Henry. *Van der Meer de Delft*. Paris, 1888

Herbert, Zbigniew. *Still Life with a Bridle*. London and New York, 1991

Hertel, Christiane. *Vermeer: Reception and Interpretation*. Cambridge, 1996

Hofrichter, Frima Fox, and others. *Leonaert Bramer 1596–1674*. Milwaukee, 1992

Houbraken, Arnold. *De groote schouburgh*, three volumes. Amsterdam, 1718–21

Houtzager, H.A., editor. *Kruit en Krieg*. Amsterdam, 1988

Houtzager, H.A., and others. *Kaart Figuratief van Delft*. Delft, 1997

Huizinga, Johan. *Dutch Civilisation in the Seventeenth Century*. London and New York, 1968

Huygens, Constantijn. *A Selection of the Poems of Sir Constantijn*

Huygens; trans. P. Davison and A. van der Weel. Amsterdam, 1996

Israel, Jonathan. *The Dutch Republic*. Oxford, 1995

James, Henry. *Transatlantic Sketches*. Boston, MA, 1875

Jonge, C.H. de. *Dutch Tiles*. London, 1971

Kilbracken, Lord (John R.G.). *Van Meegeren*. London, 1967

Kirk-Smith, Harold. *William Brewster: His Life and Times*. Boston, Lincs, 1992

Koning, Hans (as Hans Koningsberger). *The World of Vermeer*. New York, 1967

Lairesse, Gerard de. *Het Groot Schilderboek*, two volumes. Amsterdam, 1707

Liedtke, Walter A. *Architectural Painting in Delft*. Doornspijk, 1982

Maarseveen, Michel P. van. *Vermeer of Delft*. Delft and Amersfoort, 1996

Malraux, André. *Tout Vermeer de Delft*. Paris, 1952

Monconys, Balthasar de. *Journal des Voyages*, three volumes. Lyons, 1665–6

Montias, John Michael. *Artists and Artisans in Delft*. Princeton, NJ, 1982

Montias, John Michael. *Vermeer and his Milieu*. Princeton, NJ, 1989

Nash, John. *Vermeer*. London and Amsterdam, 1991

Painter, George D. *Marcel Proust*, two volumes. London, 1959 and 1965

Pavord, Anna. *The Tulip*. London, 1999

Pepys, Samuel. *Diaries*, ed. Robert Latham and William Matthews, eleven volumes. London, 1970–83

Proust, Marcel. *À la Recherche du Temps Perdu*, eight volumes. Paris, 1913–27 (I have used, and occasionally slightly altered, translations by C.K. Scott Moncrieff and Andreas Mayor, revised by Terence Kilmartin, published in 1981 in London by Chatto & Windus and in New York by Random House.)

Rosenberg, Jakob, with Seymour Slive and E.H. Ter Kuile. *Dutch Art & Architecture 1600 to 1800*. Harmondsworth, Middlesex and Baltimore, MD, 1966

Sandrart, Joachim von. *Teutsche Academie*. Nuremberg, 1675–9

Schabaelje, Jan Philipszoon. *Historisch Verhael van het Wonderlick en Schrickelick opspringen van 't Magasijn-huis.* Amsterdam, 1654

Schama, Simon. *The Embarrassment of Riches.* New York and London, 1987

Schama, Simon. *Rembrandt's Eyes.* New York and London, 1999

Schierbeek, Abraham, and M. Roosenboom. *Measuring the Invisible World – the life & work of Antonie van Leeuwenhoek.* London, 1959

Sebald, W.G. *The Rings of Saturn.* London and New York, 1998

Slatkes, Leonard J. *Vermeer and his Contemporaries.* New York, 1981

Snow, Edgar. *A Study of Vermeer.* Berkeley, CA and London, 1979

Steadman, Philip. 'In the Studio of Vermeer.' See Richard Gregory, editor. *The Artful Eye.*

Steadman, Philip. *Vermeer's Camera.* Oxford, 2001

Strien, C.D. van. *British Travellers in Holland during the Stuart Period.* Leiden, 1993

Sutton, Peter C. *Pieter de Hooch.* Oxford and New York, 1980

Swillens, P.T.A. *Johannes Vermeer, Painter of Delft.* Utrecht and Brussels, 1950

Visser, P.C. *Delft – bladzijden uit zijn geschiedenis.* Delft, 1969

Wheelock, Arthur K., Jr. *Perspective, Optics, and Delft Artists around 1650.* New York, 1977

Wheelock, Arthur K., Jr. 'History, Politics, and the Portrait of a City, Vermeer's *View of Delft*'. See Susan Zimmerman and R.F.E. Weissman, editors. *Urban Life in the Renaissance*

Wheelock, Arthur K., Jr. *Vermeer and the Art of Painting.* New Haven, CT and London, 1995

Wijbenga, D. *Delft – een verhael van de Stad en haar bewoners*, Volume Two, 1572–1700. Delft, 1986

Wilenski, R.H. *Dutch Painting* (1929); revised edition. London, 1955

Zimmerman, Susan, and R.F.E. Weissman, editors. *Urban Life in the Renaissance.* Newark, NJ, 1989

Zumthor, Paul. *Daily Life in Rembrandt's Holland.* London, 1952; New York, 1953

Exhibition Catalogues

Delftse Meesters (Delft Masters – Vermeer's Contemporaries). Prinsenhof, Delft. Zwolle, 1996

Der Stad Delft: cultuur en maatschappij van 1572 tot 1667, two volumes. Delft, 1981

Johannes Vermeer, ed. Arthur K. Wheelock, Jr, with contributions by Wheelock, Albert Blankert, Ben Broos, and Jorgen Wadum. National Gallery of Art, Washington, DC, and Mauritshuis, The Hague. New Haven, CT, London and Zwolle, 1995

Pieter de Hooch, ed. Peter C. Sutton. Dulwich Picture Gallery, London, and Wadsworth Athenaeum, Hartford, CT. London and New Haven, CT, 1998

Rembrandt and his Age. National Museum, Stockholm. Contains article by Walter Liedtke, 'Vermeer teaching himself'. Stockholm, 1992

Periodicals

Artibus et Historiae, no. 6 , article by Arthur K. Wheelock, Jr and C.J. Kaldenbach, 'Vermeer's *View of Delft* and his Vision of Reality', 1982

Boston Globe, various articles on the theft of *The Concert,* 1990–9

Burlington Magazine: six articles by W. Martin on methods of Dutch artists, 1905–7; article by Jean Decoen, 'Vermeer of Utrecht', September 1935; article by Abraham Bredius on a new Vermeer, November 1937; article by Michael Kitson on *St Praxedis,* June 1969; article by Walter Liedtke on Carel Fabritius's *View in Delft,* May 1976

Evening Standard, London, article by Luke Jennings on the Kenwood House theft, 'Every Picture Tells a Story', 3 December 1999

Gazette des Beaux-Arts, Paris, vol. 21, articles by E.J.T. Thoré (William Bürger) on 'Van der Meer de Delft', pp. 297–330, 458–70, 542–75, 1866

Hollandse Mercurius. Haarlem, 1676

HP/De Tijd, article by Erik Spaans, 'Vendetta voor Vermeer', 13 May 1994

Oud Holland, no. 3, review by J.M. Montias of D. Haks, and others, *Dutch Society in the Age of Vermeer*, 1997

Theoretische Geschiedenis, no. 19, article by J. van der Waal on Vermeer's civic guard service, 1992

Index

An asterisk indicates an entry that refers to a footnote in the text.